Aubrey De Vere

Recollections of Aubrey De Vere

Aubrey De Vere

Recollections of Aubrey De Vere

ISBN/EAN: 9783337217792

Printed in Europe, USA, Canada, Australia, Japan

Cover: Foto ©Thomas Meinert / pixelio.de

More available books at **www.hansebooks.com**

RECOLLECTIONS

OF

AUBREY DE VERE

EDWARD ARNOLD

NEW YORK
70 FIFTH AVENUE

LONDON
37 BEDFORD STREET

1897

University Press

John Wilson and Son, Cambridge, U.S.A.

PREFACE

" RECOLLECTIONS " and " Autobiographies " are very different things; and this book belongs to the former class, not to the latter. We have seen persons and places which have amused or interested us, and it occurs to us that if accurately described they might amuse or interest others also; but this is a very different thing from writing one's biography, with which the world has little concern. Moreover, Self is a dangerous personage to let into one's book. He is sure to claim a larger place than he deserves in it and to leave less space than their due for worthier company. Several of the portraits drawn by me are prevented by lack of room from taking place in the present volume, amongst others those of Ambrose de Lisle, Kenelm Digby, Sir John Simeon, the Baron Theodore von Schroeter, Maurice FitzGerald Knight of Kerry, and Father Faber of the Oratory. I should have wished to describe Maurice FitzGerald as known to me in the days of my youth, with his

> " Lofty port and spiritual eye,
> Like some embodied dream of chivalry," [1]

if only as a type of the old Irish Norman noble, corresponding to that of the old Gaelic chieftain presented in my sketch of the late Sir Edward O'Brien. Another volume may, however, remedy such deficiencies. The chapter on the great Irish Famine (1846 to 1850) is but one of two projected. The second, intended to describe more largely the severer part of that awful calamity, is deferred both from lack of room in the present volume and in the hope that if read at a later time the facts recorded may be less subject to unjust misrepresentations. Such were the charges brought in recent times against the Government existing at that of the Irish famine as if several mistakes into which it fell had been acts proceeding from negligence or from evil design. Charges equally untrue have been as recently made against the Irish proprietors in those terrible years (many of whom fell victims to their labours for the poor), charges in direct contradiction to the impartial evidence of a strong Irish Liberal, A. M. Sullivan, Esq. He censures the absentees; but he says also " The bulk of the Irish landlords manfully did their best in that dread hour. . . . Cases might be named by the score in which such men scorned to avert by pressure on their suffering tenantry the fate they saw impending over themselves. They went down with the ship." [2]

It is only just to remark that charges as untrue, or as exaggerated, have often been brought by a very different class of accusers against

[1] " The Lamentation of Ireland," by the late Sir Aubrey de Vere.
[2] " New Ireland," 1878.

the great mass of the Catholic clergy in Ireland in later years.
Violent expressions used by some among them, and probably long
since regretted by many, have been quoted as if they represented
the language of the majority; and few have taken the trouble to
enquire what proportion of the Irish clergy joined in the recent agitation, and how many abstained from doing so.

The marvel is surely not that many of the clergy in all denomi-
nations should be unskilled or heated politicians, but that trained
and experienced statesmen, whose studies included History, Political Philosophy and Political Economy, should so often in late years
have extemporised political principles or defended political courses to
the full as Jacobinical as any of those promulgated at those meetings
so justly condemned. But there is another side to this matter which
it is both our duty and our interest not wholly to ignore. What
would have been the condition of Ireland by this time if the Catholic
clergy of Ireland had not during the whole period of Irish agitation
from first to last denounced the Secret Societies and refused the
sacraments to those who joined them? It was thus lately, and it was
thus long since. The Secret Societies will not soon forget the great
Bishop Doyle, who waged against them an incessant war, or his last
appeal to them shortly before his premature death, " My people, you
have broken your Bishop's heart."

There are few in connection with whom I have so many Recollections as with the earliest of my friends and my near kinsman, Stephen
Spring Rice. I see from the window at which I write, the trees which
we used to climb together as boys. I have been allowed to grace
one of my volumes with not a few of his Sonnets. Many of them
abound in poetic merits, but, to those who knew and loved him, their
highest charm will be the vividness with which they recall the many
beautiful qualities of head and heart which were combined in him
with a rich imagination and a profound sense of social and political
duty.

In the Memoirs of Lord Tennyson, Lord Houghton and Sara
Coleridge, are many Recollections embodied in letters of mine to
their respective biographers. Additional personal Recollections will
be found in my literary critiques on the poems of Wordsworth, Sir
Henry Taylor, Archbishop Trench, Coventry Patmore, Landor and
Sir Samuel Ferguson.[1]

                                        AUBREY DE VERE.

Curragh Chase.
June, 1897.

[1] " Essays in three Volumes " (Macmillan).

Contents

Recollections of Aubrey de Vere

CHAPTER I

CHILDHOOD AND BOYHOOD

Rural Dances at the Avenue Gate — Duels the favourite Irish Sport — My Grandfather's Ways — He made his Son, when only five years old, a Captain in a Regiment of Volunteers which he had raised — The condition of the Poor was that of a merry misery — A large Emigration wisely assisted by the State was the necessary Preliminary to serious Improvement — Neither English Statesmen nor Irish Proprietors saw this in time — My Father was strongly in Favour of " Catholic Emancipation," and in his Politics generally a " Liberal Tory " or " Canningite " — A Summer on the Shannon — A Residence in England from 1821 to 1824 — Richmond Hill — The Sunsets from its Terrace — Ham House and its Groves — My Father's early Dramas — Our first Tutor, William St. George Pelissier — Pleasant Christmases at Adare — Adventure on Knockfierna, or the Hill of the Fairies.

MY earliest recollections are of our Irish home, Curragh Chase, and I always see it bathed as in summer sunshine. It was not once, however, as it is now. At the bottom of the lawn there now spreads a lake, but at that time it was rich meadow land, divided by a slender stream, with fair green hills beyond. The pleasure ground now blends insensibly with the lawns and woods; but it had then a wall around it, which, as my father's old friend and schoolfellow, the then Sir Thomas Acland, said on visiting us, when both had left youth behind, gave it a look of monastic seclusion. It was then divided into four grassy spaces,

as smooth as velvet, and bright with many a flower-bed.
I can still see the deer park, and the deer bounding from
brake to brake of low-spreading oak and birch; the gathering of the poor on Sunday evenings at the gates of the
long ash avenue for their rural dance; and the gay,
though half bashful, confidence with which some rosy
peasant girl would advance, and drop a court'sy before
one of our party, or some visitor at the "big house,"
that court'sy being an invitation to dance. There was
also a little open space in the woods in which the neighbours danced; nor have I yet forgotten the vexation with
which I found myself once snatched up and carried home
to bed by one of those " merry maids whose tresses tossed
in light," and who lost little time in returning to the revel.

It was a time at which opposites of all sorts oddly combined. The country gentlemen were then looked up to as
so many little princes, and the poor would have gladly
adopted them as chiefs, like those of old, had they cared
to accept that position; yet there was great familiarity in
the intercourse of classes. It was all strangely mixed with
simplicity of life. My grandmother drove about the park
with her four greys and an outrider, while my father, with
whom she lived, had his four blacks and an outrider; yet
dinner, which was at five o'clock, would have been far
from satisfactory to a diner-out of the present day. What
a stranger would have thought ostentation was often a
necessity, for the roads were often carried over high
hills. I well remember my grandmother's beautiful but
melancholy black eyes, her ways at once authoritative and
affectionate, and the reverence with which she was regarded
by all. Nor have I forgotten her good-night to us chil-

dren: "God bless you, child, and make a good man of you"; nor the loud laugh once when the youngest of us, not to be outdone in civility, responded, "God bless you, grandmother, and make a good woman of you."

We cared less for my grandfather, for though Curragh Chase, his chief residence, had always been our home, he lived much elsewhere. He was regarded as a man of remarkable ability, which he seldom turned to serious purpose. That ability was early marked, and Lord Shelburne, then high in office, when on a visit at our house, was so much struck by the boy that he turned to his father, and said: "Place that boy in my hands! I will give him a political education, get him into Parliament on his coming of age, and he will turn out a great man." The offer, however, was not accepted, and accordingly the boy was brought up to be an Irish squire, at a time when England may have "expected every man to do his duty," but Ireland expected every man to do, possibly, some other man's duty, but, in any case, whatever amused him — ride well, stand by a friend, say good things and fight duels.

In those days a duel was the most mirthful of pastimes, and in Dublin there still remains a tradition of two lawyers, — one the biggest, and the other the smallest, man in Irish society — who met in the Phœnix Park, just after sunrise, to indulge in that amusement. As they approached each other, the big man set his glass to his eye, and exclaimed: "But where is my honourable opponent? For I really cannot see him."

"What's that he's saying?" demanded the little man.

"I just remarked," replied the big man, "that I am so large that if you miss me, you are like the man who, when he took aim at the parish church, never succeeded in hitting the parish."

"What is that big 'Golumbus' of a man babbling about?" was his small antagonist's rejoinder. "That I can't miss him and he cannot see me? Let his second get a bit of white chalk, and draw my exact size and shape on that huge carcass of his; and any bullet of mine that hits outside that white line shall not count."

My grandfather had no taste for duels. At a great public dinner, among the "healths" proposed was that of Lord Castlereagh, to whom my grandfather, then a member of the Irish Parliament, was known to have a special aversion. All looked toward his seat, wondering how he would meet the dilemma; for the refusal to drink to a toast could then be expiated only by a duel. The glasses filled, he was the first to rise; he lifted his own and said: "Here's to the health of my Lord Castlereagh!" adding with a significant expression of face, "the Lord be troublesome to him!"

My grandfather always gave the sagest advice to a friend, but generally acted himself from whim. Once when walking in a London street, he passed a room in which an auction was going on, and, attracted by the noise, entered it. The property set up for auction was the Island of Lundy in the Bristol Channel. He knew nothing whatsoever about it, but when the auctioneer proclaimed that it had never paid either tax or tithe, that it acknowledged neither King nor Parliament, nor law civil or ecclesiastical, and that its proprietor was pope and emperor at once in his own scanty domain, he made a bid, and the island was knocked down to him. It turned out a good speculation. It paid its cost by the sale of rabbits; and whenever its purchaser chanced to have picked a quarrel with England and Ireland at the same time, it was a hermitage to which he could always retire and meditate. He planted there a small Irish colony, and drew up for it a very compendious code, including a quaint law of divorce in case of matrimonial disputes. In money matters he was adventurous and unlucky. He lost about £15,000 by cards, and then renounced them. He is said to have also lost about half the family property through some trivial offence given to his father. In other matters he was more fortunate. During the war he raised two regiments consisting of the sons of farmers, his own tenants and those of his neighbours, and bestowed a captain's commission on his only son, then a boy of five. I remember my father describing the pride with which he strutted about in his scarlet uniform, when the general rode out to review these regiments. " But where is the captain? " exclaimed the veteran. " Here I am," shouted the child. " But, my little man, you are too young to fight! " " Not at all," was the answer; " let the French land, and " — waving his sword in the air — " I will cut off their heads! " Alas! the hard-hearted Englishman " disbanded the captain," as the poor people described his act, and the youthful warrior lost for ever the opportunity of humbling that " Corsican adventurer," who had called England a " nation of shopkeepers," and affirmed that the lions on her standard were only leopards.

My grandfather was the most popular of our country gentlemen, because he had a great love for the poor, and always helped them at a pinch. A very old tenant once

told me many stories illustrating this side of his character.
Here is one of them.   A young man was tried for murder,
having killed a member of a rival faction in a faction-fight.
The judge, reluctant to sentence him to death, on account
of his youth, turned to him and said: "Is there any one
in court who could speak as to your character?" The
youth looked round the court, and then said sadly: "There
is no man here, my lord, that I know." At that my grandfather chanced to walk into the grand-jury gallery.   He
saw at once how matters stood.   He called out, "You are
a queer boy that don't know a friend when you see him!"
The boy was quick-witted; he answered, "Oh, then, 't is
myself that is proud to see your honour here this day!"
"Well," said the judge, "Sir Vere, since you know that
boy, will you tell us what you know of him?"   "I will,
my lord," said my grandfather, " and what I can tell you
is this — that from the very first day that ever I saw him
to this minute, I never knew anything of him that was not
very good."   The old tenant ended his tale by striking his
hands together and exclaiming, "And he never to have
clapped his eye upon the boy till that minute!" The
boy escaped being hanged.   Such traits make a man
popular in Ireland; and it is said that at his funeral the
keening (funeral wail) for many a mile was such as had
rarely been heard.   Not long ago I came upon a letter
from an English minister of the day, informing him that
the patent for his peerage, an English one, was ready. It
seems, however, that at the last moment he changed his
mind and declined it.   Possibly there was some one to
whom " he would not give so much satisfaction " as that
of seeing him take a peerage.

The poorer class in those days seldom wore shoes or stockings. That they did not count a hardship. On the contrary, they found these appendages irksome; and at a later time often carried their shoes in their hands till near a town. Many of their houses were but hovels without chimneys or windows. The real patience, or rather cheerfulness, with which such hardships were borne, should be recollected by such as justly complain of more recent violences committed in retaliation for imaginary wrongs. At that time the mass of the people spoke Irish, not English, habitually. They did not read; and if they had read they would have found no publications that preached Jacobinism. They were faithful, notwithstanding, to their political traditions. No one could keep an orange lily in the garden, though planted by known enemies of the Orange party. It was sure to be thrown over the wall, while we were informed that there were some "bad mimbers" in the neighbourhood whom no vigilance could keep from stealing. We had at one time an excellent gardener, but he was an Orangeman from the "Black North." He had brought with him a large blunderbuss for the pacification of the South; and he boasted much of its capabilities. One night a number of men with blackened faces burst open the window of his bedroom, which was on the ground floor. The family were then in England, except two young lady relatives. One of them hid in a garret, the other made her appearance on the field of action, attended only by two maids, without fear and without cause for fear. The men listened to her rebuke with respect, and spared the life of the Orange gardener, after making him, however, swear to return forthwith to the

North. They took away his blunderbuss, but a few days later wrote a letter stating that it would be found under a particular tree; and there it was found.

The extreme poverty here described will suggest the thought that the proprietor class had been very remiss in the discharge of their duties. This charge would be only partly true. They did not feel that poverty as much as they ought to have felt it; but neither did the Irish poor themselves, in ordinary times. The penal laws were still sufficiently recent to live on in their consequences; and one of these was, as Edmund Burke affirmed, a legislative mandate, "Thou shalt not improve." In prohibiting property to the mass of the people they had proscribed industry; but they could not prevent early marriages; and the consequence was that between the huge population and the scanty means of support there existed no proportion. The problem had become too vast to be solved by any efforts of individual proprietors, had they been ever so dutiful, able, and wealthy. The farms were too small for scientific cultivation; and if they had been consolidated, multitudes must have been deprived of all support. The farms were not, it is true, laid out for cultivation at the landlord's cost, as in England; but if they had been, wherever competition for land existed, those improvements must have been paid for by a rent proportionately increased, as in England. Neither the proprietor nor tenant possessed the capital necessary for such improvements, but the poor man's capital was his labour, and the system which grew up in Ireland was the best at that time, not only for the landlord, but even more for the tenant, because he had thus his earnings at once as a farmer and as a labourer. Again, the labourer's pay was deplorably low; but the work given for it was proportionately low. That arrangement also grew naturally out of the circumstances of the country. If the rate of wages had been higher, the labour would then have been unproductive; and half the labourers must have been thrown out of employment, since even at a low rate of wages there was not work for the labourer for more than half the week. The low rate of wages simply distributed a small labour-fund among a large number of half-labourers. A philanthropist who doubled the rate of wages would only have increased the evil in the long run: for he would have drawn in upon a small neighbourhood a double population with an artificial and therefore ephemeral support. Eventually the Irish population, wholly unemployed during a large portion of the year, was reckoned at two millions. A remedy for all this was indeed most necessary, but it did not rest with the individual proprietor, but largely with the State also. It must have begun with a system of State-aided emigration to the colonies, where aids, both before and after their arrival, should have been provided for the early settlers. The work would have been costly, but "these are heroic works and worthy kings." Ireland had early done what unaided energy could do in the way of emigration; but the effort was wholly insufficient, while also attended by needless suffering and a scant reward at best. Such State aid was a debt of honour on the part of the State; but the impulse thus given to the growth of her colonies, and the extension of her markets, would have eventually repaid that cost, a large proportion of which might have been justly charged upon the Irish property thus rendered capable of indefinite improvement. The land-laws in Ireland would have worked as they did in England when the pre-condition had been fulfilled, — that is, a state of things substantially similar in the two countries. But this would have demanded assisted emigration, and such aid to industrial enterprises at home as the legislation of past times had rendered necessary.

The disproportion between the vast population and the slender means for their support continued to increase year by year. I remember hearing, in my boyhood, my father frequently lamenting the blindness of statesmen who paid no serious attention to it. His political predictions generally turned out true. " We sit in a boat the gunwale of which is nearly level with the water," he used to say. " How will it be when the waves rise? " The waves rose in the famine of 1847–50 and his words recurred to me. They would have been heard often and far if he had had a parliamentary career. Unluckily he stumbled at its threshold. He stood as a candidate for his county at the election of, I think, 1820. At that time, to represent a county was a great distinction, and one sometimes sought from lower motives. My father stood for his county because he wished to benefit his country. But he stood a week too late; and the clouds of letters sent daily to the post were often answered by regrets that the votes of the writers had not been asked until they had been promised to another.

Elections then lasted for a fortnight in Ireland, and were times of fierce excitement, though politics had little to do with it. My father was strongly in favour of Catholic Emancipation, and was popular among the poor.

He was popular also among the country gentlemen. Every day the excitement increased. I can also remember being frightened by hearing that if my father were beaten it would be by the votes of "dead men" — that meant, of deceased freeholders whose names remained accidentally on the registry lists, and who were personated by impostors. One of these impostors had but a few years before won his niche in the temple of local fame. He had voted, but saw no reason why he should not vote a second time if he could do so without detection. Accordingly he left the court, had his head shaved, substituted a red wig for his own black hair, and got three of the most prominent teeth in his upper jaw knocked out. He then returned to the court, and, recognized by none, voted for the rival candidate, with whom he had made his bargain!

In the case of my father's election the contest lasted long. At last it was decided after an odd fashion. A country gentleman with whom my father had always been on the friendliest terms, and who had waited for the last day of the polling in order to impart a more emphatic character to his proceeding, rode into Limerick at the head of his numerous tenantry, and voted against him! Between the two there had never been a coolness, but many years before he had had a quarrel with my father's uncle, the Earl of Limerick; he had vowed revenge, and the opportunity had come. My father was a man of great magnanimity, and never resented injuries. Somebody once said of him, "Others forgive injuries, but he entirely forgets them, and that very soon." His conduct to the friend who had thus deprived him of a

political career illustrated the old saying, "It takes two
to quarrel." The intercourse between the families continued as before. Our vindictive neighbour was a friendly
man when not crossed, one of high breeding and great
abilities; though, being, like most Irish gentlemen, without ambition, he never turned them to account. I remember seeing him walk up and down our library years
afterward, with his hands locked together behind his back,
his head bent low before him, and his long white hair
streaming back over his shoulders, and hearing him say :
"It is a great thing to be able to look back on a long
life, and record, as I can, that never once did any man
injure me but sooner or later I had my revenge." What
he thus recorded he certainly regarded as a merit. An
evil tradition had generated a "false conscience." He
was like an Indian chief who had never forsaken a friend,
or complained of a pang, or left a scalp on the head of
an enemy of his tribe.

This disastrous vindictiveness is often found in races
whose sympathies are no less keen, but who have only
half emerged from an early stage of civilisation; and it
may then be combined with the most sensitive heart,
and the strongest spirit of self-sacrifice. It is the barbaric element surviving in a society in which the Christian element may also be strong in many hearts, but into
which the conventional ingredient of civilisation has not
yet entered. In Ireland the faction fights, then so common, witnessed to the intensity of a perverted fidelity.
They were regarded as a just retribution, avenging a
wrong inflicted perhaps a century before. Neithér the
civil nor the ecclesiastical power could restrain them.

I remember a good old priest describing one of these faction fights to me. When the day appointed for the terrible yearly rite had arrived, the two factions met at the place usually set apart for it, and stood face to face with a considerable space between them. The priest rode along the line, dismounted, knelt down, lifted his hands, and solemnly adjured both factions in the name of God, to depart, and not imbrue their native land with the blood of brothers. They thanked him with great reverence, and then requested him as he had acquitted himself of his duty, to take his departure. He mounted and rode to the top of an adjoining hill, on which was stationed a considerable body of cavalry and several magistrates, one of whom, a venerable old man, beckoned him to his carriage window, and said to him with great agitation, "Sir, this is a dreadful sight!" "I pitied him," said the priest to me, "and desired him not to take on in that way, since there was no help for it." Then the two factions raised a great shout, and met in the middle space; the next moment the cavalry charged down the hill, and rode right over both.

I remember a touching incident in connection with the faction fights. While the agitation for repeal was going on, O'Connell, both on religious and political grounds, made a great attempt to put them down, for he was quite sincere in his frequent assertion that "he who commits a crime is the enemy of his country." With the aid of the Catholic clergy he induced the rival factions in many parts of Ireland to meet at their parish church, renounce their ancient enmities, and shake hands. A relative of mine then travelling through the country observed a great crowd around a village church. He got out of his carriage, and entered the church. It was a "reconciliation" meeting. Two old grey-haired men, leaders of two rival factions, advanced slowly, with several halts, from the opposite ends of the church to the middle, stood there silent, face to face, and at last shook hands. The next moment one of them dashed himself down on the stone pavement, and cried aloud, "O my son, my murdered son! I have clasped the hand that shed the last drop of thy blood!"

The earliest political event which I remember is the death of King George III. We children were all great loyalists; on this occasion we were put into mourning, and I believe that our grief on that occasion was very real, though not very lasting. Soon afterward we migrated to Mount Treachard, the residence of my maternal grandmother, on the banks of the Shannon. Many a day was spent sailing in a little open boat, with three masts and four sails, now by the ivied cliff and fair wooded shores of Cahircon, now among the islands at the mouth of the Fergus, now beneath the heathy hills that overhang Foynes. I well recollect my father's characteristic remark on the far nobler view we should have had, if only on one of those hills there had chanced to stand another castle like "Shania," a ruined keep of the Desmonds, which crowned an eminence a few miles inland. He pointed also to Knock-Patrick, and told us how from its summit Ireland's great apostle had sent his benediction over all the lands to the south and west. Sometimes we made our way down the river, past Glin, Tarbert, and Kilrush, and saw near its mouth the island of Scattery, the lonely hermitage of St. Senanus, and the long line of Ballibunion's cliffs, with their submarine palace of caves, the sound of which, after a storm, was heard, in a strong west wind, thirty miles off. I have never since felt anything like that terrible sense of loneliness which penetrated my whole being on the evening of our arrival, when I was left for an hour alone, and looked westward over "the spacious Shannon spreading like a sea" and diversified only by a few black-sailed turf-boats far apart.

The next year we went to England. We travelled in a very large old family coach with our own four black horses. It took us four days to reach Dublin, and twice as many more to reach London. On the second evening, at Maryborough, we were informed that we should have an interesting sight the next morning at breakfast, as a man was then to be hanged on a platform just opposite our windows. We started accordingly an hour earlier than had been intended. Steamboats were then in a very early stage of their existence, and seven hours were dolorously spent before we landed at Holyhead. The slow rate at which we travelled showed us, however, many fair sights which the traveller now misses.

I remember vividly the interest with which we saw King George IV., drawn by six cream-coloured horses, in his state coach, with the Duke of York beside him, and the Duke of Wellington opposite, on the occasion of a dissolution of Parliament. I remember no less, as in duty bound, our French governess, who told me, then eight years old, that I should never forget her, because she had taught me to write. She had, I believe, but one fault, namely, that, though not pretty, her man-

ners were so perfect, and she was at once so brilliant
and so "spiritual" that at evening parties she attracted
more attention than any other lady in the room. She
was an ardent Bonapartist, and her sister had married a
brother of the Emperor Napoleon. At one time there
was on a visit to us a young French lady, an equally
ardent Legitimist, and I used to hear people marvel at
the skill with which, in their passages-of-arms, the two
politicians united the extreme of politeness with sarcastic
bitterness.

During our residence in London my father published
his first drama, "Julian the Apostate," and also his second, "The Duke of Mercia," both of which were highly
praised in the periodicals, though neither had a large
circulation. One of these critiques affirmed that "Julian
the Apostate" was a drama of a higher order than any
which Lord Byron had given to the world; and I have
reason to hope that that critique was written by Hartley
Coleridge, then a young man. No poet was then popular
except Byron, who must have deprived the world of as
much poetry as he ever produced. I remember asking
my father whether Byron or Scott was the greater man,
and his answering, "Scott, because he is as great, and
he is a good man also."

We passed a delightful summer on Richmond Hill, in
a house then adjoining the "Star and Garter." We
daily watched the sunsets from Richmond Terrace, with
the Thames, reddened but glassy still, winding away
among leagues of rich lowlands, "a haunt of ancient
peace"; the hedgerow trees crowding so closely together at a distance, that the rich pasture-lands and

stately homes embosomed in them seemed destined to be reabsorbed into the primeval forest which still waged a peaceful war with that "sweet enemy," modern civilisation. Still more charming to my imagination were the long avenues and solemn groves of Ham House, within whose inclosure the venerable mansion looked content to stand half hidden and guarded by its grim iron gates. I did not associate it with the historical events which it records, but with a German fairy tale about a witch whose delight was to entice young lovers into her forest, then change them into birds, and hang them up in the cages that lined the corridors of her palace prison. Every year I revisit those scenes, and wonder at the recollection that our parents, with whom we first enjoyed them, seemed then to us to be elderly persons. On the contrary, they were young. They had married at eighteen and seventeen.

Next summer was passed by us in a place called Ruxley, near the village of Esher. It had a small but lovely lawn, in the middle of which stood two venerable cedar-trees. Beyond it was a wood, and on the other side a common, where we played cricket. In the neighbourhood we visited many beautiful places, especially Hampton Court, with its palatial gardens and priceless cartoons; Bushey Park, with its vast horse-chestnut avenue; Claremont, Kingston, and Boxhill, with its box-trees, in some cases, nearly as large, if I remember aright, as birch-trees. Close to us was a high hill, from which we used to fly our kites, instructed in that art by our tutor, William St. George Pelissier, the descendant of a French family exiled by the revocation of the Edict of Nantes.

He was a very remarkable man, judging him by the impression he made on others as well as by my own recollections. He had a massive intellect, vigorously trained and richly stored; high principles, both moral and religious; a lofty sense of honour, perhaps too much self-confidence, which some would have called self-assertion, for he habitually spoke, though never discourteously, with the tone of a superior. He was a great classical scholar, and well acquainted with the best literature of modern countries, especially the chief English poets and theologians. In person he was short and thick, with strong features, and a fine forehead, which I remember describing as "bursting with sense," for I had an enthusiastic admiration for him. That sentiment he was very far from reciprocating; for, so slow was I at my Latin for a boy of ten years, that he desired me to discard it altogether, inasmuch as I was an idiot. I asked him what, that being the case, I was to do; to which he replied that I might cultivate the moral faculties, since I had not the intellectual, and also make traceries of maps, laying them level upon glass. I asked next whether the moral faculties or the intellectual were the better; to which he replied that the moral were, seeing that good men took such with them to heaven, whereas the intellectual faculties underwent some strange revolution after death — an answer which entirely contented me.

A few weeks afterward my father asked me some questions respecting my studies, and I replied that I had abandoned them all by my tutor's advice on account of being an idiot, and spent my time tracing maps on glass, and cultivating the moral qualities. With this state of things my father was far from being contented, and he told my tutor that the more stupid I was, the more trouble he should have taken with me. My Latin grammar was resumed, and when one day at our historical lesson I repeated to my tutor by heart the speech of Scipio Africanus to Hannibal before the battle of Zama, in place of giving merely the substance of it, he seemed surprised, and confided to me his opinion that possibly I might one day cease to be an idiot. Probably his earlier impression was not far astray, for when I began with arithmetic, several weeks elapsed before I could understand the process of "carrying," at the end of a line of figures in addition.

He accompanied us when we returned to Curragh Chase, and there continued to read aloud to us the plays of Shakespeare, as he had previously read them, to our intense delight, at Ruxley. He was a magnificent dramatic reader, and these Shakespearian readings were perhaps the most stimulating part of our education. In about a year more he left us and settled at Carnarvon, a grievous loss to us, as I have always believed. He was careful of our religious instruction after a certain "high and dry" fashion, and constantly inculcated on us rectitude, purpose, and energy, his praise of the last being expressed in the saying, "There are three letters of more value than all the rest in the alphabet, namely, N R G." We had many later tutors, but none like him. The best of these was Edward Johnstone, a most kindly, upright, and religious man, who afterward became a clergyman. He was an ardent admirer of Wordsworth, and the first to point out to me the extraordinary merits of his "Vernal

Ode." One of our tutors I remember chiefly from his oddness. He used to ride with me, but never would leap a wall on a Sunday, because as he remarked, " If I were killed while riding on a Sunday my friends would not pity me."

Some four or five years after our return to Ireland passed away in a quiet routine of studies, wanderings in the woods, occupation in the garden, in which each of us had a little territory of his own, and pleasant readings aloud in the evening, our book being generally one that combined instruction with amusement, such as travels or biographies, seldom a novel, except when Walter Scott had brightened all the households in the land with another of his delightful romances. Sometimes a speech of Brougham's, Plunket's, or Canning's was read aloud; some of which had passages which strongly moved our youthful imaginations, such as Canning's celebrated boast in connection with his recognition of the independence of the South American republics — " I called a new world into existence to redress the balance of the old." It would have been difficult not to have caught a portion of the enthusiasm with which Canning was at that time spoken of by his friends (while even his enemies often contented themselves with calling him " a splendid Evil "), and of their delight when, on the death of Lord Liverpool, King George IV. reluctantly made him prime minister. On the other hand, the fanatics of the day abhorred him, and all the more for having allied himself with the leading Whigs, and discarded Lord Eldon and the high Tories. Unhappily he died too soon to carry Catholic Emancipation, which in that case would not have needed to be carried through intimidation, and by statesmen who on principle had always resisted it.

When the "Clare Election" was won by O'Connell, my father expressed his certainty that Catholic Emancipation must follow inevitably. It proved so. Before another year had passed (that of 1829) the hills were covered with bonfires celebrating the passing of "The Bill." I was then fifteen, and I well remember climbing to the top of a high pillar on the summit of a hill opposite our house, though how the feat was achieved I cannot conceive, and standing upon it for many minutes, waving a lighted torch round my head in the gathering darkness. Alas! like the concession of "Grattan's Parliament," in 1782, it had been a concession to fear, not to principle; it included, in deference to unworthy prejudices, several provisions of a petty and offensive character, and for forty years it continued to be unaccompanied by that which, thirty years previously, Pitt had perceived to be its necessary supplement, namely, religious equality. The ancient religious patrimony of Ireland continued to be the endowment of a small minority, and "Protestant Ascendency" continued to maintain in Ireland a war of religion, where otherwise the old war of races would soon have been forgotten.

When Catholic Emancipation was conceded, half the political world thought that Ireland was to become a paradise, and the other half, that it was to become a pandemonium. They were both mistaken; for several years there was no very marked change. In it two antagonistic parties had long been accustomed to quarrelling, and when there was nothing to quarrel about, life seemed a little

dull; and each of them would have been in sympathy with
Paley, who, when the Archbishop of York boasted to him
that he and his wife, though married for fifty years, had
never had a difference, replied, "Mighty flat, my lord,
mighty flat!"

Our home life pursued the even tenor of its way. We,
the three elder brothers, worked at our classics in the
morning, and in the afternoon took a long walk or a long
ride, for each of us boasted a horse, though we seldom
rode together; and in the evening there was often music,
especially when Lord Monteagle was with us, for he and
his sister, my mother, had been used to play duets from
Mozart in their youth, he on the flute, and she on the
pianoforte, and they continued the habit in advanced life.
At Christmas we used to visit at Adare Manor. It was a
gay as well as a friendly and hospitable house; after dinner
we had private theatricals, games of all sorts, dances, and,
in the daytime, pleasant wanderings beside the beautiful
Maique, which mirrored, in waters that even when swiftest
seldom lost their transparency, as stately a row of elms,
ninety feet high, as England herself can boast, and the
venerable ruins of a castle which belonged to the Kildares,
— though islanded, as it were, in a territory almost all the
rest of which belonged to the Desmond branch of the same
Geraldine race. Adare, then as now a singularly pretty
village, had for centuries been a walled town. It had seen
many battles, and had been more than once burned down;
but it was famous chiefly for the number of its monastic
institutions, still represented by the ruins of a Franciscan
convent, as well as by one of the Trinitarian and one of the
Augustinian order, the churches of which have been re-

stored, and are now used, one for Catholic and the other for Protestant worship. The Knights Templars once possessed a house at Adare; but its site cannot now be discovered.

Among our Christmas holidays at Adare there is one which I am not likely ever to forget. About eight miles from the village rises a hill eight hundred feet in elevation, with a singularly graceful outline, named "Knockfierna," or the "Hill of the Fairies," because in popular belief it abounded in the "Good People," then universally believed in by the Gaelic race in Ireland. We set off to climb it one day soon after breakfast — *we*, meaning my two elder brothers and I, and the son of our host, Lord Adare, afterwards well known as Earl of Dunraven, the author of two valuable works, "Memorials of Adare" and an excellent book on Irish antiquities. Two other members of the exploring party were our tutor, and a friend of Adare's several years older than he. It was hard walking, especially after the ascent of the hill began; we had to climb many walls and ditches, and to force our way through many a narrow lane. We had brought no luncheon with us, and before we reached the summit the winter sun had sunk considerably.

We walked about the hill top for some time admiring the view, a very fine one, though, like many Irish views, somewhat dreary, from the comparative absence of trees, the amount of moorland intersected by winding streams, and the number of ruins, many of them modern. All at once we discovered that we were faint with hunger, and so much fatigued that without refreshment we could hardly make our way home. Half-way down the hill stood a

farmhouse.   The farmer was most courteous, but, alas!
there was not a morsel of food in his house.   What he
had he gave, and that was cider, for which, like the Irish
peasant of that day, he would take no payment.   Each of
us drank only one cider glass of it, and we took our departure, cheered, but by no means invigorated.   After the
lapse of some ten minutes one of us became so sleepy
that he could hardly walk, and his nearest neighbour at
once gave him an arm.   A little later the same complaint
was made by another of us, and the same friendly aid was
forced upon him.   But in a few minutes more not only
were we unable to walk, but we were unable to stand, the
only exceptions being the two among us who were no
longer boys — our tutor and Adare's friend.

Never shall I forget their astonishment first, and afterwards their vexation.   They were in some degree in charge
of us, and the responsibility seemed to rest upon them.
The Christmas evening was closing around us; there was
no help near, and apparently no reason why our sleep
should not last till sunrise.   They argued, they expostu-
lated, they pushed us, and they pulled us; but all would
not do.   I was the last to give way, and my latest recollection was that my second brother had just succeeded in
climbing to the top of a wooden gate, but could not lift
his leg over it, and lay upon his face along it.   Our tutor
stamped up and down the road indulging largely in his
favourite ejaculation "Gracious patience! gracious patience!" to which my brother replied, with his last gleam
of wakeful intelligence, "There is one very amiable trait
about you, Mr. Johnstone: you are never tired of toasting
your absent friends."   The next moment he rolled over

and slept beside us in the mud. The cider had affected
our brains because our stomachs were empty. In about a
quarter of an hour the trance was dissolved almost as suddenly as it fell on us; and we walked forward very mirth-
fully, reaching home just in time to hear the dressing bell
ring. Only one light shone through the mullioned windows of the manor-house; and I remember Adare's remark
as we drew near: "Beside that light my little sister sits
weeping. She is sure that I am dead." At dinner we told
the story of our adventures, and it excited much laughter.
Lord Dunraven "moralised the tale." "You see, young
gentlemen, each of you undertook to support and guide his
neighbour, though not one of you could take care of
himself. That is the way of Ireland. You will help your
neighbour best by taking care each of himself." His
advice was like that of another old Irish gentleman, a
relative of mine, whose "good-night" to his grandchildren often ended with this counsel, "Take good care
of yourself, child; and your friends will love you all
the better."

Lord Dunraven was certainly one of the most sagacious
and remarkable of those whom I associated with those old
days. He had represented our county in the House of
Commons in three successive parliaments, and was by
many regarded as the best speaker among the Irish members, though so sensitive was his temperament that to
address a board of magistrates or of poor-law guardians
was to him a painful effort. It was in conversation when
he forgot that he had an audience, and was only thinking
aloud, that his keenness of wit, discriminate selection of
language, force and felicity of illustration, made them-

selves felt. He was much given to reflection on practical, not abstract, subjects, and held strong opinions
on the ethics of life, which challenged attention all the
more because it was never as the preacher or the moralist
that he spoke, but as one recording what observation or
experience had impressed upon a clear intelligence. I
well remember his once saying, while a pale blue eye
kindled with conviction: " Some people do wrong because they regard that as a proof of their cleverness.
Their cleverness is the cleverness of an old Irish beggar
woman who has dreamed that she found a crock of gold
in some particular spot under the wall of a neighbouring
ruin. She rushes to it, kneels down, and drags at the
loose basement with her withered old hands till the stones
higher up get loosened, and tumble on her head. Nothing that is wrong is ever a success except for the moment.
The nature of things is against it. The man who undertakes the enterprise is contending against a law or a fate
that is irresistible."

CHAPTER II

YOUTH

Gerald Griffin — His early Writings — "The Collegians" — He renounces Literature and joins the "Christian Brothers" — My Father was educated at Ambleside — Sir William Rowan Hamilton, Astronomer Royal of Ireland — His splendid Career — A Day with Him among the Wicklow Mountains — The rising up of the Repeal Agitation — The great "Limerick Election" — The Landlords deserted by their Tenants — The defeat of the Earl of K. and its consequences — O'Connell a Repealer and a Democrat, but wholly opposed to Jacobinism and Socialistic Principles — Neither of the great English Parties were sufficiently in sympathy with Ireland to be just to her in time.

GERALD GRIFFIN, a friend of mine in youth, lived about four miles from us in a village called Pallas. He was a man of remarkable genius, and of a character yet more remarkable, though his life was too short to allow either to be recognised widely. He was the youngest of four brothers, whose parents had emigrated to America. As a boy he lived with two brothers, both of them physicians whose talents and conduct eventually made them eminently successful in their profession; but in early years their career was a struggling one. The boy had a high spirit of independence. He resolved to be no longer a burden to them, but to cast himself upon the huge world of London and make his way as he might. Knowing that his brothers would not sanction a design apparently so hopeless, he took his departure without an adieu; and for a considerable time they did not know where he was. At first he supported himself by reporting for newspapers, and afterwards by writing short dramatic pieces for the small theatres. He could thus, however, win but a precarious existence, and during several years seems to have been in danger of starving, for he never allowed his brothers to know of his difficulties. Later, he wrote tales illustrative of Irish life in the lower and middle classes, entitled, "Holland Tide," "Tales of the Munster Festivals," etc.

All at once, to his great surprise, his little spark of local reputation burst out into a flame. His "Collegians" appeared; it met with a great and immediate success. Some of the critics pronounced him the best novelist of the time next to Sir Walter Scott; his publisher sent him £800, and he despatched the whole of that sum at once to his parents in America. "The Collegians" has been fre-quently reprinted, and presents the best picture existing of Irish peasant life — at once the most vivid and the most accurate. Its comic parts are the most comic, and its tragic the most tragic, to be found in Irish literature. The tale is founded on a terrible crime perpetrated in the county of Limerick early in this century. A young man of gentle birth fell in love with a beautiful and virtuous peasant girl, married her secretly, got tired of her, and drowned her in the Shannon. For a considerable time it was impossible to arrest the murderer; his capture was described to me by a near relative of mine, the magistrate who arrested him. He had received secret information, and led a body of police to the house of the murderer's parents at a late hour of the night. Apparently there had been a dinner-party in that house, for on the door being

opened, after a slight delay, he was received in the hall by
its mistress, a tall and stately lady in a black velvet dress.
She addressed him with quiet scorn, informed him that
her house, a hospitable one, had been favoured by many
guests, but none resembling those who had come at that
unusual hour to visit it; that she knew his errand; that
her son had not been in that house for many weeks; but
that he was welcome to search for him as he pleased.
They searched the house in vain: they next searched the
offices. When on the point of retiring, one of the party
remarked a ladder within the stable, the top of which
leaned against a small door in the wall. The policemen
refused to mount it, for they said that if the murderer was
hid on the premises he must be behind that door and
would certainly stab the first to enter. The magistrate
mounted. The search was again in vain, and all had
descended from the loft except the last policeman, who,
as he approached the door, carelessly prodded with his
bayonet the straw with which the floor was covered. A
loud scream rang out from beneath it, and the murderer
leaped up. He had been grazed, not wounded, and if he
had held his peace must have escaped. His scream was
almost immediately re-echoed by a distant one louder and
more piercing. It came from one who knew her son's
voice well. The magistrate told me that the most terrible
thing he had ever witnessed was the contrast between that
mother's stately bearing at first and the piteous abjectness
of her later appeals as, on her knees, she implored him to
spare her son.

The guilt was conclusively proved, and the murderer was
sentenced to be hanged; but in those times justice was

not always impartially administered, and the peasantry
were certain that a gentleman would never be hanged.
He requested that he should be taken to the place of execution in a carriage, but his crime had excited universal
abhorrence, and none of the livery stables in Limerick
would supply one. A vehicle was procured from a distance on the morning of the execution, and the unhappy
man entered it. On the middle of the bridge that spans
a small arm of the Shannon, the horses stopped, and no
efforts could induce them to go farther. The crowds
were more certain than ever that somehow there would
be an escape; a gentleman could not be hanged. The
horses plunged more and more furiously, but would not
advance. The murderer fell into an agony of terror.
He exclaimed, " Let me out, and I will walk!" He
walked to the place of execution, and was hanged.

The " Colleen Bawn," which had an extraordinary success at one of the London theatres, was a dramatic con-
densation of " The Collegians." I went to see it, but
could not remain for more than ten minutes. All the
refinement which, not less than strength, marks the original, and especially the scenes that describe the Irish
peasantry, had vanished, and a vulgar sensationalism had
taken its place. This vulgarity has been so common in
the delineations of Ireland, whether in novels or on the
stage, that the ordinary English conception of the Irish
peasant is the opposite of the truth in many cases; at
least it wholly ignores that delicacy, pathos, and sympathy
which characterise the humbler and the better among
them, and remind us that manners are a tradition, and
that, in the centuries gone by, many a political convul-

sion had placed nobility "in commission" among the poor. In Gerald Griffin's day, when, whatever crime might be stimulated by violent passions, or whatever exaggeration might mingle with a generous "Nationalist" enthusiasm, the preaching of that vulgarest of all things, Jacobinism, had never been heard, and a man of genius like him could not fail to feel the charm both of the Irish character and the Irish manner, a thing then so much valued that "bad manners to you" was an ordinary malediction. Many of his poems illustrate Irish peasant life with singular grace and pathos; and to become the Irish Burns, as he once told me, was long the great object of his ambition.

After the publication of "The Collegians," Gerald Griffin took up his abode once more in the small dispensary house of his brother at Pallas. My father thought that he would there find little room for his books, and many interruptions of his studious hours. He invited him to pass the winter at Curragh Chase, placing two rooms at his disposal, and telling him that he would find quiet in the woods, and a large command of books in the library; but Gerald declined the invitation. He built an arbour in his brother's garden, and there, I think, made a study of Homer. He had a great knowledge of early Irish history, and we all expected from him a long series of historic romances illustrating Ireland as Scott's had illustrated Scotland. An unexpected obstacle frustrated that hope. He was a remarkably religious man. Prosperity, which weakens religion in many Irishmen, deepened it in him. Whatever ambition belonged to him in youth left him early; things spiritual remained to him the sole realities, and literature was of worth only so far as it reflected them. He startled his

friends by asserting that strong passion, one of the chief
attractions in imaginative literature, did little but mischief.
It was in vain that those friends, clerical as well as secular, maintained that in wise hands it should have an ele-
vating tendency; he clung to his doctrine all the more
because it involved self-sacrifice, well aware that it must be
fatal to the success of literature such as that for which his
gifts and his experience had especially fitted him.

He wrote no more popular novels, though a later production, " The Invasion," recording one of the Danish
piratical descents on Ireland, is full of admirable description.   One day his brother found the fireplace black with
the cinders of papers recently burned.   He had just destroyed the whole of his manuscripts, verse and prose
alike, and answered all inquiries by stating that he had
devoted the rest of his life to the instruction of little
peasant boys, as one of the " Christian Brothers " — the
humblest of all religious communities.   He laboured assiduously for a few years at Cork; and there, some years
later, I saw his grave, and heard his fellow-labourers declare that if Ireland had ever had a saint, Gerald Griffin was
one.   No doubt his choice was the best, not only for himself, but for the children who came under an influence so
benign.   But the country he loved so well lost its chance
of an Irish Burns, or an Irish Scott; and the unfriendly
critic will say, " So fares it with Irish gifts: the lower hit
their mark, the highest miss it, sometimes by going to one
side of it, and as often by going above it! "   Macready,
later, brought upon the stage a drama called " Gisippus,"
written by Gerald in early youth.   I think it proved a
success, and the £300 paid for it brought out a new edi-

tion of Gerald's works. In his religious retreat he found a peace and solemn happiness of which he wrote in rapturous terms. In person he was dignified, and his face was eminently handsome, as well as refined and intellectual.

My recollections in connection with these, my early years, are chiefly rural and sylvan. They come to me fragrant with the smell of the new-mown grass in the pleasure-grounds, the breath of the cows as they stood still to be milked, rolling their eyes in quiet pleasure, with a majestic slowness such as the Greeks attributed to the eyes of Juno. No change was desired by us, and little came. The winds of early spring waved the long masses of daffodils till they made a confused though rapturous splendour in the lake close by, just as they had done the year before: and those who saw the pageant hardly noted that those winds were cold. Each spring the blackbird gave us again his rough, strong note, and the robin's, as the season advanced, gained a roundness and fulness like that of the thrush. Each year we watched the succession of the flowers, and if the bluebell or the cowslip came a little before or after its proper time, we felt as much aggrieved as the child who misses the word he is accustomed to in the story heard a hundred times before. Each spring there came again the contented cooing of wood-doves far away, and that tremulous pathos of the young lamb's bleat, which seemed hardly in harmony with his gladness as he bounded over the pastures illuminated by the sudden April green. Each year the autumn replaced the precipitate ardours of the spring with graver joys and more sedate fruitions — its golden harvests, and all those darker colours which decorate, though sadly, the funeral feast of the year. The maple slowly as of old relinquished its fires, and there was the falling leaf and the frightened flutter of the poplar's gilded tablets, in place of the thickening leaves and deepening shadows of the vernal woodlands: but beyond these woodlands a remoter landscape was once more seen through clearer air.

In youth the enjoyment we derive from nature is less consciously the enjoyment of its beauty than it is in later life or in memory. We then think, perhaps, less of the scene than of the incident connected with it — less of the tree than of our triumph when we first climbed it — less of the flower than of the one for whom it was gathered; but beyond all these incidental joys associated with nature there is an unconscious joy in her beauty — the better, no doubt, for being unconscious. In the home of our childhood there was all the more of this incidental enjoyment, because, owing to its size, there was always so. much of labour going on in it. One of its approaches was three miles long, and it passed three lakes, one surrounded by meadows, pastures, and groves, another by woods which had never been planted by man, though perhaps often cut down and successively renewed — a portion of ancient Ireland's "forest primeval." Through those woods my father was never tired of making new drives and walks. The most interesting of these was the "Cave Walk," so called from a deep cave retiring back from a long line of cliff crowned with wood, matted over with ivy, and so perpendicular that it looked like the walls of a castle. I used often to descend into that cave merely in order to enjoy, on reascending, and approaching its mouth, the embalmed and delicious air into which the breath of unnumbered flowers and leaves and streams, seen or invisible, had been melted down. One felt as if life required nothing more for its satisfaction than the quiet breathing of such air — a healing bath to body and spirit alike.

With my father, landscape gardening was one mode of taking out the poetry which was so deeply seated within him; and if he had lived in a garret he would probably have written more verse. His love of nature was one of his strongest instincts, though hardly stronger than his love of really high art. Most of our enjoyments cost us much, and most of our affections, whether associated with the household life or with our country, cause us so much pain, either in the way of regret or of anxiety, as abundantly to remind us that they were accorded to us even more as a school of duty than as a source of enjoyment. But Nature is a very disinterested benefactress — she gives much and demands little; she touches the human heart with a hand of air so light that it leaves behind no burden of responsibility. The fallen tree seldom has a tear dropped on it; the faded flower never — or never for its own sake; and in our wanderings from river to river, or from vale to vale, we never reproach ourselves with inconstancy. There, at least,

"We've but to make love to the lips that are near."

For that reason a wise man should put a finer edge upon his appreciation of nature than on most of his sensibilities.

My father probably owed much of this, the most unalloyed of his enjoyments, to his mother's generosity, amounting, as it did, to a self-sacrifice almost heroic. She had seen how much boys, and especially an only son, as my father was, suffer from the influences of home, enervating when unmixed, and when the adulation of dependants, never so seductive as when it comes (such was then the case in Ireland), not from self-interest so much as from affection. She sent her only child, then about ten years old, to the charge of a tutor on the banks of Windermere. All the night before his departure the boy heard his mother's sobs; but she persisted, and, when the years of separation were past, reaped the reward. His tutor was not much of a scholar, but he was dutiful, upright, and brave, and he instilled those virtues into his pupil or protected their growth in him. The wild and witching scenery all around taught him another lore. Gleams from Windermere, always his favourite among the lakes, were probably with him amid the less striking, though still lovely, scenes among which his mature life was chiefly cast, gleams that may without his consciousness, have interpreted them to him. Nature's grander features create in a responsive imagination those great ideas of loveliness and of sublimity which, once elicited within us, enable us to detect and enjoy those natural attributes wherever they exist, though less strongly manifested.

The improvements which my father was always making in his country seat were stimulated also by his desire to do good. They gave a very large amount of employment to the poor, who regarded him in return with reverence and gratitude. We young ones became also much more widely acquainted than we should otherwise have been with the humbler class, and many a remembered and

often quaint incident brings back that intercourse to me.
I may as well mention one of them. At one time the
work in progress consisted in the removal and planting
out of large trees under the superintendence of a certain
Ulysses D——, who in that art was a specialist, though
without education. Once he remarked to me: "It is
a pleasure to find that the older we get the better we
get. When I was a young man I was continually cursing,
and now I curse mighty little. Neither priest nor parson
could make any hand of me. It was a lady that cured
me — Mrs. Aldworthy. I was planting a tree, and a big
one, and was after saying to the men, 'Three bounces
each man round that tree, to stiffen the earth!' Now
there was a labourer among them who could not bounce
rightly because he was wearing a greatcoat. Then I
began to curse him most terribly, and never heard Mrs.
Aldworthy coming up behind me. Said she, 'I've heard
great cursing in my life, but I never heard cursing like
that!' I was greatly frightened, and answered: 'Sure,
ma'am, it is only for his own good, and for the good of
his innocent children that I am cursing him; for if Mr.
Aldworthy saw him working in a greatcoat he'd turn
him out of the concern, and they would all starve together.' Then she gave me a wonderful answer: 'Sir,'
she said, 'it's a wonder to me that you would not think
more of your own soul than of another man's body!'
Since then I've been dropping the fashion."

Our store of amusing incidents was always increased
when my eldest brother returned from Cambridge at
vacation time. We used to hear much of two among
the younger Fellows who united great scholarship with a

strong sympathy with the undergraduates. These two were Julius Hare, the great friend of Walter Savage Landor, and Connop Thirlwall, afterwards Bishop of St. David's, the latter of whom I never think of without a grateful recollection of the grief which I heard him express at the destruction of the monasteries in England. It was a sentiment which I had not expected from one who was opposed to the traditional and ecclesiastical school of English theology. Some of the anecdotes which I then or later heard respecting Cambridge matters related to the head of one of her chief colleges, a man justly honoured for his learning and piety, but often criticised for the prosaic character of his mind and for a certain minuteness which petrified his erudition. Two of the undergraduates were discussing his "dryasdust" ways in the college library after a fashion a little irreverent, when a Fellow walked up to them. He was a somewhat pompous man, and his reproof was true to his character. "You are probably ignorant, young gentlemen, that the venerable person of whom you have been speaking with such levity is one of the profoundest scholars of our age — indeed, it may be doubted whether any man of our age has bathed more deeply in the sacred fountains of antiquity." "Or come up drier, sir," was the reply of the undergraduate.

Another anecdote indicates that the venerable man's simplicity was equal to his scholarship. After fifty years' seclusion within the walls of his college it struck him that it was time for him to see a little of the world, and he accepted an invitation from an early pupil who was entertaining a large party in a great country-house. At dinner he sat next to the young lady of the house. Their conversation fell upon baths, and she happened to mention that she took a shower-bath every morning to invigorate her system, adding, when he inquired what a shower-bath was, that it resembled a very small round room; that the bather stood in the centre of it, and upon pulling a string was at once drenched by a sudden flood of water from above. Next morning the recluse rose at his usual hour, six o'clock, and, being of an inquisitive temper, thought it well to explore carefully what he had never seen before, a large country-house. On pulling open a door he found himself at the entrance of a very small circular apartment — one of those in which housemaids store away old brushes and household articles past their work. In the centre of it stood a plaster cast of the Venus of Medici. The venerable man recoiled, closed the door, and walked in the park till summoned by the breakfast bell. He took his seat, and his host asked whether he would have tea or coffee. But he had reflected on what good manners imperatively required; and his answer was: "My lord, I can neither partake of tea, or coffee, or any other refection, until I have first tendered my humblest apologies to the interesting young lady whom I now see dispensing the chocolate, and on whose sanitary ablutions this morning as she stood in her shower-bath I was so unfortunate as unwittingly to intrude."

It was in the earlier half of September, 1831, that I met first the man of the greatest intellect that I have ever known, and between whom and myself there sprang up what may be called a friendship at first sight, he being then in the twenty-seventh year of his life, and I in the eighteenth of mine. My new friend was Professor Hamilton, better known as Sir William Rowan Hamilton, "Astronomer Royal" in the Dublin University. I had often heard of him as the prodigy of that university, one who on entering it had sent in an essay written in fourteen or fifteen different languages, most of them Oriental, Greek being the latest which he had learned; and who during his course at Trinity College had successively carried off every prize open to his competition, whether in classics or in science. At the age of twenty-two he had published a mathematical essay, "Systems of Rays," of which one of the chief men of science then living pronounced that "it had made a new science of mathematical optics."

It was impossible for the most careless observer not to be struck by him at once. One's first impression was that he was a great embodied intellect rather than a human being. Wordsworth wrote of Coleridge as "the rapt one of the godlike forehead," but it could not have been more marvellous than Hamilton's. The moral expression of his countenance corresponded with the intellectual. What it indicated was, when there was nothing to disturb him, an unbounded reverence. It was as if his constant recollection of what is above us rendered him but half conscious of the things around. The nobility of his forehead, which alone arrested one's attention, imparted a grandeur to a face otherwise not remarkable. There was also a dignity about him which came from his entire unconsciousness. His voice was a singular one, generally low-toned, but leaping up occasionally into a higher key upon some slight excitement.

It need hardly be said that with his habitual reverence there went a corresponding humility as regards himself, and an invariable courtesy in his intercourse with all others. He seemed always to think it likely that he might be mistaken, while in every neighbour, however full of infirmities, it was the human being that he saw, and one invested with all the rights and dignities which belong to humanity. Another quality which belonged pre-eminently to him was his absolute absence of all disguise. Some one remarked of him "Hamilton is simply transparent; his thoughts are as visible to you as the leaves of a tree close by and sun-smitten. It would be impossible for him to tell a lie even if he wished to do so, and he could no more conceal a thought than he could tell a lie." In that entire unguardedness there was something both attractive and pathetic; it was like a fragment from a world higher than ours — a virtue hardly suited to a world like ours, in which the unprotected must so often become the prey of the fraudulent and the wicked. Of Sir William Rowan Hamilton I may state Wordsworth's opinion. One night, while we stood beside his little domestic lake, Rydal, as it glistened in the beam of a low-hung moon, Wordsworth said, "I have known crowds of clever men, as every one has; not a few of high abilities, and several of real genius; yet I have only seen one whom I should call wonderful — Coleridge." He then added: "But I should not say that; for I have known one other man, a fellow-countryman of yours, who was wonderful also — Sir William Rowan Hamilton; and he was singularly like Coleridge."

One of the things most remarkable in Sir William Rowan Hamilton was the combination of qualities mental

and moral, seldom united.   In Coleridge the metaphysical
power existed in not less strength than the imaginative;
and though, no doubt, he owed great duties to so great a
faculty, and effected much to spiritualise the metaphysics
of his age, every lover of poetry must lament that he did
not for another dozen years give himself mainly to poetry.
Wordsworth once said to me that Coleridge's twenty-sixth
year was his " annus mirabilis," and that if he had not then
suffered himself to be drawn aside from poetry he must
have proved the chief poet of modern times.   But Sir William Rowan Hamilton's combination of the mathematical
gift with that for languages, and of both with the metaphysical, was a union more rare.   I used to see him reading the most arduous works of Plato in the original Greek,
wholly unconscious that the room was dinned by a somewhat noisy company.   When he had soared into a high
region of speculative thought — and it was there only that
he was quite at home — he took no note of objects close
by.   A few days after our first meeting, we walked together
on a road a part of which was overflowed by the river at
its side.   Our theme was the transcendental philosophy, of
which he was a great admirer.   I felt sure that he would
not observe the flood, and made no remark on it.   We
walked straight on till the water was half-way up to our
knees.   At last he exclaimed: "What's this?   We seem
to be walking through a river; had we not better return to
the dry land?"

Both at Adare and Curragh Chase I used to sit up with
him in his bedroom till near sunrise, while he held such
discourse as, I suppose, was the best compensation I could
have had for never hearing that of Coleridge.   His mirth-

fulness, however, was almost as strong as his speculative power. Once, just after he had admitted that some passages in Coleridge's writings were as obscure as they were profound (adding, however, that by patient attention he had found out the meaning of those passages, excepting one in "Aids to Reflection") I answered: "I know a lady who seems to have found no difficulty in his works, — Mrs. ——, that very gay and fashionable person you met lately. She spoke of the 'Aids to Reflection,' and I replied that it was a great book, I believed, but a long and difficult one. She answered, 'I will take it up to my room after breakfast.' She did so; brought it down at luncheon time, and told me she had read it, thought it a very pleasant book, and had found nothing difficult in it." He laughed till he could no longer stand. I early observed that his abstracted habits, while they kept him as ignorant of the world as he was indifferent to it, did not prevent his occasionally exercising a keen, if fitful, appreciation of character. He would refer to past incidents, which at the time he had not seemed to remark, with a singular, though never uncharitable, insight. His absence of self-confidence, as regards judgments on all subjects, was indicated by some unconscious modes of expression such as "I seem to myself to think."

His profound convictions respecting the Christian revelation, and also the truths of a spiritual philosophy, acquired an additional force from their contrast with his self-distrust in lighter matters. To all reasonable objections he listened with a deference which looked like a provisional and tentative consent. He approved strongly of Coleridge's revival of the scholastic terms "subjective" and "objective," though perhaps he would have been more careful than Coleridge was that the larger and more solid prerogative of the objective, where the latter was not confounded with the merely material, should not suffer from the aggressions of the subjective. I remember his once saying: "It is no conceit in a poet if he sees much more of interest in his own poetry than others see; with his associations it must possess more; but he should remember that the merit which it possesses at once for himself and for others is all the merit that belongs to it objectively." Theology interested him quite as much as philosophy, and at a somewhat later time, when "Church principles" began to be strongly asserted, he said that on philosophical grounds they had great claims on our religious consideration, and that he hoped to write an essay showing that, on the reasoning of Butler's "Analogy," they were in affinity with Christian ideas. When, however, some of those who had adopted High Church principles had made their submission to the Roman Catholic Church, he seemed to me to turn his attention away from that subject. His early training had, I think, given him in some degree the traditional prepossessions against the Roman Catholic Church common among Irish Protestants, not unconnected with past or present political conflicts. These I did not share, being already an ardent disciple of Edmund Burke, who asserted that there was no religious body in Europe which represented or at least resembled the early Christian Church so much as the Irish Catholic Chuch of his own day. I looked upon her as deeply wronged in the past, and as placed by the conse-quent political agitations of recent times under circumstances unfavourable to a right estimate of her religious character.

I could not, of course, but be drawn yet nearer to Sir William R. Hamilton by the profound affection which he felt for my sister almost from the first time that they met, a love recorded in several poems included in the admirable life of him by the Rev. R. P. Graves. His sympathies were perhaps at first attracted to her by the discovery that she had for several years felt the same enthusiasm for Coleridge as a poet which he himself had felt for him as a philosopher. If reverence, gratitude, and a cordial friendship could have been an adequate return for love, he might have been well satisfied; but we must remember Leolf's reply to Elgiva [1] when she had asked, "Is gratitude, then, nothing?" It was this: "To me, 'tis nothing, being less than love." Such love as his, however, whether fortunate or unfortunate in its immediate issues, could not but in the long run have proved "its own reward." She survived him for many years after he had entirely fulfilled the early promise of his youthful genius, and enjoyed a long career of deserved admiration and ennobling happiness; and to the end she retained the same gratitude for that early affection which I also felt at the time, and have never ceased to feel. She only met him once after he returned from Adare to his labours at the Observatory. I was more fortunate, and frequently visited him there, especially during my undergraduate course in the Dublin University.

When each examination was over, I hurried to the Observatory, and soon found the philosopher in his study,

[1] Sir Henry Taylor's "Edwin the Fair."

or in his garden, laid out by Bishop Brenkley, his predecessor, of whom he always spoke with a filial reverence.
"I am afraid I offended him," he said, "the first time we
met. I, then a youth of eighteen, sat next him at some
public luncheon. We did not speak, and I felt as if good
manners required that I should break the silence. My eye
happened to rest on a large map of Van Diemen's Land,
which hung on the wall. I turned to him and said 'Pray,
my lord, were you ever in Botany Bay?' The Bishop
turned half round to me with a displeased look, and only
replied, 'Eat your soup, sir, eat your soup!' He evidently thought I was inquiring whether he had ever been
transported. Such a thought had never entered my
head."

Sir W. R. Hamilton kept a headstrong horse, to which
he had given the name of "Comet," and used to gallop it
in circles, or perhaps in ellipses, round the lawn. On one
occasion he mounted him in Dublin, just after a curious
mathematical problem had suggested itself to him. The
horse took a mean advantage of his abstraction, and ran
away. "When I found it impossible to stop him," he
said, "I gave him his head and returned to the problem.
He ran for four miles, and stood still at my gate — just as
the problem was solved!" Another time, when the
country was disturbed, I found him practising with a
pistol. "It occurred to me," he said, "that if the Observatory were attacked, I ought to know how to defend it."
He had fixed a deal board on the garden wall, traced a
black circle on it, and marked the centre of that circle by
a blue periwinkle stuck in a hole. "Now you shall fire,"
he said, "and we shall see which of us can get nearest to

the mark." I had never fired a pistol before, and fired almost at random. By an odd chance the bullet went through the heart of the periwinkle, leaving the outward leaves stuck upon the board. We were both amazed, and I considered myself a heaven-born genius in regard to this new accomplishment. Why will not the successful stop in time? I fired again and again, but never could hit the flower, the circular space, the board, or, I believe, the wall itself!

The Royal Astronomer did not look through his telescopes more than once or twice a year! He used to say, "That is my deputy's business. The stars move all right; but what interests me is the high *mathesis* that accounts for their movements." He was so much occupied with the purely abstract part of science that its material phenomena interested him only so far as they revealed laws. This characteristic was remarkably illustrated by one of his best-known discoveries, that of "Conical Refraction." He read a mathematical paper before the Royal Irish Academy, demonstrating that under certain possible circumstances beams of light would be refracted, not as had ever been previously observed, but in the form of a cone. His statement was heard with wonder, and he was invited to verify his discovery by the aid of some instrument invented for that purpose; but he declined to make such an attempt, remarking that no experiment could add a certainty to mathematical demonstration. A considerable time afterward the desired instrument was constructed by Professor Lloyd, and after the discovery had been forgotten by most of those who had heard it announced, the radiant stranger leaped into palpable existence. When informed of the fact, Hamilton dryly made answer, " I told you so."

It was on the heights of mathematics that he breathed freely, and I used to see him writing his calculations from morning till late in the evening, almost without stirring from his chair, as rapidly as another could have written notes of invitation, and flinging each of the long foolscap sheets on the ground beside him. I have been assured by competent authorities that there existed but few mathematicians in Europe capable of reading and under-standing what had thus been so easily written. Many volumes of those compositions are said to exist in an unpublished form. I remember his telling me that on one occasion he had escaped from a fit of severe depression by resolutely rising into those regions of what he called " planetary contemplation." But I believe that on that occasion his meditations had belonged to the metaphysi-cal yet more than to the mathematical order.

His domestic life was brightened by children to whom he was devotedly attached, though his devotion to them sometimes combined with it an odd form of speculative interest. " That little boy," he once said, pointing to a boy of about five or six years old, " ran up to me the other day, and cross-questioned me about the mysteries in the doctrine of the Trinity. ' How,' he demanded, ' can there be three, and yet only one?' I answered, ' You are too young for such matters; go back to your top.' He flogged it about the passages a score of times, then returned to me and said, 'I have found it all out — this is the explanation,' and propounded his theory. 'You are wrong,' I answered; 'you are too young to

understand the matter; go and play.' He returned
three times more, successively, and each time propounded a new explanation, and received the same answer. But now listen! His four explanations of the
mystery were the four great heresies of the first four
centuries! He discovered them all for himself. I did
not give him the slightest assistance. What an intellect!"

The next year I repeated my visit, and Hamilton told
me another tale of his boy, but with less of paternal
triumph. 'I said to him last night when he was going
to bed, 'To-morrow Aubrey de Vere will be here; shall
you not be glad to see him?' He mused for some
time, and then made answer, remorsefully, 'Thinking of
Latin, and thinking of trouble, and thinking of God, I
had forgotten Aubrey de Vere.'"

In those days I saw Hamilton under various circumstances. On one occasion we made an expedition
together among the "wooded walls" of Wicklow's mountains, and ended by drinking their health. Then did our

> . . . flowing cups run swiftly round
> With no allaying Thames,

though we brimmed them frequently and only in part
from the Powerscourt cascade. When he looked at the
mountains he made as good remarks on them as Wordsworth could have made; when he was soaring in the
region of mystical philosophy, he saw them no more
than if he had been tracking the Sahara sands; and when
I told him amusing stories he flung himself on the heather
in convulsions of laughter. Our wanderings ended at the
hospitable country house of the Provost of Trinity Col-

4

lege, at Killiney, after leaving which he addressed to me a sonnet commemorative of them, of which I was very proud, and which included this striking line on music,

Problems of harmony proposed and solved,

which confirms the assertion often made that between music and mathematics there exist important relations. He introduced me to various friends worthy of his friendship. One of these was a lady who sang with remarkable pathos. She boasted to me that when she sang her first song to him he paid her no compliments, but stood listening while the tears ran down his cheeks. Another of these friends was the Irish poetess Felicia Hemans, whose poetry, rich in felicitous diction and metrical harmony, and always sustained by high thoughts and sentiments natural and elevated, if not now remembered as it deserves to be, was honoured by the praise of Wordsworth. He assigned to her a place among the poets whose successive deaths are the theme of that " Extemporary Effusion," which stands high among his later poems. She had passed a summer at Dove Cottage, close to Windermere, and there seen much of him; and when we called on her in Dublin she had just received a manuscript copy of his " Yarrow Revisited," copied for her by Wordsworth's daughter Dora. She read it to us, not in the musical chant which to him was natural, but with singular sweetness, significance, and an especial pathos when she came to the passages which marked that love borne by the poet, himself neglected so long, for him who had been from his youth " the whole world's favourite."

But a time was approaching in which themes such as occupied the great mind of Sir W. R. Hamilton were to lose their interest for all except a few, and all other utterances to be lost in one great political battle-cry. The cry was "Repeal of the Union." The great democratic battle had begun.

The low rumbling on the horizon became louder by degrees, and the interval between the flash and the sound became shorter. When, at the Clare election, a late surviving Irish chief, one of the largest of the Irish proprietors, and passionately loved by his tenants, saw them for the first time voting against him, and the other tenants follow their example, he declared in amazement that the country was "not fit for a gentleman to live in."

"The old order changeth, yielding place to new," was a warning more loudly proclaimed as the Repeal agitation went on. An election took place in the county of Limerick, and both sides prepared for the conflict. Nearly all the proprietors were banded together against Repeal and O'Connell, including the few who had advocated Catholic Emancipation. The candidate on the opposite side was a man of ancient family, excellent character, and not, I think, a Repealer, but it suited the Repeal game to support him, in order to separate the tenants from their landlords. Of these the most powerful by far was a certain nobleman, the Earl of K——, whose territories, 60,000 acres, with a rental of £46,000 per annum, extended through a large part of three counties, and included much of those Desmond lands, some 600,000 acres of which had been confiscated by Queen Elizabeth in a

single day. He was also, I believe, descended in the female
line from the "White Knight," to whom that title had been
given, after a battle fought many centuries previously, by
the then "White Knight's" father, the Earl of Desmond.

The despotic temper of the Earl of K—— was no doubt
increased by scenes which he had witnessed as a boy.
When he was but fourteen, during a great social gathering at his father's residence, a profligate neighbour, one
of the county gentry, though a married man, induced a
daughter of the house to elope with him. The moment
the crime was discovered, the Earl, accompanied by the
boy, went in pursuit of the criminal. After several days'
pursuit, the outraged father arrived, late in the night, at
an inn which the fugitives had reached a few hours previously. He got out of his carriage, accompanied by his
young son, and with a pistol in each hand mounted the
stairs. A door was pointed out to him. It was locked;
but the Earl kicked it open. A man rushed forward; the
Earl fired two pistols, and the betrayer fell dead at his
feet. The Earl was arraigned for this act before the Irish
House of Lords, and made no defence. The peers walked
processionally in their robes, and each as he passed the
throne, laid his hand on his breast and pronounced the
verdict, " Not guilty, upon my honour." A few years
later the boy witnessed another important event. He had
become a young officer; the Irish rebellion of 1798 burst
out, and with several other persons of importance he was
suddenly captured, and detained as a hostage. When
fortune turned against the insurgents, in the first rage of
disappointment a massacre ensued, and he had a narrow
escape from death.

When the family estates had become his own, the Earl is said to have ruled with a sway almost as absolute as that of one of his forefathers, who, as was reported, transported several persons to America on his own sole authority. The later Earl also was impatient of "the law's delays," and it was rumoured that if a tenant had in his opinion seriously misbehaved, he simply gave directions that his house should be pulled down about his ears. Notwithstanding, he was regarded as a "beneficent despot," and the handsome houses of his tenants, whose rents were never called exorbitant, excited the envy of all the neighbouring farmers. He built two churches in the neighbouring town — a Catholic one and a Protestant one — and near them stood a "hospital for decayed gentlemen and gentlewomen," supported by a charge on the estate of £1,200 per annum. He gave an immense amount of employment, and was honoured proportionately by the labouring class. He had been for a long time kept out of the family residence by the protracted life of his mother. On her death he sent at once for an architect. "Build me," he said, "a castle. I am no judge of architecture; but it must be larger than any other house in Ireland, and have an entrance tower to be named the 'White Knight's Tower.' No delay! It is time for me to enjoy." When the castle was half finished, a wealthy manufacturer built a huge chimney in the square of the town, which crouched beneath the hill on which that castle stood. The Earl sent him orders to pull it down or depart — two invitations which the man of business declined. The Earl drove down into the town, and, as usual, a crowd collected about his carriage.

He said: "I am come to wish you good-bye, boys. This place is but a small place, and there is not room in it for me and that man (pointing to the factory). He says the law is on his side, and I dare say it is. Consequently, I go to England to-morrow morning." During the night the lord of industry received a visit from uninvited guests; the next morning no smoke went over the the towers and the woods, and on the third day he had taken his departure. The great castle was finished, and there was one great house-warming.

No gathering of the sort ever succeeded in those stately halls. What succeeded was the Limerick election. As that election drew near, a rumour grew up that the fidelity of the tenants was not to be relied on; but few believed it. A neighbour of ours, himself a nobleman of large landed possessions, went to the new castle to consult with its lord, who greeted him with the inquiry, "Is —— in the field?" "No," was the answer; and the questioner resumed, "Then I set up my old friend M——," naming a popular country gentleman worth £10,000 per annum, who had lately built a house suitable to that income, on visiting which his friend at the castle commented on it thus: "The house is pretty; but what is the use of it? It is too large to hang at your watch-chain, and too small to live in." When the two peers had discussed the political symptoms of the day, the Earl of K——, dashing his hand loudly on the table, exclaimed: "Sir, I will tell you the simple truth of the case. The Irish people are gone mad! My father returned fourteen members of Parliament (he meant the Irish Parliament), and it is with difficulty that I return eight!" The loyalty of the tenant-vote was next touched upon. "That matter is settled," the Earl replied. "I have sent orders that the whole of my county of Limerick tenants shall ride into Limerick on the first day of election, and be the first to vote. Once they have set the example, the other fellows of course will follow it. I shall go into Limerick myself." He did so two days before the election, and each day he gave a banquet to the neighbouring gentlemen.

The Earl occupied the house of his friend, Lord Limerick, which, with the palace of the Protestant bishop, occupied one side of a court opening into a wide street. At the open window the Earl sat with the candidate he favoured. They were big and burly men both, and in high good humour, now quaffing a bottle of champagne, now leaning out and chaffing with the city mob, which cheered them to the echo, for it united the old Irish taste for chieftainship with the novel aspiration after democratic power. The rest of the room was filled with a fluctuating throng of country gentlemen, who brought in the latest news, and then amused themselves with the humours of the crowd. The appointed hour was sounded from the bells of St. Mary's Cathedral as merrily as on that morning when Sarsfield crossed the Shannon and burst the Dutch cannon. In mile-long cavalcade the K—— tenantry rode down Limerick's chief street; another and larger crowd cheered them and their fine horses, and doubtless that acclaim sent an exhilaration into their heads as potent as the fumes of champagne could have created there. After an hour or two a dulness began to spread over that gay apartment, and many talked in whispers. The Earl soon perceived that all was

not right, and its usual sternness returned to his strong
face. "You are hiding something from me," he exclaimed; "something has gone wrong; what has happened?" After a pause a gentleman moved forward and
replied, "My lord, what has gone wrong is this; the
K—— tenantry have voted." "What of that?" "My
lord, they have voted with the enemy to a man! The
other tenants are following their example. The election
is lost!"

I record these things as they were described to me
by those who witnessed them. The Earl travelled back
to his castle all night; at early dawn he reached it; but
it is doubtful whether the White Knight's Tower, as he
drove beneath it, smiled upon a defeated chief. During
the whole of that day he sat alone, speaking to none,
and seen by none. Late the second night the bell of
his bedroom rang without intermission, and a short time
afterward mounted couriers were scouring all parts of
his estates, commanding the attendance at a certain spe-
cified hour of all the tenantry in occupation of its 60,000
acres. When the appointed hour arrived, he sat enthroned on the dais, at one end of a gallery a hundred
feet long: his official persons were ranged near him in
a line at each side. What he intended to say to his
tenants has often been guessed at, but will never be
known. The tenants thronged in at the lower end of
the gallery, advancing nearer each moment, as their numbers increased, to where the Earl sat. His eye was fixed
upon them with that look for which it was famed, but
he spoke no word. Suddenly its expression changed;
he leaped from his seat, raised his arms on high, and

exclaimed: "They are come to tear me in pieces; they are come to tear me in pieces!" The next night but one he was in a madhouse. There he continued to live for many years, faithfully attended by a devoted wife; but he is said never to have had a lucid interval.

Thenceforth O'Connell became the one great power in Ireland. In his day he was in some respects misunderstood. Though a Repealer and a Democrat, he was the determined enemy of Jacobinism and all that warred against property law, or what has been called the "hierarchy of society." He had been educated in a French religious college during the French Revolution, and had early imbibed a lifelong abhorrence of Socialistic and Communistic principles. But while the movement for Catholic Emancipation had been a distinctly religious movement, and only after the long failure of pacific methods had thrown itself upon a stormier form of agitation the Repeal movement had from the first been a democratic one. If Catholic Emancipation had been conceded before the Waterford and Clare elections had shown the people their power, tenants might have continued to vote with their landlords for many a decade. But the lesson once taught could not be untaught; and as the proprietor class were almost all opposed to Repeal as dangerous to the unity of the Empire, so the Repeal agitation was from the first opposed to their political influence, while fully recognising their prescriptive proprietary rights. Year after year the most precious opportunities for cementing a "union of hearts" between the two countries were allowed by both the great English political parties successively in power to slip by. Both those parties wished well to

Ireland, and both passed measures for her benefit; but neither of them had sufficient sympathy with her to be wholly just. A chronic poverty weighed down a vast population wholly out of proportion to the means of subsistence; a "heroic" measure of State-aided emigration could alone have met that evil, and created in Ireland a clear stage for the ordinary operation of ordinary laws, social and economical; but the strong head and the strong hand needed for such a work were not found; and if they had been found, the rivalry of parties insensibly changing into factions would hardly have allowed fair play to such an enterprise.

I have already recorded the foresight with which my father prophesied the consequences of that neglect. On another subject he was not less clear-sighted, namely, the necessity, political at once and moral, for the creation of religious equality in Ireland, and that not by levelling down, but by levelling up. He would have had no secularisation of Church property—the patrimony of religion and of the poor—but he would have placed the Catholic clergy of Ireland in a position of entire equality with the Protestant, including the dignity and the security of their respective endowments. Till then, he maintained that there must ever remain a root for social and political uneasiness, a mutual jealousy which must vitiate the operation of the justest laws. So it turned out. The creation of the Queen's Colleges was a thoroughly well-intended measure, but its chief effect was to add to the Irish battles one more—that between "mixed" and "denominational" education.

CHAPTER III

IT was about in my eighteenth year that I began to
write poetry, though without any thought of publication, but with a wish to preserve a record of reflections on occurrences that had interested me. The subject
of these poems was seldom personal: some were de-
scriptive, some meditative, some political, as, for instance,
one suggested by the Reform Bill of 1832 — of which I
could then have been no judge.

My early poems were often cast in the sonnet form,
partly owing to my admiration for Wordsworth's, which,
if less stately than Milton's, seemed to me more thoughtful and wider in their sympathies. One of my earliest
was addressed to Coleridge. About the same time I
wrote an "Ode to Wordsworth," which affirmed that
there went forth from his poetry a mastering spirit that
pursued the reader long after he had laid down the book,
moulding his mental processes, as the murmur of the
sea pursues a man for hours after he has walked inland.
Boys take in with almost equal facility the most opposite
impressions. Only a year previously I had fallen in with
Byron's poetry, and read it for about a month. At the
end of that time, an inmate of the house said to me,
"What has flung that cloud over your face?" It was
the Byronic sulk! Wordsworth exorcised it.

I had happened to say to my father, "I suppose every
one knows that Byron is the greatest modern poet?"
He answered very quietly, "I do not know it." "Then
who is?" He replied, "I should say Wordsworth."
"And, pray, what are his chief merits?" He answered,
"I should say, majesty, and pathos, as, for instance, in
his 'Laodamia.'" I read 'Laodamia,' standing, to the
last line, and was converted. I seemed to have got upon
a new and larger planet, with

> "An ampler ether, a diviner air,
> And fields invested with purpureal gleams."

Shelley's poetry also had helped to deliver me from the
influence of Byron's. Our excellent tutor, Edward Johnstone, had written a critique on it. It was full of dis-
crimination, and did full justice to the poet's genius,
while deploring his religious errors. It made also large
quotations from his finest poems, including his "Hymn
to Intellectual Beauty," a confession of faith which occupies a position in Shelley's works analogous to that
which the "Ode on the Intimations of Immortality"
possesses, *mutatis mutandis*, in Wordsworth's. Soon
afterwards a present from an unknown donor was made
to my sister, a copy of "The Beauties of Shelley," with
her initials, E. de V., glittering on its green morocco
cover. She read aloud the "Ode to the West Wind,"
and a few evenings later, by the last light of a summer
evening, his "Adonais." About the same time I became
acquainted also with the poetry of Keats, Landor, and
Coleridge. We used to read them driving about our
woods in a pony carriage. The pony soon found us

out, and we had many hairbreadth escapes. Sometimes we read them by night to the sound of an Æolian
harp, still in my possession.

On one of those nights a boat lay on the lake at the
bottom of the lawn; I lay down in it, allowing it to
float wherever the wind blew it. Sometimes it got en-
tangled in weeds, and sometimes it was captured by a
woody bay. There I lay half asleep, till a splendid summer sunrise told me that it was time to get to bed. It
was all Shelley's fault. His was a sleepless spirit — the
worse for him, and probably for his poetry.

CHAPTER IV

OLD TIMES AND NEW [1]

IN a London club I once found myself ruminating thus: Everything here is very luxurious, doubtless, but the top of an Irish mail coach, even in winter, had something to say for itself. It was rich in discomforts, but we had a faculty that ignored them; and we were easily amused. Here everything is perfection; but perfection is often "mighty flat," as Paley remarked to the Archbishop of York. By degrees I fell into a reverie; and a day spent on the top of the coach between Limerick and Dublin, a bitter day in early March, presented itself to me again in all its quaint details. What is now a warm railway journey of about three hours, was then one that began at half-past seven in the morning, and ended at half-past ten at night.

The company on the coach's roof was a large one. Among the passengers was a gentleman with a merry eye and courteous demeanour, and two men of the farmer class, one apparently prosperous and a little sleepy, the other apparently unprosperous and somewhat bewildered. There was a pretty girl of about seventeen with a gladsome face and the manner of an Irish girl, at once trusting, modest, and shyly amused. There was an old priest reading his breviary, but glancing off it occasion-

---

[1] Recalled to my memory in part by old letters. With my Recollections connected with this particular drive, a few others may have mingled.

ally, unconsciously attracted by the humours of the road.
There was an old woman with an enormous basket of
eggs; there was a Protestant clergyman full of observation and vivacity; and there were not a few besides,
among others an English traveller with a well brushed
coat, and polished boots. A young attorney, with evidently strong political feelings, asked him many questions
as to what he had seen in Ireland. The questioner
affirmed that in Limerick the two things most worthy of
being seen were a pair of Limerick gloves, thin enough
to be crammed into a walnut shell, and the "Great Stone."
"The capitulation of Limerick was signed on this latter,"
he added, "solemnly promising Ireland a number of
grand privileges; but the promise has not been kept.
O'Connell and the Clare election cured all that, but
O'Connell's popularity will soon be a thing of the past,
for he has just refused to fight Lord Alvanley, who had
been defamed by O'Connell, and had sent him a challenge.
That challenge O'Connell has declined. His excuse was
as follows. 'Once when I was a young man I killed a
man in a duel; and I am sorry for it, for it was a sin,
and, besides that, I am now too old for such things. I
am also a family man with a wife and daughters, who would
have reason to complain of me if I was killed in a duel.'
The day after O'Connell's letter appeared in the newspapers, Dublin was placarded all over with this poem: —

"'O'Connell, averse to all slaughter,
    Exceedeth the Lord's command;
  For he honours his wife, and he honours his daughter —
    That his days may be long in the land!'

O'Connell's game is played out now!"

"That's a lie for them that say so!" exclaimed a shrill voice from the hinder part of the coach. "It will not be long before he gets the Union for Ireland, that is, I mean, Repale."

"And if we got Repale itself," murmured an old woman, "what good would that do to poor people like ourselves?" To which her neighbour replied, "Whist, you old ignoramus; sure you know well that if we got Repale on Saturday evening, tea would be down to one-and-twopence on Monday morning!"

A short time before there had been a fiercely contested Parliamentary election in Limerick. The Repeal party had recently met many successes on those occasions; but on that one it had sustained a defeat. There had been a division among its ranks; and I remember a clergyman, I will not say of what denomination, express-ing sad forebodings: "Our candidate is a fine fellow; but when the question is as to the price of a vote I am afraid he is a trifle *parsimonious.*" Votes went high. Earlier a freeholder had managed to get paid twice over. He had *plumped* for one of the candidates, and perhaps received what he regarded as the value of one vote only, not of two. He left the court, got three front teeth drawn, had his head shaved, put on a red wig, returned so disguised that nobody recognised him, and voted for the rival candidate.

Multitudes of election stories amused the company on the roof of the coach that day. One of those recorded how the foremost among a line of benches had been cov-ered with pitch and tar before the court was opened, and how, after the crowd rushed in pell-mell, the witless occu-

pants of that seat found it impossible, when the proceedings were over, to extricate themselves from it.
How, wherever they went, it followed them; while, of
course, they could not get through the doors, wedge
themselves sideways as they might, so that the cham-
pions of liberty had to present themselves in a very
undignified condition of partial undress to the mob in
the streets. While one of the two rival candidates was
" polling his good baronies," all depended on the celerity
with which he was able to register the favourable votes,
because the hour for closing the court was approaching.
The attorney at the opposite side interposed a dozen times
and successfully interrupted the proceedings, in spite of
the presiding magistrate, who threatened to send him to
prison, amid shrieks of renewed laughter. Some of these
interruptions were comical, especially the last. A freeholder had stood up to vote. The attorney at the opposite side sprang forward, and solemnly demanded of the
presiding magistrate, whether money might be lawfully
offered to voters in open court. " I must be brief," the
obstructionist continued, " for the time runs by. As yonder miserable man moved slowly to the place of his shame,
a well-known member of the landlord party, who stands by
the window behind the presiding magistrate, ostentatiously
took out his watch. It is a silver watch, but its internal
works are gold: he opened it deliberately; he caught
upon it the last beams of yonder descending luminary;
he flashed them into the eyes of that pallid wretch who
forgets that he has a country and remembers only that he
has a starving family — flashed it upon the gold, suggestive of a bribe!" In vain the magistrate rose to assert

the dignity of the court. The clock struck six and the proceedings broke up. On a later occasion the successful candidate, my brother, was congratulated after an odd fashion by an old friend. " I was the most vehement of your opponents, but as you have succeeded, and as we are old friends, I hope you will make me at least a resident magistrate." He was the fattest man in the county. His " old friend " regarded him from broad shoulder to shoulder and answered, " Make *you* a resident magistrate! I will make you *two!* "

" At all events," said the young attorney, " the popular party did their best. When they heard that the strongest tenantry in the county were coming into Limerick at six the next morning, they sent six " side-cars " to meet them with two orators on each, and two pipers pledged to set up their pipes whenever an opponent began his oration. They sent also a young clerk connected with the chief bank in Limerick, who was charged to say nothing, but to keep his eye fixed long on tenant after tenant. Those tenants knew well that he knew well how much cash each tenant had in the bank, and how many were well able to pay their rents."

Here began a political discussion which lasted an hour. And somebody averred that if, as their enemies asserted, the Irish had unnaturally hard heads, that was because the English had kept pounding their ancestors' heads for centuries. A story was here recounted of Sir Lionel O'Malachi. He was a member of the old Irish House of Commons, and had been stoned three times, but ineffectually, his skull having but become the harder on that account. On one occasion he was sitting under the gallery of the House while a stranger sat in it just above him. The stranger had brought a large wet umbrella, which projected beyond that gallery. During a great flight of Mr. Flood's eloquence the stranger kicked the umbrella and it fell, its sharp point striking perpendicularly on the centre of Sir Lionel's bald head. An Englishman must have perished on the spot. Sir Lionel only leaped up in a rage, and exclaimed, "Mr. Speaker! There's beastliness in this House, Sir! A gentleman in the upper gallery is after spitting on my head!" A loud laugh put an end to the stormy debate.

Soon afterwards a short delay took place. The hat of an old gentleman was blown off. He quietly put a skullcap in its place; but a young man who venerated age, jumped down, pursued the fugitive, and restored it with a low bow. The horses had not enjoyed standing still in the wind on the top of the hill. When we moved on again they ran away. A week before, a coach on the same road had suddenly divided into two parts, the hinder one falling upon both the legs of the coachman and pinning them to the ground. He died before it was possible to release him, but not before he had exclaimed, "Let them send after Mr. Bourne's horses; they will be destroyed if they are not stopped!"

In the meantime an intermittent conversation had arisen between the prosperous and the unlucky farmer. The latter complained that his landlord, "a fine, easy-going, gentleman," had recently sold a part of his estate to a retired shopkeeper, who at once doubled his rent. The other farmer said that he had told such a story of his distress to his landlord that his rent had been reduced by one-third, though he was bound to admit that it had always been a low rent. "Now," he said, "I can walk about the fields at my ease; I need never take my hands out of my pockets." "The end of that," said the attorney, "will be that in ten years more you will have nothing but your hands to put into your pockets."

At that moment the pretty girl with the modest but arch eyes, took out her rosary and began to say her beads. A Protestant clergyman beside her thought the opportunity a happy one for her conversion. "What is the name of this large bead?" he said. "A Pater Noster," she replied. "And what is the name of this small one?" "An Ave." "And those priests make you say ten Aves for every one Pater! Now you see how much more they think of Mary than of her Son! What but idolatry is that?" "Well," the girl answered, "I always thought that any one, even a parson himself, knew that one Pater was the equal of ten Aves any day." There was another laugh, and the controversialist took to studying the signs of the weather.

But the winds of controversy, once roused, are not quickly lulled. On this occasion it took a bantering turn. The old priest asked the controversial clergyman "Did you ever hear of the penal laws? An old Irish gentleman once told me how his family became Protestant. It happened thus. An infant was born in that household. His father said, 'We have fought the battle of religion for many a generation, and in consequence we have lost nearly all our property. If we continue the battle we shall lose the rest of it. Little Tom shall be brought up a Protestant. He will commit no sin, for he will only believe what he is taught; and I will commit none, for I shall die in the true Church.'" "This gets too serious," exclaimed the man next him," I will tell you a livelier story. There lived a poor groom in Dublin Castle. They insisted on his attending some religious service in the Castle chapel. The clergyman had reached a prayer to the effect that the magistrates might all administer justice indifferently, and that all the Lords of the Council might always hang together 'in accord and concord.' Poor Paddy forgot where he was, clapped his hands, and exclaimed at his loudest, 'Oh, then if I could see them hanging together in *any cord*, 't is myself would be satisfied."

The gladsome hour at last arrived, and we stopped to dine. We resumed our way. Our dinner had made us all so comfortable that polemics long kept at a distance. All our views of things were indulgent and hopeful. "What an improvement has been going on even in our time," somebody said. "In the last century nearly every gentleman was put to bed drunk. You had either to fight a duel or drink as others drank." I then remembered my father's once telling me how, when he was eighteen years of age, after a day's hunt, he had only avoided intoxication at dinner, by watching till the others were beginning to get tipsy, and after that, pouring each new glass of wine down his neckcloth, then worn so large that the chin was buried in it. When the last of the topers lay under the table, he rushed to his bedroom, took a bath, dressed again, and joined the ladies at their twelve o'clock tea. The next morning at breakfast, all the gentlemen rose when my father entered and received him as if he had been a prince. They had heard that he had been unaffected by the wine, and considered that so strong a head was entitled to the highest honours.

A member of our party enlarged on the improvement as regards cursing and swearing, and told how a highly respectable old clergyman, parson and squire in one, when his son was departing on the grand tour of Europe, admonished him thus: "Remember, Jack, your religious duties in whatever country you may be: that's a good plan, and a damned good plan;" and how the young jackanapes had responded, "Thank you, sir, I'll put a knot on my pocket-handkerchief that I may never forget them!" The execrations then common came from all classes. On one occasion he had himself heard a man in authority hurling on the head of a poor labourer, for some trivial offence, such maledictions as made his blood run cold; all present had trembled except the man on whose head they alighted. He answered very meekly, "Well, long life to your Honour; and I'll be praying that if your Honour does ever die, you'll go to Heaven!" "Why so?" said the offender, wiping a heated face with a dirty handkerchief, and a little touched. "Oh, then, because if your Honour does go to Heaven, it's a sure thing that we'll all go there!" A rapid smile passed from face to face except that of the girl with the rosary, whose thoughts had been wandering. "I wonder," she said, "where I will find my mother when we reach Dublin." "Do you not know where she is living?" "How would I know it?" Here there was a loud laugh, and an exclamation. "It will take you some years to find a poor woman in Dublin. Dublin is a big city!" "Well! God is good," was her reply.

Here the polemical clergyman made another attack on the girl with the rosary, but she found a zealous protector in an old humourist who evidently thought that his best means of dealing with such assailants lay in turning the attack against the aggressor's camp. He did so valiantly on this occasion, but as his stories carried with them a strong polemical animus, I do not think it necessary to repeat them at large, though some of them would illustrate the period I record. He ended thus: "Why do you gentlemen of the 'new light' always address your efforts to the starving poor, not to our celebrated divines? Was I not myself in that famous island of the West in which, as you affirmed, such a number of conversions had been made? There was only one respectable name among all the converts, and he was not a convert at all as it turned out. His own father had declared, it is true, that he would probably become one, but that was only because the young man had not only drained two wet fields, but also built a pigsty, and turned the pigs out of the kitchen. Now, what was the end of this renowned enterprise? When the original Protestants had heard that the new missionary was giving large sums to starving Catholics for professing to be Protestants, perhaps in part himself taken in, they went to him and said, 'What a cruel taste you have for bad Protestants! It seems that you think nothing of us who are the real Protestants, and stuck to our faith in the worst times. Not one of them has ever seen a penny of your money! Tell us at once what you are going to give us for *remaining where we are!* But perhaps you do not think that we and our little families are worthy of any consideration at all!' This adventurer had made such a reputation for conversions that he could not afford to lose it by desertions. He had in the end to pay the rogues — first one and then another — three times as much for remaining where they were as he had paid to the bad Catholics for changing; and yet he had nothing to show for his money. In the end he found himself a ruined man and had to fly from the island leaving his debts unpaid ! "

The next story, told by the sharp young attorney, was unpolemical. " I have heard it said that during the earlier part of what is facetiously called the Irish Rebellion of '98, some of the King's troops in Ireland did not fight particularly well. General T—— was named among these. It may amuse our distinguished English guest to hear a story connected with him. When that war was over, and all went gaily as a marriage bell, the lord and lady lieutenant gave a grand party in the Phœnix Park. All the nobility were there; but of course none of the poor people. Notwithstanding, a beggar woman forced her way into the circle, asking for charity, which General T—— regarded as unseasonable. To his admonitions she replied, ' It is I that am proud to see your Honour here in the red coat you wore the very day when you saved the life of my boy, little Mickie ! ' ' Indeed ! ' replied the General, not sorry to hear anything to his credit on such a distinguished occasion, ' I had forgotten all about it. How did I save his life ? ' ' Well, your Honour, when the battle was at the hottest, your Honour was the first to run ; and when me little Mickie saw the general run, he ran too, and only for that he 'd have been killed ; and many an honest boy was killed there that day, the Lord be praised! 'Nonsense!' said the coachman, 'there was no danger that day!' The old beggar was of a different opinion. 'No danger,' she repeated, 'what can be more dangerous than death?'"

All stages of civilisation have their own advantages and disadvantages. When I was a youth, the hall door of our house was left open all night, and property ran no danger. Not very long ago I passed a night in a country house a few miles from Bath. The party consisted largely of elderly ladies. An hour or two after they had retired to rest I observed that the moonlight lay in extraordinary beauty upon the pleasure ground. I could not resist the temptation of walking up and down the sward, and tugged at the lock of the hall door. In a few minutes more, innumerable bells began to clang in all parts of the house, high and low. A short time more, and numberless bedroom doors opened, and shouts were heard of " Fire " and " Robbers." The ladies had not given themselves time to add much to their night apparel; and for the most part their merits did not consist in youthful beauty. It was an awful sight! All this confusion was my doing! That one luckless tug had set a ramification of bells, extending all over the house, into a storm of action. Yet this protection against robbers was needed in the most civilised of lands. " O Ireland," I exclaimed, " barbaric Ireland! How little were thy merits appreciated in the days before railways! "

But to return to old times — I must admit that coaches too had their imperfections. It had become quite dark, and again the horses ran away. We were approaching the bridge of Naas, which is a singularly dangerous one even in broad daylight, the scene, indeed, of many a sudden death. We heard the coachman say to the gentleman next him, "Please, sir, place both your hands strongly outside mine: my fingers are getting numbed. I hope we shall not go over a stone." Fortunately the horses thought better of it before they had reached the bridge. Persons who had ceased for ten minutes from loquacity became eloquent again: persons who had heartily forgiven their enemies, or sincerely, though silently, asked forgiveness of any whom they had ever injured, cheated, maligned, disedified, or otherwise offended, retracted rash vows and reasserted their natural liberties. Conversation was resumed. The first subject discussed was why, after the calamities of so many centuries, the bridge of Naas had not been reformed in this age of "improvement." Nobody knew.

It had rained severely for the last two hours, and I heard the cracky voice of an old gentleman saying, "Sir, I request. that you will remove the iron rib of your umbrella from between my neckcloth and my neck." Next a loud rattle revealed to us that the drag had got loose. The guard crept under the coach to replace it. We soon heard him at work; but the rain being now very heavy, we could not but think him rather long about his labours. So thought the coachman, who thrice shouted to him, "Pat, are you ready?" and received for answer, "Wait a minute, Jack," with a renewed clattering of the drag-chain. At last the coachman's remonstrance took a more reasoning tone. "Well, Pat, if you got down under the coach that you might shave yourself before driving into the great city of Dublin, it's a wonder to me that you would not wait till you could get a little soap along with the water."

At last we were driving into Dublin. As we passed from the dusky suburbs into a well-lighted street, some one exclaimed, "I am sorry for that poor motherless girl who does not know where to find a roof over her head this wet night!" As he spoke a cry of delight was heard. "That's mother! I saw her face in the window: let me down!"

The coachman stopped, and within a minute more the girl was in her mother's arms. The great clock of the post office struck half-past ten as we drove into the central court. A shout rose from the crowd assembled there. The guard made the response, "Now that you have seen the great Limerick coach come in, you may go to bed with a good conscience; and if you are wet, I give every man of you liberty to drink my health in three tumblers of whisky-punch — at his own expense!"

CHAPTER V

MY SISTER'S MARRIAGE — 1835

My Sister's Marriage — Dromoland — The O'Brien Race — Sir Edward
O'Brien, the direct Descendant of Brian the Great, King of all Ireland
— The Parish Priest wins his " Little yellow Pony " — Sir Edward takes
great Offence at being told that he is likely to live longer than his
Ancestors — The last Irish Chief — His Character — " The pleasant
Dromoland Days " — A remarkable Conversion — The Clare Coast —
Miltown Malbay — Kilkee — The. Cliffs of Moher — The Caves of
Ballibunion — Augustus Stafford O'Brien — The good Priest, and the
young Man who had committed a Murder and resolved to surrender
himself to Justice.

IN the year 1834 my only surviving sister was married
to Robert O'Brien, the fourth son of Sir Edward
O'Brien, of Dromoland, a marriage to which she owed
the chief happiness of a long and happy life, for he was
worthy of her, and possessed all the qualities most useful
for the husband of one whose fine sensibilities and un-
certain health rendered protection especially requisite.
She was too much wrapped up in others to be a protector to herself; but whatever she lacked in that respect
was made up to her by the vigilant tenderness of her
husband, by his sound judgment, his energy, high principles, and manly cheerfulness. His sisters also were as
devoted to her as she was to them. They were all of
them delightful in their respective ways, and one of
them, Mrs. Charles Monsell, became in her widowhood
well known as the foundress of the Anglican Sisterhood

of Clewer, and of very numerous Houses connected with it in several parts of the British Empire and America.

But the most original and remarkable of the family was the head of it, Sir Edward O'Brien. He was the direct descendant of Brian the Great, King of all Ireland, who at the Battle of Clontarf put down for ever the dominion of the Danes in Ireland; and he was therefore the chief representative of a family which, for many centuries before either Dane or Norman had trodden Irish soil, had held sovereign rule over Thomond, or Northern Munster. After the sovereignty had long ceased, the chieftainship had remained; it was as an Irish chief that Sir Edward O'Brien was regarded by the masses in Old Thomond, and I have seen no other who reminded me so much of one. I sketched his character in one of my "Legends of St. Patrick" under the name of "King Eochaid." The combination in him of qualities often antagonistic must have struck any one at once on meeting him. His manner was at once authoritative and good-natured. He was habitually frank; yet he could be reserved too with those whom he distrusted; he had great acuteness, and it amused him to shew it. He had a great love for his country; but much of its noisier political life he regarded as more often a mixture of the game and of the jest than as the serious expression of political convictions. He had a child's simple respect for religion, but a great dislike to those controversies which had so long inflamed the animosities of race or class in Ireland; and when he spoke on religion, he sometimes said: "I never feel so devout as when I hear a ripening corn-field murmur in the wind;

it makes me say to myself, 'God is preparing bread
for His people.'"

He was ardently attached to his family, and especially
to his wife, who was devoted to him, though she could
not understand his not sympathising with the zeal with
which she strove to diffuse her Evangelical opinions,
both by speech and pen. With her active mind and
benevolent heart, she long had "judged the Israel of the
County Clare," as some one remarked, and probably much
increased the seriousness, if not the orthodoxy, of its
higher class; but her proselytising efforts among the
poor were ineffectual. They respected her motives, and
were grateful for her generosity; but preferred their an-
cestral faith to hers. I remember an amusing instance
in which her zeal produced an effect very different from
that intended by her. A neighbouring Catholic priest
had heard that Sir Edward O'Brien intended to sell his
"little yellow pony," and had called at Dromoland in
the hope of being allowed to buy it. As Sir Edward
and he sat together, Lady O'Brien came into the room
with a number of tracts under her arm, and demanded
of the priest what he considered that St. Paul had meant
by a certain text. The priest replied with perfect respect
that he would rather not engage just then in a theological
argument, having other things on hand, and indeed better
things. Lady O'Brien asked another question, producing
one of her tracts, and received a similar answer. Sir
Edward then interposed a little warmly, — "Lady O'Brien,
I beg you will let this gentleman alone! He did not
come here to chop texts with you, but to see if he could
buy my little yellow pony!" The lady, however, was

not to be daunted. Again and again the attack was renewed, and again the battle was respectfully declined. At last Sir Edward jumped up and exclaimed, "Now, Charlotte, I'll tell you what it is! This reverend gentleman, as I informed you before, did not come here for a controversy with you, but to buy my little yellow pony; and he has been worried and molested in my house; and now I will not let him buy the pony, for I will make him a present of it. He shall not pay me a farthing!" The lady departed with her tracts, and the priest with the little yellow pony — the latter probably the better contented of the two.

Everybody who knew Sir Edward respected and loved him. His tenants adored him, and never married a daughter without asking his consent, which he always gave, and a wedding gown besides to the girl. He was full of little oddities; but what would have given mortal offence from another, gave none from him. Once when, in a fit of irritation, he had spoken roughly to some labourers, a certain formalistic relative reproached him. "You speak to them like dogs!" His answer was: "And don't you think they would rather be treated like dogs by me, than like gentlemen by you?" Sir Edward was full of quaint wilfulnesses. One day, as we sat after dinner over the wine and walnuts, he remarked, "I have just been thinking that this is the year that I have to die in." My father replied: "Nothing of the kind, Sir Edward; I never saw you better. You will probably live another dozen years." Sir Edward was highly provoked. "Do not say that, Sir Aubrey," he rejoined; "the head of our family always dies at the age I have now reached.

It is our way; and I don't want to change it." Soon afterwards he spoke with more interest on some trivial topic of the day.

His death occurred that year as he had predicted. It was attended with little suffering, and as little alarm on his part, a circumstance which reminded me of a remark which I had once heard made, namely, that although in his youth a very lax and unscrupulous sort of society had largely prevailed in Ireland, there had always remained a singular innocence about him. The morning of his death he read his county newspaper at the usual hour. Later, he lay with closed eyes upon his pillows, murmuring at intervals, "His mercy endureth for ever." At last he passed away without a struggle. During several days the poor trooped up to the Castle from all parts of his wide estates; and leaving their shoes outside the walls, mounted the stairs in silence, drew near to the bed in reverence, and bade their last adieu to one so many years beloved and revered. They bent and kissed him on brow and breast; and, departed, whispering, "The Lord be merciful to him!"

I shall never forget Sir Edward O'Brien, or meet another like him. His stature was low, and his eye of the paler Irish blue, his accost abrupt but friendly, his questions innumerable, his sympathies ready, and he harboured malice against none. In his own neighbourhood he found himself accepted as a sort of prince; but if he therefore regarded himself as one, it did not make him vain. One virtue often ascribed to princes he had in an eminent degree; that of speaking his mind to every one, high or low. When the Marquis of Anglesea, then Lord Lieutenant, paid him a visit, the first thing

he did after welcoming him to Dromoland, was to read
him a sharp lecture on his misgovernment. "Several of
our country gentlemen have seen their lawns turned up
by wild marauders, and potatoes planted in them; how
would you like to see Beaudesert treated in that fashion?"
I well remember my own first meeting with him when I was
about twenty years of age. He was seated on a sofa, after
returning from his daily ride, a little tired, with his left
foot unbooted, and tenderly nursed on his right knee.
As I entered he addressed me. "I suppose you are
Aubrey; I am told you write poetry. Is that a fact?"
I assented, and he continued: "I have no opinion of
you minor poets! I respect Pope, and Dryden, and
Milton; but that is because they have received the
sanction of public opinion. I think very little of you
minor poets."

For several years after my sister's marriage, Dromoland
was her home. That circumstance, and the great love
borne to her by all its inmates, caused an unusually warm
affection to spring up between the two families; — such an
intimacy as could not have continued long, if our new
friends had not been among the most genial and true-
hearted of human beings. Every few months we used
to rejoice at the sight of the huge old Dromoland landau,
with its four horses, making way up our approach after
a journey of above thirty miles; and the visit was always
soon returned. I used to read poetry to the young people
nearly every morning; and each afternoon we had a long
ride over the roads that wound among the craggy hills of
Clare, with their vivid Irish green over-blown by salted
breezes from the sea, and their numerous ruined Border

6

towers. These rides were often to the country seats of the neighbouring gentry, nearly every one of which boasted a lake, pronounced by the geologists to be the crater of an extinct volcano — the land itself having thus, apparently from the first, partaken of the "perfervidum Scotorum ingenium." Those happy Dromoland days remained till the family dispersed on the death of its head; but the recollections connected with them are bright still.

One of the incidents connected with those days was a remarkable one, and one which at the time excited a wide interest. Edward, the third son of Sir Edward, a lawyer, was a man of very striking qualities. His character was one of singular benevolence and candour; and his intellect possessed a remarkable speculative activity. He had a strong tendency to doubt, though fortunately one not proceeding from pride of intellect; and his life at Cambridge had not diminished that tendency. A few years later, when practising in Dublin at the bar, he lost his faith altogether, that is as far as a man can be said to have lost a faith which he laments to lose. Though that loss had been a gradual one, he had neither the hardness nor the levity of those who incur it almost without feeling it. He wrote to many among the ablest of his friends, and to several remarkable men besides, such as Southey, Archbishop Whateley, and the Archbishop Trench of a later day, asking them what help they had to give him; and the correspondence was a very interesting one. He still believed that Christianity was a great support to the moral law and to human happiness; yet, notwithstanding, he could no longer believe in its divine claims.

After the lapse of a considerable time he met at Dromoland an old friend, and they conversed one evening on the subject of Christianity. There being little time for a theme so vast, they agreed to confine their discussion to a single point. Edward's friend admitted the difficulties of Christian theology when regarded from the standpoint of the human understanding alone, but remarked that Christianity itself admitted, or rather asserted as much, and distinctly affirmed that it could only become intelligible when "spiritually discerned" through the joint action of faith with the higher reason and conscience. Why should not these faculties co-operate, and thus enable us to reach heights which neither could reach by itself? In science, the lower faculty, the experimental, suffices to enable us to deal with mechanics and chemistry, but we could never have soared to the Copernican astronomy unless the intuitive or mathematical faculty had co-operated with the lower or experimental one.

Now comes the marvel. Any one can use the expression "spiritual discernment," but no one, even if he possesses it, can impart it to another. Edward was too philosophical to deny the possible existence of an unknown faculty; but from the moment when he heartily accepted its possibility, that possibility changed with him to probability, next to certainty; and then he began apparently to use it. He had fortunately early acquired an intimate acquaintance with the Holy Scriptures. Successively he began to quote passage after passage, illustrating them as seen from a spiritual point of view. Each of them shone out on him with an unsuspected radiance, and flung that radiance upon another passage. Doctrine after doctrine disclosed a meaning wholly distinct from that one which lay upon its surface, and each meaning seemed in entire harmony with the other. After a time, in place of saying "the inner meaning *may* be this," the phrase changed to " *must* be this."   By degrees he seemed to discover that he had been living in two worlds at the same time — a Christian world, and a natural world that hung over the Christian world like a mist; now hiding it, now in part disclosing it. One of the things that seemed to surprise him most was the absolutely new meaning which the Christian creed imparted to the Humanities. All the ties of life seemed, he said, to speak of higher ties. Every moment, as the cloud lifted, he spoke with a stronger insight, but not with the slightest excitement; on the contrary, there was a still and grave self-possession about him.   In the meantime that higher world seemed by no means to hide the lower. The strange thing was that it should itself have been so long hidden.

His friend could only listen and wonder. The teacher had become the taught and had learned much more respecting " spiritual discernment " than he knew before. He also understood better than before the full meaning of the assertion, "Religion and Reason are alike *their own evidence* " — that is, principally, not exclusively.

At last the sun rose, and the friends retired to rest. That morning there was a something in Edward which his family had never seen in him before — a perfect placidity, a perfect content, and an unusual affectionateness.   He told them of the entire change in him on the question of religion.   That change seemed to extend to everything touched by it. Not only all the ties of human life, but much besides seemed to bear for him a symbolic moral significance. This was the more remarkable because he had always professed to be, and was regarded by others, a man essentially unimaginative. If any friend doubted whether a change so rapid was likely to be permanent, that doubt could not have lasted long. The new conviction was one plainly proof against everything. His nature had been an anxious one; but all anxieties passed away and never returned. Soon after that change there occurred to him what in past times would have been a great calamity. He seemed hardly to feel it. Yet he showed no tendency to religious excitement. All the great doctrines of the Apostles' Creed he held with an unwavering faith. Notwithstanding, Edward was no mystic. It was chiefly in its most practical point of view that he looked upon Christianity—as the help of the helpless, and the hope of the hopeless, as that Truth and Righteousness in which each man should walk and aid his neighbour to walk. He had little confidence in anything that can be effected by argument; but he witnessed faithfully and simply to what he knew and felt of Truth. He wrote a remarkable work entitled "The Lawyer," in opposition to those disingenuous, forensic arts, practised by many in deference to the traditions of the legal profession. He devoted himself to charities, and established, through his ceaseless labours and large pecuniary aid, a "Night Refuge" for the destitute poor in Dublin, many of whom then passed their nights in the streets; and one that, after the lapse of more than fifty years, continues to shelter the roofless. He married, and had a happy home. Soon afterwards he died of a fever, most likely caught in his charitable labours. Some will perhaps smile at such a conversion; but his were the qualities, especially those of good-will, simplicity, and an ardent search after truth, to which truth is promised, and by which, when won, it is used aright.

After one of our visits at Dromoland we passed to Miltown Malbay, a spot on the Atlantic coast celebrated for its strengthening breezes, and thought likely to benefit my mother's health.   There we found a very large hotel, then inhabited chiefly by the winds.   The scenery was, though forlorn, yet of pathetic beauty.   The sea was of the deepest purple.   Along the coast there extended a long range of sand-hills that strangely mingled the melancholy with the sublime.   Those sand-hills were warmed by the sunbeams, and brightened by small yellow pansies and violets.   We found a sleepy pleasure in walking among them, and listened to the whispering of the mighty sea beyond, waxing stronger as we ascended them, and lessening as we descended.   Several miles from us was a scene of a very different character, namely, the cliffs of Moher, compared with which those of Kilkee with their darksome masses of marble, their cave, and their reefs, were trivial things.   The cliffs of Moher are six hundred feet in height, commanding for about five miles a view of Galway's glorious bay and Arran's saintly isles, still true to the memory of St. Enda.   My father wrote, in connection with the cliffs of Moher, of Kilkee, and of Miltown Malbay, not a few of those sonnets which Wordsworth praised so highly.   Here is one of them: —

> " And O ! ye solitudes of rocks and waters,
>   And med'cinable gales, and sounds Lethean !
>   Remote from strife, and fratricidal slaughters !
>   Have I not sighed to hear your mighty pæan

Reverberating through the empyrean!
And yearned to gaze while your white-throated surges
Leap and dissolve in air, like shapes Protean
That sport in the sunset as the moon emerges
Over the sea-cliff? Have I not felt the longing
Then most intensely when the storm-steed rushes
O'er the wild waves tumultuously thronging:
Smiting their wan crests—scattering as he crushes—
To stand on some lone rock; and hear from under
Its caverned base the Ocean's melancholy thunder?"

The largest sea-caves in the neighbourhood are those
at Ballibunion, near the mouth of the Shannon — there
eleven miles wide — which divides the counties of Limerick and Clare. No single one of those caves is nearly
as large as Fingal's Cave at Staffa, but the number of
them atones for this defect. It is a submarine palace,
consisting of multitudinous halls, opening out each into
another, as one's boat glides along under roofs now green
as grass in the sun, and now blood-red. The visitor
needs a good guide, for the labyrinth of caves is an intricate one. The sea is insidious in its ways. On one
occasion, soon after a party had entered, the boatman
suddenly shouted, "Bend down your heads for your
lives!" No one saw any danger, but the boatman felt
the placid water insensibly rising, and knew that the tide
had turned. At last the visitors knew this too; for it
was not till the boat had ascended to within a few inches
of the roof, that it began to descend. "Pull your best,"
exclaimed the man at the helm; "if the second wave
reaches us we are lost." But before the second wave
had reached the cave they had issued from its mouth.

There is one old friend who always has a part in my

recollections of Dromoland, namely, Augustus Stafford O'Brien, called later O'Brien Stafford. His family came from the Dromoland stock, but had long resided at one of their English homes, Blatherwick, in Northamptonshire, which for several years he represented in Parliament. When in Ireland, he was always a welcome guest at Dromoland, to which his joyous spirits and brilliant wit added an additional brightness. In societies of the most different sorts he was a favourite, as he had been at Cambridge, especially among that body quaintly named "The Apostles." Of these, Richard Monckton Milnes was perhaps his closest friend; but closeness sometimes produces friction, and so it happened to them. They used to quarrel and make friends; but the friendship lived on, though it lived an uneasy life, and I remember some one amusing Milnes by inquiring, "Does that old friendship between you and Stafford continue to rankle on still?"

Of R. M. Milnes I have written in his published biography. Augustus Stafford made one of the most admired speeches in opposition to Sir Robert Peel's great Free Trade measure in 1846, and on the accession of the Tories to power, he was made Secretary to the Admiralty. Soon afterwards he was violently assailed for requiring, on behalf of the Government, the votes of a certain class of officials in the dockyards. The same claim had always been made and conceded previously, but just then one of those sudden accesses of virtuous indignation to which public opinion is liable fell upon it; and the storm raged. Immediately Milnes was found at his old friend's side, shouting "Hypocrites!" The onslaught

was taken philosophically by Stafford; and his unpopularity was of short duration. The Russian war broke
out not long afterwards, and later the cholera raged
fiercely in the Crimea, and especially in the French
ships. Stafford, then in the East, ministered assiduously
among their sick crews, at the imminent risk of his own
life, having previously handed over whatever money he
had at his disposal for the increase of their comfort.
The poor fellows were very grateful to him, and always
called their English benefactor " ce cher Monsieur
'Damn me.'"[1] The French Emperor wrote him a hearty
letter of thanks; and on his return to London he found
himself one of the most popular men there. If he had
lived, he must have risen high in the political world.
His extraordinary brilliancy, versatility, and wit, made
him much sought in society, including Royal society, and
especially his skill as an amateur actor; but he was beginning to be tired of gaiety, and daily gave himself
more to business, serious reading, and practical kindness
to his poorer Irish neighbours at Cretloe. He stood
once for the county of Limerick, but lost the election.
He had singular beauty of face and person, and, besides
being rich in accomplishments, possessed a rapidity of
mind I have never seen equalled. His life was spotless,
and his religious belief strong—that of the High Church
school. That belief seriously affected his literary tastes.
He was a passionate admirer of Wordsworth; while of
Byron he wrote to me: "Is it not deplorable to think
what mischief Byron did to that noble thing, the Youth
of England?"

[1] Their name for an Englishman.

Among my Recollections associated with the wild
Atlantic coasts, I must include one connected with a
priest, who may be regarded as no inapt representative
of a large class among the Irish Catholic clergy of that
day, and one perhaps not easily met out of Ireland. He
was not a politician, and he was the last man to claim
for himself the title of a saint. Neither, probably, did
he expect that his parishioners should be all saints; but
he required that they should be good Christians. He
was also very zealous as to their education, especially in
the case of some among them for whom he gave it a
certain scientific tinge. I will record an incident in his
career told to me by the person to whom he narrated it
(seeing nothing remarkable about it), as they drove on a
" side-car " beside Dingle Bay in a storm of rain.

He had attended a fair, in a village not far from his
abode. Some one had just bought a horse at it, and
the priest, who rode well, was urged to show off its action,
and ride it over a wall that divided the village green from
a low-lying bog. He did so, but as he dropped into
the bog a pallid and haggard youth, leaped up almost
from under the horse's feet, and fixed his eye upon its
rider. The priest looked steadily at him in turn : " Are
you not the boy that I used to take out shooting with
me so long ago to carry my game? — the boy I taught
to shoot?" " I am," was the answer; " and bad luck to
the first day that ever your Reverence taught me to fire
a gun. I am the man that shot Mr. ——, the agent, a
year ago. The police have been hunting me ever since,
but they have never come upon me. It's small trouble
I'll give them in future. I'm better pleased to die than

to live. I'm tired out; and I can't bear the pain I have in my heart any longer; and I'm come here to give myself up."

"Is it to be hanged you have come here?" said the priest. "It is, then, to be hanged, your Reverence." The priest replied: "My boy, it is a very serious thing to die, and meet one's God. I'm afraid it's a long time since you were at Mass and that you have forgotten your religion. Let me hear now if you can say the Apostles' Creed." The youth strove to recite it, but failed. "This is a strange thing," the priest rejoined. "Here is a man who does not know a B from a bull's foot, and yet he thinks he is fit to be hanged! Where are you living, my boy?" "I am living down there, your Reverence, about a mile to the west." The priest answered, "I will go to you every night about ten o'clock; I'd be afraid of going before it is dark, for I might be hanged myself as an accomplice; and as it is, that's likely enough, if they come upon us." Every night the priest visited the self-condemned youth, and taught him the fundamental truths of the Christian faith, adding this promise: "As soon as ever I find you are fit to be hanged, I will tell you so. Till then, don't dare to do anything of the kind."

Many nights in succession the priest visited his penitent, many more, it is likely, than were necessary, but after the forgotten religious knowledge had been restored (the faith had never been obliterated) his spiritual adviser was solicitous that sufficient time should elapse to allow that restored knowledge to ripen into the corresponding spiritual dispositions, and that repentance which is but remorse to pass into that true Christian repentance which rises out of love and is consoled by love. It is probable also that he had become much attached to the friend whom he was daily helping, at the risk, as he believed, of his own life, and did not wish to hasten the moment of their separation.

One night, however, before giving the youth his usual parting blessing, he said: "I promised, my boy, to let you know when I considered you fit to be hanged; and now I have the satisfaction of assuring you that I never knew a man fitter to be hanged than yourself. But first I have another thing to tell you, which I did not tell you before now, for reasons. You are not obliged in duty to go and inform against yourself at all. It is the duty of the police to arrest you, and they are paid for it. At the same time, my boy, you have to understand that if you choose to give yourself up and suffer for your sin, there is no crime in that, but rather a merit; as in that way you will be giving a warning to all poor foolish boys to mind themselves and not fall into any sin, and especially any grievous sin. So, you see, you are free and can use your own discretion." "I'll give myself up, Father, on Monday, when the magistrates meet, in the name of God." "May the Lord strengthen your heart, my boy, in that hour. You know in whom is all our trust — the Redeemer of the World."

The youth gave himself up. He was transported, not hanged.

CHAPTER VI

ADVENTURES IN SWITZERLAND IN 1839

Hairbreadth Escapes, and quaint Incidents — Perilous Places and no Guides — Black Night in a Forest — A broken path on a Cliff-side during a midnight Storm — The Lake of Brienz — Interlaken — A storm on Monte Moro — Lost in the Snow — Tempest — Saved I never knew how — A patriotic Irishman's Depreciation of Switzerland — The Lake of Tegernsee — Misfortune in a Hotel from Ignorance of German — Unexpected Aid at the last Moment.

DURING my wanderings in Switzerland I never took guides. They would have cost much, and interfered with my liberty, for they have their own notions as to the paths which orthodox travellers should take. The same remark applies to mules. I will not affirm positively that they are judges of the picturesque: but the spots where the views are finest are those where they rest while the traveller admires, and if I had passed such spots by, I had no doubt that they would have looked upon me as an idiot. I everywhere walked alone with a pocket-handkerchief in my hand holding my guide book and a change of linen. This mixture of parsimony and independence on one occasion very nearly cost me my life. A long walk had taken me to Brienz on my way to Interlaken, a distance of about seven miles. After I had time to rest and dine I got all the information that seemed necessary and set out once more. Before I had walked far I found myself in a huge wood, darkened yet more by

the approach of night. Occasionally I met a peasant, but
not one of them could speak a word of any language save
German, of which I was totally ignorant. I should otherwise have speedily discovered that I had made a serious
mistake. I was on an old road, long since discarded, the
later road being at the other side of the lake! The clouds
descended upon the forest; it became too dark for me to
walk quickly; the rain began to fall heavily, and several
times I had thought of returning; but I did not like to be
defeated. The road grew rougher and rougher; ere long
it became a walk; the walk grew narrower and narrower;
and the onward rush of a torrent indicated that near me
there was a precipitous descent.

At last I could see nothing, and had to track my way
by closing my umbrella and then trailing it along the right
hand side of the walk, which had become a very zigzag
one. The walk ended in a plank crossing the stream. It
was impossible to know either whether the plank was a
reliable one, or whether the walk was continued at the
other side. It was not a time for long deliberation, and
I stepped upon it, feeling my way as before by trailing my
umbrella. It turned, and I fell; but at that spot the
chasm was not deep; I clambered out of it, and found the
path again at its remoter side. At last I learned from the
sound of the waves that I had come upon the lake, and
that the path thenceforth skirted the precipice which over-
hung the waves. The rain had now ceased; but in place
of it a tremendous storm was raging, the thunder echoing
from mountain to mountain. Every two minutes the lake
burst into sudden illumination from the successive flashes
of lightning; and the sudden glare was more trying than

the preceding darkness. But something more uncomfortable than either soon made itself plain. The path was narrowing. At last it shrunk from one apparently about two feet wide to much less. There was still room for my feet, but hardly for my shoulders. Every new flash made it more plain that a change was necessary; it was now too late to turn and retreat, and I had to advance sideways with my face to the cliff, sliding the palms of my hands against it. I had a faint hope that the path might widen again. A change came, but not one for the better. I reached the end of the cliff, and found myself on what is called in the Cumberland lake-land a "shilly-bed," in other words a downward slanting mass of stones and gravel sometimes dropping to the edge of a precipice or to the margin of a lake, and occasionally intersected by a loose path. In such a path the one I had long trod terminated. There, however, it was no longer possible for me to trail my umbrella; and I had to grope my way with my feet, till the next lightning flash enabled me to see my way.

All this time I found myself annoyed by a constant iteration in my brain of the words, "What a pity! What a pity!" words which we commonly use in connection with the misfortune of another, not one's own. In a few minutes stones of, as I guessed, considerable size came down from above, passing me by: and I had become enough of a mountaineer to know that a few such stones often set a whole shilly-bed upon its downward way. Soon it was plain that the whole shilly-bed was descending, though not rapidly, and that path there was no longer any. I remember saying to myself: "If I have nearly reached the remoter side of the shilly-bed, and if I can keep my foot-

ing I may escape yet." In a few minutes more the shilly-
bed was in rapid motion, and finding that to avoid falling
was no longer possible, I flung myself forward extending my hands. They were grappling with bushes and
brambles, to my great joy.

I was now once more on terra firma, but I had drifted
too far down to leave any chance of finding my path
again, even if any such path existed. I was again in a
wood. A complete darkness had closed round me; but
I felt the storm less. On the other hand, my strength
began to give way, and, drenched as I had been for hours,
the cold made its way into my bones. Every moment
I knocked against a tree or tumbled from a rock, but
not a high one. I struggled on, however, not in the hope
of finding my way; but from a belief that if I yielded to
weariness and slept, I should never wake again.

At last I could fight it out no longer, and lay down in
a space in which the trees seemed less thick than elsewhere. How long I lay there, I cannot guess; but at
last it seemed to me that I descried something white like
the first gleam of dawn far before me. I rose and walked
towards it. At a few steps' distance I distinctly felt a
stone wall! "If this is a chalet for cattle," I said, "it
will be locked, and I shall be none the better for it." I
coasted it, and turned a corner. Still all was darkness.
I turned another; and a light shone from a window. An
old man and his old wife received me kindly. Soon
afterwards they roused a young man from a sleep doubtless well earned; and there was one word out of my
small German vocabulary which he managed to understand — "Interlaken." He lighted a lamp and beckoned

me to follow him. Soon afterwards we were again on the borders of the lake. There I encountered again that awful path! When he showed it to me with his lamp, at the worst spots I found it much more difficult to make my way along it than when the darkness prevented me from seeing how formidable it was. How often, in the moral sense, we may be unconsciously traversing such passes without knowing it!

When we reached Interlaken, the storm had blown over; the village wore its usual festal aspect, and the dancing still went on, though it was half-past one in the morning. The landlord of my hotel was standing at its door, and gave me a genial welcome. He asked me many questions — amongst others, why I had not come in a carriage. When he heard from me and my boy companion how I had come, he could hardly believe us. The track I had taken had been abandoned many years before; and even the mountain shepherds seldom used it. He showed me my room, and left me a blanket with which I at last rubbed myself dry. I then went to bed. He soon returned with excellent tea and abundant bread and butter — the best meal, I thought, which I had ever enjoyed. My only remaining misfortune was that my guide book and the linen which I carried in a parcel in my left hand were drenched. My umbrella, that faithful friend, was uninjured.

When I woke in the morning the sun was shining brightly and all was as still as if nature were incapable of storm. Later in the day I went up the lake in the steamboat. It passed near that cliff with which I had made so close an acquaintance the night before. High

above the water that narrow and broken pathway was
distinctly visible; but the sight made my brain reel, and
I felt certain that, in the daylight, I could not have
trodden a dozen paces on it. Suddenly I heard again
that strange iteration which had worried me during
the night — "What a pity!" but this time it was explained by a corresponding spectacle which rose before
my eyes as I had seen it nearly ten years before. A
beautiful child lay drowned on the strand beside the
Shannon. Many stood or knelt beside her, loud in grief.
A physician bent over her; and as each new effort to
restore animation successively failed, he reiterated in a
low voice, "Too late! What a pity! What a pity!"

I had few perilous adventures among the Alps, for I
soon learned prudence; I will record only one more. It
happened many years later, and on that occasion I had
two guides with me besides a friend of high Alpine experience. I had heard much of the Pass of Monte Moro,
one of the highest, I believe, then known in the Alps, and
one commanding a marvellous view chiefly of the Monte
Rosa's ranges. It was very much too late in the year
for such an expedition; but I met an old friend who
was travelling, and since he, as well as a skilful guide,
regarded the expedition as still practicable, I joined them.
We started early from Saas, and the weather was pro-
pitious till about two o'clock in the afternoon, when we
fell in with a travelling pedlar who was in the habit of
carrying his wares over that pass. He joined himself
to our party, so that we had the benefit of his experience as well as that of a local guide. Soon after he
joined us we reached the steeper part of the ascent, up

which the path ascended in curves. Suddenly we encountered a tremendous storm of snow which, though to us it seemed a sudden one, may have been raging there for several days. The storm was master there; and we were intruders. We struggled against it, my friend keeping somewhat in advance of the rest. Soon I found that I could not breathe without keeping my mouth open, in which case the snow made its entrance, the hard breathing changed to suffocation, and I fell to the ground and lay there panting for a couple of minutes. This happened several times. The guides urged me forward, telling me that we were still far from the summit, and that if we did not reach it before the light left us, we were lost. Every moment, however, the sense of suffocation increased, and I could not advance more than a few paces without falling. During the last of these seizures they told me, with much courtesy, that they could wait no longer, and took their departure along the path then nearly invisible. They had each a strong alpenstock; I had had none, and in place of one, I had carried a heavy knapsack; and thus had laboured under a double disadvantage. I walked again. Each time that I fell, the sense of suffocation was all but intolerable. I felt a strong belief that, when the snow was dissolved by the summer heat, my bones would be found on the spot where I had fallen last.

After a certain lapse of time my breathing power seemed to improve slightly and I thought I should at least make one more effort, however hopeless, to reach the summit. The path was soon wholly lost; but it seemed as if my best chance consisted in taking what seemed the shortest upward way, even if it was the steepest also. Probably the storm was then less directly in my face: for I certainly made some upward progress, though after every few paces, I fell again, and lay on the snow in agony. "At this rate of progress," I said to myself, "it would be impossible for me to reach the summit for many hours. I do not think I could have thus struggled on for one hour or made a furlong's progress, when I heard voices above me in the fog. I recognised them. I made a last effort upward, shouting in my turn. In a few minutes I was on the summit, in the midst of my recent three companions! They had reached the crest of the Monte Moro Pass some considerable time before; but fortunately the two guides could not agree upon the road down. Each stormed at the other, and the loudness of their controversy, perhaps also the frosty air, had made them audible to me. It ended by our taking our downward way at hazard, each with the one before him at a slight distance. At last we heard a triumphant shout from the guide farthest in advance. He had suddenly found himself at the outside of the cloud: we were not long in joining him. Below us lay our resting-place for the night, Macugnaga, and a dozen miles of its exquisite valley bathed in the splendour of the setting sun. Probably the whole snowy range of Monte Rosa was in sight; but just at that time I was as cold to mountain snows as they had been to me; and my eyes were bent on the lowlands. Neither my old friend nor the two guides made any allusion to my temporary absence — neither did I.

I asked my friend to order our dinner, and lay down on my bed till it was ready. I fear I felt very cross with our two guides when they left me — an impatience the more unreasonable because each of them had offered, before the snowstorm gnashed its white teeth against me, to relieve me from the knapsack which I carried on my shoulders.

I was punished for not having looked at the Monte Rosa range when it was in sight, for the next day as we walked 30 miles down the valley of Anzasca the mountains were hidden by unceasing rain. We saw instead, however, all day long, one of the loveliest of the young maidens whom that valley boasts with their beautiful faces so modest and so frank. My friend lent her his umbrella all day, and refused her offer to restore it in the evening, when she pursued her wet journey alone. Doubtless she was glad to meet companions of her way. The valley of Anzasca was then almost unknown; and its inmates were said to know no sin graver than that of kicking their pigs as they drove them to market.

Nowhere do the extremes of the grave and the gay, the tragic and the comic meet, more strangely than in the high Alps. I have just recorded two very serious incidents of mountain travel — the only serious dangers I ever encountered there. Incidents of a quaint character often retain not less tenaciously a place in our memory. I had been standing long before what many consider the finest torrent in all Switzerland, the Handeck Waterfall, and the sound was still in my ears as I walked back slowly to my hotel. In its *salle à manger* I found a traveller who, as his conversation suggested to me, might have been a Dublin shopkeeper resting himself after his labours by a holiday. If so, he was a very patriotic Irishman. Whatever I said in praise of the scenery around us he seemed

to regard as a distinct aspersion on Ireland. " What can
you compare here," he demanded, " with the mountains
of Wicklow ? "   " Perhaps," I replied, " one might name
the mountains of the Mont Blanc range."   " Oh ! " he
replied, " they are out of all reason !   I am after walking
along the Chamouni Valley for three days, and I only saw
four of those mountains !   Sure in Wicklow I have counted
as many as eight of them in three hours ! "

" Have you seen this wonderful waterfall within half
a mile of you? " I asked.   " I have not seen it, and I am
not going to see it," was his answer.   " Have I not seen
the O'Sullivan Cascade at Killarney?   Down it comes
from such a height that you don't know from Adam where
it comes from !   Down it plunges, thundering and bellowing, sometimes as black as ink, and sometimes as white
as milk, dashing itself against the right-hand rocks and
smashing itself against the left-hand rocks !   Indeed,
indeed, you would not give a pin for it before ever it
reaches the ground !   What is your Handeck Fall compared to that? "   " Some persons would answer," I suggested, " that the waterfall here is about ten times as
high, and six times as broad."   " Oh ! " he replied, " the
O'Sullivan Cascade is not big enough for you !   And
tell me this now !   Could not you take a magnifying glass
to it ? "

The guides of Switzerland were as little to his liking as
the mountains.   " There was a rascal among them that
promised to take me up to the top of a first-rate mountain easily, a week ago.   Before we got up half the way
I was near knocking him down !   I daresay it was the
English in the hotel that set him on me.   If I had gone

the other half of the way I must have died of the heat I
was in! Besides that, as we went down the mountain
he drenched me in a thunder shower. I was as wet as
the River Rhone after it has flowed through forty-eight
miles of the Lake of Geneva!" As soon as he discovered
that I too was Irish he took me under his protection, and
on learning that I was on my way to Rome, gave me
a letter to a friend of his there, telling me first to read it.
It ran thus: "The bearer is a countryman. Give him all
the help you can at Rome; and show him all the curios-
ities of the place."

I may here record another of those quaint accidents
with which fortune sometimes regales those who have set
out on their travels in the belief that they are to meet
nothing on their way except the sublime. I had seen
something of the Swiss and the Italian Alps, but nothing
of the German, and I resolved to see them too. An
obstacle presented itself in my ignorance of the German
language; but I took for granted that wherever I went I
should find hotels in which French or Italian was intelligible. At Argolis I had got on without speaking Greek
and why should I not fare as well if I went to see the
beautiful lake of Tegernsee? Near it were the baths of
Kreuth, and in the hotel there I felt sure that I should
be received with acclamations if I only announced that
I had an incurable complaint in my little finger. I hired
a small carriage driven by a wild youth instructed to
drive me to Kreuth. The shores of Bavarian Tegernsee,
seemed to me almost as lovely as those of an Italian lake;
and I passed a heavy poetic malediction on the first
Bavarian king who had changed its magnificent mon-

astery into a royal palace; but I had eaten nothing all
day, and smelt far off the luxurious *salle à manger* of
half the world's valetudinarians. As we approached the
Paradise of the infirm, the lights shone through its many
windows, and sounds of all manner of instruments were
heard. It was a festival. A wealthy lady who had
nourished three serious maladies there during the last
fifteen years had driven away a week before — another
benevolent lady, with six, had that day taken her place,
and the villagers had come to welcome her.

Could I have a bed? No! Could I have my dinner
at least? No! What was I to do? Take a place in a
diligence which left that hotel at six in the morning for
Munich. I must sleep that night at another hotel only
a mile off. They would put my heavy luggage on the
diligence; and I might drive on with the lighter. I
reached it soon; but no one could understand a word
I said. I walked into a large room with a large table
crowded by a multitude of hungry servants and couriers;
but nowhere could I find any one whose language I understood. I took possession of a vacant bedroom and soon
afterwards the wild boy came up with my lighter luggage;
he put out his hand for his fare, but, alas, my hat-case was
wanting, and I could not make him understand my wrong.
He stamped fiercely up and down the room; but I was
resolved not to pay till my property was restored. The
tumult became so loud that many persons rushed into
the room just as I was preparing to go to bed. At last
they found a lady's maid who not only spoke French, but
was able to understand mine. The hat-box was found;
the wild boy grinned with a savage delight when I paid

him his fare, and the lady's maid ordered a dinner for me explaining that I was to be called early as I was going on to Munich. Very early the next morning I rose; but no one could I find to take down my luggage, or to stop the diligence as it passed the gate. The hour for its arrival had nearly come when in my despair I knocked at the door of the French maid's room which I had observed as she bade me a courteous good-night. The answer was a very sleepy "*Entrez!*" I did so. The late sleeper's eyes were very sleepily lifted; so were her arms, two very splendid bracelets falling far back down them as she asked with a look of surprise what "Monsieur" required.

I answered that what I required was that she should get up as fast as possible, and give such directions as would enable me to pay my bill, and get upon the diligence, which must otherwise carry off my luggage to lands unknown. She promised that she would do all this "if Monsieur would leave the room as propriety demanded." I did so; and within five minutes she made her appearance as gaily dressed as if for a ball! She offered to order breakfast for me; but I thought it safest to walk on and meet the diligence. Before long I saw it advancing rapidly and I rejoiced. I raised my hand: I hailed it. I saw my portmanteau on its roof: I ran beside it bellowing — it was in vain: on it passed: it did not stop a moment at the hotel. The French maid told me that there would be no other diligence for several days: that the landlord could not help me: but that if any return carriage for Munich passed by I should be duly apprised.

About two o'clock that afternoon a return post-chaise drove up, and I hired it. The day was hot; the road dusty; I felt very foolish and very cross; and the boy who drove me knew no more of any language I knew than the wild boy of the day preceding. At last he jumped down and addressed me. The word *Gasthaus* made me know that he enquired to which of the Munich hotels he was to drive me. I wanted "The Golden Stag," and did not know its German name. I ruminated, and then began a series of experiments. I bleated like a sheep, and the boy shouted "Yaa, Yaa," but I shook my head. I then neighed like a horse; and again he shouted "Yaa," and again I shook my head. I next barked like a dog, and he shouted as before; but by this time he had taken up the idea of the animal races into his head. I next raised both hands to my forehead, parting my fingers so as to make them as like horns as was practicable, and the boy shouted. I nodded and took out my watch, and showed him the case of it, which was silver; he shouted, and I shook my head as before. Lastly I opened the watch and showed him the interior, which was gold. I nodded, slapped his shoulder, made him a complimentary speech in English, and left him to meditate. He mused for a few minutes, then laughed loud, clapped the carriage door to, and leaped on the box, and in another half-hour put me down at the doorway of "The Golden Stag." My success with the boy made my blunders of the preceding day seem pardonable, and I ate my two days' dinners in one! The next day I visited the churches and the palaces, and was greatly gratified at seeing that a new school of Christian art had risen up in Germany. The art there seemed to me true-hearted, though of course it lacked the inspiration of an earlier day. I remember writing a sonnet in honour of the king who dined on five francs a day, and had already made his metropolis worthy of being called the Gate of Italy.

CHAPTER VII

EARLY YEARS IN ENGLAND — 1841-45

Journey to England in the Spring of 1841 — I see something of O'Connell — His view of Legal Practice — Tintern Abbey and the Wye — My Delight at Oxford (1841) — Bolton Priory — Visit to the Cumberland Mountains — Miss Fenwick — Wordsworth (1842) — Hartley Coleridge (1844) — Debates in the House of Lords — Lord Derby's Attack on Earl Grey — Mr. Shiel (1848), and Fergus O'Connor — Henry Taylor's Family — Mrs. Edward Villars — Grove Mill, Cassiobury.

AFTER a year and a half of pleasant wanderings in the south and east, I returned to Curragh Chase about midsummer, in 1840, and found its inmates all well. The rest of that year was spent in " domestic dissipation " and in literary pursuits. In the spring of 1841 I returned to England by a circuitous route, selected for its beauty — one by Waterford and Wicklow to Dublin. The Wicklow valleys, with their " woody walls " and small, darksome lakes, their rocks and their ruins, delighted me, and I was reminded of them later when visiting Bolton priory ; while, on the other hand I was struck by the great dissimilitude between the Wicklow mountains and those of Cumberland and Westmoreland.

There are many spots in Wicklow lovelier than " The Meeting of the Waters," made famous by Moore's " Irish Melody " ; but *vates carent.* On arriving in Dublin I visited John Anster, who told me that he was going to translate the second part of Goethe's " Faust," as he had already translated the first, and that he considered it to be a better poem. He was amusing as ever; and when I mentioned some distinguished Protestant who had lately become a Catholic, he replied: "And I met lately a Catholic gentleman who has just become a Protestant! No doubt when the war is over there will be an exchange of prisoners." On reaching London, I arranged with Mr. Pickering for the publication of my father's "Song of Faith," and "Sonnets"; and the next morning I met at breakfast Dr. Whewell, Bishop Thirlwall, Frederick Denison Maurice, and Wordsworth, who much pleased me by the warmth of his enquiries after my father, mother, and sister.

But I am forgetting the most interesting incident of my journey to England. A few minutes after getting on board the steamer at Kingstown I observed a large, strong man, whose face I at once recognised, though I had never seen it before. There it was, the eye potent, but crafty too, the large mouth, full at once of humour and good-humour, a broad, strong forehead, well adapted for thinking purposes, but better still, apparently, for butting against opponents, or pushing his way through them. His bearing had a singular confidence about it; and he wore, slightly on one side, an arrogant little sailor's cap, with a good deal of gold lace about it. It was O'Connell: I was certain of this when he spoke. "Steward, what time will we be in Liverpool?" "I expect—" "I don't want your expectations! Name an hour!" "I might deceive you." "You would not deceive me, for I would not expect the truth from you! Sure it would be hard for you to be always telling the

truth." (To the steward's boy) "Who are you, little
boy? Are you English or Irish?" "My parents are
English, sir, but I was born in Ireland." "Did you
come to Ireland purposely to be born there? You
showed your taste! Steward, you are taking me too
far: I would not give you so much trouble! We could
deliberate as well in Dublin as in Westminster; and my
son John would have as much fishing as he chose.
There's no fishing in the world like that in the streams
near Dublin! I had not such comfort in my life as I
have had since I became a teetotaller! I thought that
when hunting at Derrinane before six in the morning
the milk might miss the brandy a trifle, but it did not.
The 'Pledge' worked a miracle on Maurice. People won't
believe that he is Maurice at all now. Anthony, put away
that egg! It comes from Liverpool, and you pledged yourself to consume no English manufactures. I set up a
brewery for my youngest son. Only for the Pledge it
would have made £2,000 for him before now, and he has
not made a penny. I don't blame them, and don't grudge
it, though it's unknown what I spent on premises."

Anthony spoke next. "I'm come a thousand miles,
Mr. O'Connell, to hear this debate. Will you get me
into the House, sir?" "I will get you into the Gallery;
but I don't know whether I can get you into the body
of the House." "If you don't, sir, I'll do what I did before. I'll make my friend, Sir Robert Peel, let me in.
Billy Holmes had promised to get me in; but instead
of that the villain got sick himself, and had to race away
home. Sir Robert Peel was coming in at the same time;
and I knew him by his pictures: so I requested him to

let me in, and he did so." "That's the way with you," rejoined O'Connell, "when you've got what you can from me, you go to Sir Robert Peel. Well, come to me at the right moment, and I will see what can be done for you. You are up to anything, from pitch-and-toss to manslaughter inclusive." At that moment came up the renowned Tom Steel, "Sublime O'Connell's great head pacificator for all Ireland," solely to wish his chief good-night, which he did with a manner at once as formal and as affectionate as that of Don Quixote addressing a chambermaid. "It's time for me to go to bed," remarked O'Connell, slightly twisting his wig. "Steward, this is the most Reverend, the Bishop of Kilkenny. Take good care of him." The steward nodded jauntily; the Bishop bowed as ceremoniously as if he had been presented to the Queen; and O'Connell departed.

The next morning O'Connell was our fellow-traveller from Liverpool to London. Two little girls were put into the carriage as we started. He treated them with as much care as if they had been his grandchildren, surrendering his seat at the window to one of them that she might be able to count the sheep and cows as we passed them. He boasted that twelve of his grandchildren were to meet at Derrinane in the autumn, and described several. He told them endless stories, and repeated not a few short poems by Byron and Moore, especially Moore's lines on Emmet,

"She is far from the land where her young hero sleeps,"

which brought tears, not only into the eyes of the children but of the reciter, for a few trickled down his cheeks, both then and as he repeated passages from Emmet's speech on his trial. Somebody having complimented him on his success both in his political and legal career, he answered: "Sir, you have probably heard much more both to my credit and my discredit, than I deserve. My success at the bar was almost wholly owing to my skill in cross-examination. I never take an unjust case: it is a great sin — that is, except in defence of a man." The subject of cross-examination turning up again later, he said: "There my success is great. I force a man to contradict himself before five minutes are out, no matter how right he is. Every Irish witness is an enemy or a partisan. He is therefore most incautious, and can be easily made to contradict himself, even on oath, to bolster up an exaggeration. I make the witness think me the simplest man in the world, and particularly friendly to him. Then I make him exaggerate, and invent something to press that statement. In good time I prove his statements to be inconsistent. There is not a man in Ireland that I would not make incredible to the jury, unless he was a soldier, for they only say 'Yes' and 'No.'" The Bishop whispered to me, "You see how difficult casuistry is. Mr. O'Connell is right in thinking that a lawyer is wrong in taking unjust cases; but wrong in thinking that he has a right to make a man perjure himself in spite of himself; and you were wrong in saying that a man, when guilty, has no right to plead 'not guilty.'"

O'Connell's language, though abounding in humour and figure, was full also of force and of precision. When speaking, he worked his lips vehemently, half dropping his lids while his eyes protruded and flashed as if they had the power of making his thoughts pass before him in palpable

shape. If I had wished to make his acquaintance I had
only to tell him that I was a near kinsman of four adventurous English ladies who, travelling about Ireland, had
resolved not to leave that country without making acquaintance with its greatest man, little as they were in
sympathy with his politics. They drove up nearly to his
hall door, while he was haranguing a large body of men
who had chosen him as their arbitrator in some local dispute. He walked up to them at once, took off his hat,
and welcomed them as cordially as if they had been old
friends. Before they had got through half their excuses,
he assured them that none was necessary; that the country
was a wild one; that Derrinane was the home of every
passer-by, and that his housekeeper would show them
their rooms at once. At the dinner-table there sat about
twenty guests, most of whom asked the stranger ladies to
drink wine with them. O'Connell never touched on politics; but they heard him say in a low voice to his neighbour, "I had a letter from Normanby to-day." He was
at that time at once the chief demagogue in Europe and
the dispenser of nearly all the Government patronage in
Ireland. My English friends accepted his hospitality
during several days, and his family showed them the loveliest objects in that enchanting region, and especially that
ruined church on the seashore which O'Connell had taken
as a model for the chapel he added to his own house, and
in which he daily made his meditation. When offering
him their farewell thanks they presented him with their
cards. "I am glad to learn your names," he said, "because that makes it the more likely that we may meet
again; but I should never have asked for them."

O'Connell was a very wonderful man — one with a
nature so large that it seemed as if he was not a man,
but an epitome of many men. Ireland must be ever
grateful to him, for had it not been for him she might
have waited long for Catholic Emancipation. It must
ever be remembered that, demagogue as he was by
necessity, he was by no means a democrat; and that
he looked with horror on Jacobinism as the greatest
calamity by which his country could be afflicted and
degraded. He greatly admired the English Constitution,
and as greatly abhorred the principles of the French
Revolution; and, for both reasons, he justly resented the
more the injustice which prevented his countrymen from
sharing the benefits of that Constitution. Catholic Emancipation was his crown. His subsequent agitation for
Repeal was, as I have ever believed, an error, grounded
not so much (though Shiel called it a "splendid phantom") on an impossible ideal as on an unworthy one.
There exists a much nobler one — the Catholic ideal —
and they are inconsistent.

My journey to London was a very zigzag one, for I
hated the travelling that sacrifices the beautiful or the
historical for the sake of speed. I looked out of the
carriage at Chepstow, and the old castle stood before
me. I leaped out and got at my luggage, and, after carefully inspecting that castle, pursued my way to Tintern
Abbey with a knapsack only. The green valley and
tawny waters of the river, there nearly as yellow as the
Tiber, were flushed with the sunset lights as I passed
them, and the lowlands looked soft and luxuriant in a
degree seldom found in craggy scenery. The grey cliffs

above the windings of the river, and the chalk hills in the distance were warmed with a fainter crimson, and when I reached the crest of Windcliff, a steep of about a thousand feet in height, the windows of a distant village flashed with what seemed a conflagration. The Wye occasionally resembles the river I had last seen, though on a larger scale, except that the shelving banks of green are ridged with higher rocks and more thickly sprinkled with hedgerows, and copse-wood, while the fields, remoter from the river, exhibit as much of "the fat of the land" as Thompson would have desired for an idyll. When I reached Tintern the moon had climbed over the woody ridges, and shone on the grey walls with a brilliance that made the southern arch, seventy feet high, look as dark as the mouth of a cave. Close by the ruin stood one of those clean and beautiful little inns special to England. They gave me a well-furnished bedroom, though one so small that the honeysuckles which made their way through the open window trailed on to the bed. Very soon I sallied out to see the ruins. The gates were locked, but I was left free to walk round and round the building, and get glimpses into the interior through the long windows the traceries of which cast their ebony bars over plats of grass whitened by moonbeams. The wind sighed in the ivy, and the river murmured close by; and there was no sound beside, except that of an old white horse that cropped his meal in the churchyard, and left an occasional sigh on the sward.

The next morning I examined the interior of the buildings in the sunshine, visiting successively every spot, from the smallest side chapel to the summit of the walls, high as the towers of many a goodly church; along those walls are walks so wide that the most nervous could not feel giddy as he pushed his way through the thickets of ash and holly which murmured in the morning breeze. After climbing the steeps that enclose the valley of Tintern, I returned to Chepstow for my luggage. Thence I went to Bristol, with its old houses projecting over the streets. The rest may be given in the words of a letter, —

"I remembered what pleasure you had felt, as you told me, when, then a child, you were taken to see the Abbey church at Bath, with that famous tower, and its stone angels ascending the tower one above another, as if along the steps of a ladder. Accordingly I went there. The day was a brilliant one, and Bath laughed in the sunshine as I looked down on it from an eminence. The hills, with which it is surrounded on almost all sides, were still sparkling, after the showers of the earlier morning, with the gladsome green of spring, while the vapours which rose from them were turned by the sunbeam showers to colours innumerable. I soon found your Abbey church, your tower, and the stone angels still ascending their aerial ladder. Whatever those angels were intended to symbolise — whether the ascent of prayers, or, mystically, the upward progress of the spiritualised affections towards celestial regions, along the graduated ladder of human ties — there they stood, and there they mounted. They evidently preferred the humbler service of their feet to that of their wings ; or, as Wordsworth sings of the human affections, as illustrated by Jacob's vision, —

> " With untired humility forebore
> The ready wafture of the wings they wore."

On my way to London I passed several days at Oxford, the guest of Dr. William Sewell, who put me up at Exeter College, of which he was then Sub-Rector. He was

a singular man, one of great aspirations and great energies, but of opinions so peculiar that he never could work
long with others, and, though remarkable for the influence
which he speedily gained over young men, yet seldom
could retain that influence long. He was a High Churchman, but less, some said, on historical or purely theological grounds, than because "Church principles" were
regarded by him as practical exponents of the Platonic
philosophy, to which he was passionately attached. He
took pains not to be regarded as belonging to the school
represented by Newman and Pusey. He held the Roman
Catholic Church in great dislike, and suffered much from
the malady called "Jesuit on the brain." With his dislike
to "Rome" I was in no sympathy, though much with his
belief that High Church opinions represented a sound
religious philosophy — a belief expressed in an early work
by my friend, Frederick Denison Maurice, and held also
at one time by Sir William Rowan Hamilton, who used to
say that High Church principles might effectually be vindicated on the principles of a deep philosophy. During
the period of this visit to Oxford, and during a later one,
there prevailed a very remarkable degree of theological
excitement. It was evident to me that matters ecclesiastical were approaching a crisis, and that momentous consequences must follow whenever a plain answer had been at
last extorted respecting the meaning of certain formularies
which, by way of making them comprehensive, had been
made incomprehensible also, or equivocal in the extreme.
But, shunning the ways of controversy, which I regarded
as but a painful necessity forced on us by "private judgment," I gave myself up to the charm of a spot, to me the

most attractive in all England. I wandered about it all
day in a dream of the past, and during a great part of the
night also, favoured by a large and luminous moon; I
entered every portal, penetrated into gardens that magi-
cally combined the lovely with the venerable — the odour
of the earliest rose or the new-mown sward being wafted
to me from beyond the hoary walls which had protected
those enclosures for centuries.   On the last night of my
stay at Oxford I remember lingering long upon the bridge
close to Magdalen College, looking up at its old tower, and
wishing that I could hear the white-robed choir of boys
who still each May-morning chaunt the "Te Deum" from
its summit.   Late as it was, I found my way into the dusky
cloister, faintly lighted by an occasional lamp half lost
among the brown rafters.   I wandered on till I reached a
narrow iron gate.   I could not get through it, and stood
looking out upon the moonlit grass and the woodland beyond, out of which there softly stole a milk-white doe.   It
moved on slowly and shyly, pushed its nose through the
grating and licked my hand.   These things belong to the
days of old.   I visited Oxford last in 1895.   There were
many changes, for fifty-three years had gone by.   Newman and Pusey, Manning and Faber, and Ward and Sewell
had gone by, but they had left a great work behind.
That had its visible monuments, such as Keble College,
and a stately Roman Catholic church replacing a small
one, — in which, however, as Newman remarked, an Apostle returned to earth might possibly have found himself
more at home than in many a loftier structure hard by.
There is also the grand new chapel of Exeter College,
built after the model of the Sainte Chapelle at Paris,

and such as might have satisfied even the impassioned devotion of William Sewell to Gothic architecture. Two monuments of his noble and self-sacrificing zeal in the cause of Christian education remain — one in Ireland, St. Columba's College, and Radnor, within a few miles of his beloved Oxford. The latter of these fell at one time into great difficulties, owing to the mismanagement of the person charged with the keeping of its accounts. Sewell parted with all he had in the world to assist in paying its debts.

The attractions of Oxford detained me there long enough to incense my London friends, with whom I had engagements. Here is a fragment to appease and amuse Henry Taylor. "I can hardly write my excuses, for it is nearly twelve o'clock at night, and there is such a chiming of bells and pealing of clocks all round that I cannot collect my thoughts. What manner of discourse they are holding I cannot guess, but I am convinced that bells, like birds, have a language intelligible to themselves. Perhaps they are holding forth on the Pusey persecution, and affirming that they have witnessed nothing like it since the death of Ridley. I expect every moment to hear the great 'Tom' of Wolsey's College take up his parable thus with his dogmatic chime: 'Is any bell ignorant that I am the voice, not only of Christ Church, but of the Cathedral itself, and that no other tongue than mine is laden with scourges so ponderous for all ill spirits that throng the air.' Whatever else these bells may be saying, to me they say that the chapel doors will be opened in the morning at eight o'clock, and will fall back on their hinges at eight and three minutes and forty-five

seconds, immediately after the tide of white hoods, and
red hoods, and violet hoods has streamed past. If, from
sitting up too late over my letters, I reach the chapel door
one second too late the doors cannot be opened again
without a decree from the Convocation, and Convocation
can only be summoned by the Vice-Chancellor, and the
Vice-Chancellor is a Low Churchman, and I am probably
suspected by him of being in correspondence with the
Puseyites, who are in correspondence with the Jesuits,
who are in correspondence with the Devil. Must I stand
outside and listen when the great iron-bound books are
flung open? Will not the doctors (*domini doctores*) be
offended? the Hebrew doctor, many-wrinkled, and learned
in all the wisdom of the Egyptians; the Greek doctor
who talks Greek in his sleep; the subtle doctor who
dances on the needle-points of logical positions, the
ascetic doctor through whom the moon shines, the insane
doctor, supposed to be a great penitent, the corpulent
doctor, who sails across the courts, swaying his scarlet
gown on each side like the yard-arms of a man-of-war
going before the wind. Will not the Rector look round,
seeking in vain the guest of the college, Exeter College,
and say nothing? Will not the august Senate of the
Masters be in a maze? But I must go to bed at once
if I am to avoid creating all this confusion in 'Holy
Places.'"

In 1841 I made a delightful expedition to England's
lake-land, visiting on the way the valley of the Wharfe
and Bolton Priory. The mists hung their veil over the
woody hills which gleamed through them with a softened
lustre, the sheep on the upland lawns blending their bleat-

ing, that tenderest of nature's sounds, with the murmur of
the Wharfe, while the old Priory flung the sharp shadows
of its gables over the tombstones, striking the keynote of
a melody the pathos of which was half lost in its sweetness. We visited the far-famed " Strid " and sighed for
young Romilly's mother, and read Wordsworth's poem.
There is no "White Doe" now to wander beneath the
ruined arches of the Priory; but we contented ourselves
with the substitute for her presented by the occasional
sunbeam which made its way here and there through the
ivy-wreaths, and filled many an " obscure recess " with
" lustre of a saintly shew." The earlier and the later parts
of that poem are exquisite and carry with them a soft
perpetual autumnal melancholy dipped in autumnal sunshine. The picture also of the old knight, with his

> " Magnific limbs of withered state
> And face to fear and venerate,"

riding forth to the field with all his sons, save one, is
noble; yet I cannot think that the narrative portion of
the work adds to its value. The poem, however, has a
religious and patriotic value as well as a poetical one.
It is a reverent tribute to the memory of those true representatives of England's ancient chivalry who knew how
to die in the cause of their Faith, and, as they believed,
of their Country no less, at a time when loyalty met no
earthly reward. Three miles from Leeds is another monastic ruin of far nobler proportions, Kirkstall Abbey.
The church of that huge pile remains so perfect that to
restore it would not be difficult; but to those who look on
it and ask, " Can these dry bones live," its reply might
possibly be " Not necessary: I preach still." Later I

visited the great northern Abbey of Furness. That magnificent temple might be called the Gate of the Mountain Land. The valleys near it are themselves temples walled with rock. Those who visit them ought to pass the preceding night in Furness Abbey, like the dedicated knight of old, who passed the dark hours preceding the day of his consecration watching his arms in a chapel.

My visit to the north was spent chiefly beside Ulleswater, at Halsteads, where, through the boundless hospitality of Mr. and Mrs. Marshall, I had more than once the best opportunities for seeing that lake. Helvellyn would not then, it is true, doff his turban to an intruder; but I saw Aira Force, the most graceful of waterfalls, and the subject of one of Wordsworth's latest ballads. Near it is the green margin by which flashed so merrily the daffodils sung by him in those memorable stanzas to which his wife contributed what he affirmed to be its best line. Not far off is " The Cave of the Dying Deer," sung by Lord Houghton, who well describes the special character of Ulleswater, " Where thy black crystal sleeps without a wave."

That year (1841) I passed a week under the roof of Miss Fenwick, as, later, I passed several days under that of Wordsworth, who regarded her as the chief friend of his later years, as Coleridge had been of his earlier. Her house was within a mile and a half of his, and he passed several days with her during my visit, besides coming to her house on several other days, and taking me out walking. He showed me the scenes to which he was most attached, and recorded many incidents connected with them. In the presence of Nature he seemed to be always either conversing with her as a friend, and watching her changeful moods, or sometimes rapt, like a prophet, in mystic attention to her " oracles." It was by no means the picturesque aspects of Nature which affected him most — it was a something far more serious and absorbing. For him it was in her deeper *meanings* that the inspiring influences of Nature chiefly resided. If one had demanded of him what were those deeper meanings, it would have been as if one had demanded of Beethoven what were the deeper meanings of his grandest symphonies, which are often his obscurest. In both cases it is through the sense, not by the sense, that the meaning penetrates to the soul. In the soul only, to which the eye and ear are alike but gates, the meaning is apprehended; and it is apprehended just so far as it is felt. In both cases that which addresses the soul through the sense is itself a language, and therefore its meaning cannot be explained, for that would be to put it into another language not its own. Wordsworth might have replied that Nature's language could be learned, but could not be translated. Nature's meanings admitted of being adumbrated only; and to adumbrate what could neither be translated nor defined, was just what poetry could do, could alone do, and to do which was her highest privilege in his estimation. Another art, painting, might do nearly the same thing, and do it even more vividly; but she could not do it as nobly, as deeply, or as spiritually. During those walks Wordsworth's chief theme, next to Nature, was poetry. He did not think very highly of our modern poets, except Coleridge, of whom he affirmed that no other poet had ever had so exquisite an ear, and that if he had gone on writing poetry for ten years more he must have been the greatest poet of the modern world. For poetry itself he had the profoundest reverence as well as love. He was never tired of insisting on it that the soul of poetry was Truth.

But Truth was not the only master whom poetry served. According to him the Muse owes service to a mistress, as well as to a master. In a late sonnet he said:

> " If Thought and Love desert us, from that hour
> Let us break off all commerce with the Muse ! "

and in another poem of his old age, he says:

> " Love, blessed Love, is everywhere
> The spirit of my song."

But as the Truth which inspires his poetry is not a truth polemical or narrow, so the human love which animates it is too large a thing to spend itself chiefly in what is commonly termed " love-poetry." It was not that he was out of sympathy with such poetry; on the contrary, he told me that he had abstained from writing much of it chiefly because he feared that he might have written it with more of ardour than would have been profitable reading for the young. He considered, besides, that if he had insisted more, as most poets have done, upon what, after all, is but a single form of human love, he would have defrauded many other forms of love, not less sacred, of their due. Be this as it may, his half-dozen love-poems are of the very highest order, and of a very rare character, especially those associated with the name Lucy. They show that his eyes had rested upon creatures

> "Whom if they had not, yet they might have loved,"

to quote from Landor's " Gebir."

The absolute transparency of Wordsworth's nature imparted a delightful personal interest to our walks, while it sometimes provoked a smile by bringing different parts of his nature into a momentary opposition. Once, as we looked on a magnificent mountain view, he exclaimed: "Travellers often make their boast of Swiss mountains, on the ground of their being two or three times as high as the English; but I reply that the clouds gather so low on them that half of them remain commonly out of sight." I answered, perhaps drily, "That is true." He resumed, making the same statement several times in a different form; and I made no defence of Switzerland, remembering that if it was a folly to

> "Beard the lion in his den,
> The Douglas in his hall,"

it might be inexpedient to do battle with the prophet and priest of the English mountains as he stood on his own ground. "You cannot see those boasted Swiss mountains when the clouds hang low." "Certainly not," I answered. After a pause, he spoke again: "But I must admit, *you know that they are there.*" His characteristic veracity triumphed unaided over his patriotism — when he met with no opposition.

I passed several days under Wordsworth's roof, which I regard as the greatest honour of my life. We rose early, and went to bed early. Each night prayers were read by Mrs. Wordsworth in a voice full of reverence and sweetness. He knelt near her with his face hidden in his hands. That vision is often before me.

Before leaving Miss Fenwick, I was taken by her to Fox How, where I made acquaintance with a family to which I have ever since been much attached, that of Dr. Arnold. He was one of Wordsworth's warmest friends, though they had to exclude politics from their subjects of conversation. I also made acquaintance with Mr. Dawes, then the clergyman of Ambleside, the tutor of my father, who always retained for him a very affectionate regard. I made acquaintance also with another of Wordsworth's friends, Mrs. Fletcher, who, some fifty years before had broken the hearts of all judicious young men at Edinburgh. When I saw her she was a beautiful old lady reverenced by all.

Not long after my departure from the lake country I received the following letter from Wordsworth:

RYDAL MOUNT, Nov. 16, 1842.

MY DEAR MR. DE VERE, — Every day since I received your kind letter, I wished to write to you, and most days have resolved to do so; but in vain, so inveterate is the habit of procrastination with me in these matters. I have only, therefore, to throw myself upon your indulgence, as I am so often obliged to do with all my other friends. First, let me express my pleasure in learning that I had been misinformed concerning the article in " The Quarterly." The thing I have not read, nor probably ever shall read ; but it grieved me to think, from what I heard of it, that it should be written by any friend of mine for whom I have so much regard, and whom I esteem so highly as yourself. And I was the more concerned upon these occasions because the only disparaging notices which I have ever cared the least for, unfortunately have ever come from persons with whom I have lived in close intimacy. And this occurred in several remarkable instances. Now, though I am far from supposing that every one who likes me shall think well of my poetry, yet I do think that openness of dealing is necessary before a friend undertakes to decry one's writings to the world at large. But too much of this. Not till a couple of days ago did I hear of the volume of your poems which you designed for myself, lying at Mr. Taylor's for several months. But Mr. Quillinan will be down here in a week or ten days, to join his wife, who is here with us, and he will bring the book with him. Miss Fenwick, who is now under our roof for the winter, has read the volume with much pleasure, especially the Hymns. Upon her coming here she lent it to Mr. Faber, as we have all been paying visits up and down as far as Halsteads, and Carlisle. But then we are settling down in quiet for the winter, and your poems will be among the first I shall peruse. But, alas, the state of my eyes curtails my reading hours very much in these short days. Your father's "Sonnets," and Mr. Taylor's "Tragedy," are the only verse I have read for many months. If the expression, especially in point of truthfulness, were equal in your father's poems to the sanctity and weight of the thoughts, they would be all that one could desire in that style of writing. But in respect to your father's poems, your own, and all other new productions in verse, whether of my friends or of strangers, I ought frankly to avow that the time is past with me for bestowing that sympathy to which they are entitled. For many reasons connected with advanced life, I read but little of new works either in prose or verse. Rogers says of me, partly in joke and partly in earnest, as he says of himself and others as frankly, and has avowed in one of his letters written when he was an old man, "I read no poetry now but my own." In respect to myself, my good old friend ought to have added that if I do read my own, it is mainly, if not entirely, to make it better. But certain it is that old men's literary pleasures lie chiefly among the books they were familiar with in their youth; and this is still more pointedly true of men who

have practised composition themselves. They have fixed notions
of style and of versification, and their thoughts have moved on
in a settled train so long that novelty in each or all of these,
so far from being a recommendation, is distasteful to them, even
though, if hard put to it, they might be brought to confess that
the novelty was all improvement. You must be perfectly aware
of all that I have said, as characteristic of human nature to a
degree which scarcely allows of exceptions, though rigidity or
obtuseness will prevail more in some minds than in others. For
myself, however, I have many times, when called upon to give
an opinion on works sent, felt obliged to recommend younger
critics as more to be relied upon, and that for the reason I have
mentioned. It is in vain to regret these changes which Time
brings with it; one might as well sigh over one's grey hairs.
Let me, with Mason, the poet, say :

> " As my winter, like the year's, is mild,
>   Give thanks to Him from whom all blessings flow."

You enquire after my MS. poem on my own life. It is lying, and
in all probability will lie, where my " Tragedy," and other " Poems "
lay ambushed for more than a generation of years. Publication
was ever to me most irksome ; so that if I had been rich, I
question whether I should ever have published at all, though I
believe I should have written. I am pleased that you find some
things to like in my last volume. It has called out a good deal
of sorry criticism, as in truth happens to all my publications in
succession, and will do so as long as anything of mine comes
forth. With respect to my last volume I feel no interest but that
those who deem it worth while to *study* anything I write would
read the contents of that volume, as the prelude hints, in connection with its predecessors.

Throwing myself upon your kind indulgence for having deferred this letter so long, I remain, with high regard,

Faithfully yours,

WILLIAM WORDSWORTH.

I cannot better illustrate Wordsworth's special estimate
of Nature than by a quotation from what I have published elsewhere:

"The veracity and the ideality which are so signally combined
in Wordsworth's poetic descriptions of Nature made themselves
at least as much felt whenever Nature was the theme of his discourse.   In his intense reverence for Nature, he regarded all
poetical delineations of her with an exacting severity; and if
those descriptions were not true, and true in a twofold sense, the
more skilfully executed they were the more was his indignation
roused by what he deemed a pretence and a deceit.   An untrue
description of Nature was to him a profaneness, a heavenly mes-
sage sophisticated and falsely delivered.   He expatiated much to
me one day, as we walked among the hills above Grasmere, on
the mode in which Nature had been described by one of the
most justly popular of England's modern poets — one for whom
he preserved a high and affectionate respect.   'He took pains,'
Wordsworth said; 'he went out with his pencil and notebook,
and jotted down whatever struck him most — a river rippling
over the sands, a ruined tower on a rock above it, a promontory,
and a mountain-ash waving its red berries.   He went home and
wove the whole together into a poetical description.'   After a
pause, Wordsworth resumed, with a flashing eye and impassioned
voice, 'But Nature does not permit an inventory to be made of
her charms!   He should have left his pencil and notebook at
home; fixed his eye, as he walked, with a reverent attention on
all that surrounded him, and taken all into a heart that could
understand and enjoy.   Then, after several days had passed by,
he should have interrogated his memory as to the scene.   He
would have discovered that while much of what he had admired
was preserved to him, much was also most wisely obliterated.
That which remained — the picture surviving in his mind —
would have presented the ideal and essential truth of the scene,
and done so, in a large part, by discarding much which, though

in itself striking, was not characteristic. In every scene many of
the most brilliant details are but accidental. A true eye for
Nature does not note them, or at least does not dwell on
them.' " [1]

I was much pleased by finding that Wordsworth, a
poet hard to please, thought very highly of my father's
" Sonnets," stating that he believed they were the best of
the age. He added soon afterwards, " I need not remind
you, Mr. de Vere, that in making such a remark one
does not mean to institute anything in the way of a comparison between oneself and another writer." Wordsworth
became intimate with my father and his family in 1833.

During the latter part of 1844 I resided chiefly in our
old Irish home. Looking back from the present, with all
its anxieties, and contentions, to that light-hearted time,
the contrast seems strange. No doubt there were troubles
in those days as well as in ours; but the mirthful then
mingled with them. It was before the days of famine
or of revolution. It was the custom to look at the
humorous side of things, to amuse and be amused. Its
character in that respect may be guessed by a few extracts
from contemporary correspondence.

" Certainly ours is an odd country ! Every day one hears of
such pleasant things being said, and such odd things done, and
such wise advice being given by every one to his neighbour !
Stephen Spring Rice and I have agreed to write a great book
recording them, and to found with its proceeds a college for
the benefit of eccentric Irish gentlemen. Yesterday we heard
that three ex-officio Poor Law guardians had thrown up their

---

[1] Recollections of Wordsworth. Essays, chiefly on Poetry. Vol. II.,
pages 276–277. Macmillan and Co.

offices because they counted it 'foul scorn' that three Commissioners sitting in Somerset House should have the power of imposing a secretary on them without their having a corresponding right to send him back. When asked what they would advise in case the Commissioners prosecuted them, their answer was that of King Arthur's knights, who replied that 'Counsel they had none: but they were big enough.' The incident of last week was this. An excellent clergyman, riding near Limerick, met two men fighting. Being a man of peace, he thought it his duty to separate them; accordingly he pulled out a pistol, cocked it, and threatened to shoot them if they did not desist. His horse reared, the pistol went off, the horse was shot through the neck, the clergyman was thrown, without benefit of clergy, over his head; his own was broken; the two combatants shook hands on the spot, one of them carrying the clergyman into a neighbouring cottage while the other went in search of the lock of the pistol. Here is to-day's story: This morning a poor old woman was beaten and robbed by another old woman. She went to the 'petty sessions' for redress. There was no book on which to swear her except a large family Bible. She cast an alarmed glance on it and positively refused to swear. 'Did you not say you would swear on the Bible?' asked the magistrate. 'So I will, your Honour,' she replied, 'but not *on that Bible*. It is too big and too dangerous! I'd rather lie at the loss.' She departed, shaking her fist at her assailant and saying, 'I'll lave you to God!' I know what you will say. It is that every story one hears of the Irish proves that they are the most inefficient of men. That is because they think so much that one thought puts another out. When an Englishman gets a thought into his head, there it sticks, like a bone in his throat. He has so little to say about it that he must needs take action about it. We Irishmen discuss it from a hundred points of view and then forget it. Ireland, you say, has given Sister England a great deal of trouble, and after so many centuries has never been more than half conquered. Neither has she herself conquered. Her sons do not trust each other, for they act on their moods, and their moods change rapidly; consequently, to hold together long, is among them as difficult as to build a wall with round stones. Had they been able to unite they would have either conquered or been conquered long since."

Within another year or two I visited Miss Fenwick again near Ambleside, and again saw much of Wordsworth. I wrote thus to Henry Taylor: —

"It is delightful to see Miss Fenwick and Wordsworth together. A perpetual youth belongs to natures like theirs. On all subjects which touch their poetic or moral sympathies, he feels as he felt when he first came to these mountains; and as she listens to him she catches the inspiration, and I could fancy that those exquisite stanzas written on his daughter's picture,
> 'How rich that forehead's broad expanse,'

had been addressed to her. I never tire of hearing him recount the incidents out of which his own poetry blossomed. Not a natural object which he ever beheld can have been lost upon his mind poetic. He reminds us in one of his poems that the Muses were the offspring, not of Jove alone, but no less of Mnemosyne, or memory. Between him and you, I am beginning to transfer my allegiance from Plato and Coleridge, and to value facts almost as much as ideas."

To Miss Fenwick I wrote: —

"I wish you could get Wordsworth, in place of altering his old poems, to modernise others of Chaucer's besides 'The Prioress' Tale.' I wish also he would write down his thoughts on the poetic art, for poets alone understand the true philosophy of poetry. Mr. Wordsworth is a Protestant, but the 'mind poetic' of Wordsworth is chiefly Catholic, — as was that of Shakespeare, so far as it was religious."

One day Miss Fenwick drove me to the Nab Cottage, just under Rydal Mount, near Rydal Water, and the residence of Hartley Coleridge. She sent for him, and at once he was with us. It was a white-haired apparition, — wearing in all other respects the semblance of youth — with the most delicately-grained and tinted skin and vividly bright eyes. He could hardly be said to have walked, for he seemed with difficulty to keep his feet on the ground, as he wavered about near us with arms extended like wings. Everything that he said was strange and quaint, while perfectly unaffected, and, though always amusing, yet always represented a mind whose thoughts dwelt in regions as remote as the antipodes. After fifty years of ill-fortune the man before us was still the child described by Wordsworth in his poem to " H. C. at three years old."

> " O thou, whose fancies from afar are brought,
>   Who of thy words dost make a mock apparel,
> And fittest to unutterable thought,
>   The breeze-like motion and the self-born carol."

A few days later he dined with us, meeting a very genial and accomplished man, Edward Quillinan, the husband of Wordsworth's daughter, Dora — one of those three enchanting maidens that irradiate Wordsworth's poem " The Triad," which always looks to me as if it must have been conceived on the happiest May-day of his happy life. Quillinan and Hartley Coleridge, though they quarrelled occasionally, were old friends. On this occasion Hartley was in a splenetic mood, and talked politics in language much more radical than his serious opinions. Quillinan used language as strong in reply; and the dispute on " lib-

erty" became, as I observed, distressing to our kindly
hostess. I closed it with the help of a quotation. I said,
" I remember a definition for Liberty on which I think the
strongest zealots for Freedom or Order might agree. It
is this : —

> ' What, then, is freedom ?   Rightly understood,
> A universal licence — to be good.' "

Quillinan could make no objection, because the doctrine is
true conservatism, nor Hartley because the lines are his
own.   The combatants found themselves shaking hands
against their will, and Miss Fenwick was delighted.   She
had a great sense of humour.

It was a strange thing to see Hartley Coleridge fluctuating about the room, now with one hand on his head, now
with both arms expanded like a swimmer's.   There was
some element wanting in his being.   He could do everything but keep his footing, and doubtless in his inner
world of thought, it was easier for him to fly than to
walk, and to walk than to stand.   There seemed to be no
gravitating principle in him.   One might have thought he
needed stones in his pockets to prevent his being blown
away.   But he is said to have always lived " an innocent
life, though far astray," and he might, perhaps, have been
more easily changed into an angel than into a simply
strong man.   He was touchingly reverent when referring
to religious subjects, and in reading aloud his father's
hymn on Mont Blanc, whenever he came to the name of
God it seemed as if he could hardly pronounce it.   There
was also a great tenderness of nature about him and he
would not allow his MSS. to be taken out of his possession because many of them were written by friends now

dead. His bearing had lost nothing of its native refinement, though he had often associated chiefly with the rougher classes. His nature was plainly one of singular sweetness, yet there must have been a vein of bitterness in it also, or he could not have addressed that sonnet to his father which contains the line : —

" Thy prayer was heard — ' I wandered like a breeze.' "

Hartley Coleridge was fond of a joke. On one occasion he had listened with deep apparent interest to the voluble discourse of a well-known Irish enthusiast, who spent much of his time travelling about England, and enlightening the English mind on the subject of Popish errors, especially in Ireland. After dinner Hartley requested to be presented to a man so remarkable. On the presentation he took the far-famed traveller and philosopher by the arm, while a few of the guests gathered around, and addressed him with awful solemnity. " Sir, there are two great evils in Ireland." " There are, indeed, sir," replied the Irish guest ; " but please to name them. " The first," resumed Hartley, " is — Popery ! " " It is," said the other ; " but how wonderful that you should have discovered that ! Now tell me what is the second great evil ? " " Protestantism ! " was Hartley's reply in a voice of thunder, as he ran away screaming with laughter. His new acquaintance remained panic-stricken.

In the year 1845 I frequently attended Parliamentary debates. Here is an account of one written to a friend : —

"The Maynooth debate is over, and the majority is larger than was expected. That means Religious Equality in Ireland, if it has any meaning. Should it be followed up by that, it may

be the beginning of a peaceful time: should the implied promise remain long unfulfilled, it will increase discontent.   The
speech of Dr. Whateley, Archbishop of Dublin, was the most
striking one made, and singularly characteristic of the man.
There he stood, sometimes looking at the lamps under the
roof, sometimes at the buckles on his shoes, twisting himself into the strangest contortions, now making logical distinc-
tions, now following out a long reverie wholly unconscious of.
his audience, and yet delighting it by his brilliant paradoxes,
his sallies of wit, and his obvious sincerity.   Dr. Phillpots,
Bishop of Exeter, rose next, and before five minutes had elapsed
one discovered why he had signally failed to carry out any
authority in his diocese.   His speech was like that print
which consists of words all consisting of hair-strokes; and he
makes no allowance, either for the broad common-sense of
ordinary men, or for their instinctive feelings.   He wastes
ingenious sophisms upon men whose blunt intelligence neither
sees through them nor sees them.   There is no unravelling the
net he throws round men; but it is only a net of cobweb, and
John Bull walks through it without feeling it.   The Bishop's
face and manners are characteristic; the former is thin, sharp,
and pale, with a furtive evasive look, and keen eyes that open
out sideways.   He rose at the same moment as another nobleman; and nothing could be more edifying than the bland
urbanity and humility with which he resigned his own pretensions.   His competitor stood his ground; the Bishop sat at
the table with his hands clasped.   A smile must have lain
meekly upon his face.   Again he was called for; again he rose,
looked round him with deprecatory glance, and sank down
with a sort of court'sy.   At last he suffered himself to be per-
suaded, gradually rose, bowed gracefully towards his opponent,
and said, in the most silvery voice, that if anything could increase the diffidence with which he always addressed that House
it was the wish which that House apparently felt that the Most

Reverend Archbishop, who had last spoken, should be answered by a prelate. He then proceeded to state his unfeigned astonishment that after so many speeches it still remained for him to point out to their Lordships the one great primary error — the marvellous delusion under which both sides of the House had so long laboured. If noble Lords would only read one or two of the early documents connected with Maynooth they would learn the simple truth that what was called the Maynooth Endowment was no endowment at all. Maynooth had never been endowed. Nothing of the sort had ever been dreamed of. He then proceeded to read papers, and quote Acts of Parliament, maintaining by a series of verbal quibbles that the technical term 'corporate body' had never been formally applied to Maynooth; that the Government of the day had only experimentally given a charitable subscription to a Roman Catholic college; that the experiment had deplorably failed; and that the system pursued there was so notoriously bad that, while Protestants hated the institution, the Roman Catholics of Ireland refused to aid it, though its buildings were falling into ruins. The Bishop's movements were sometimes as graceful as those of a girl, and at other times as sharp and fierce as those of an angry sibyl; his face never lost its amenity, nor his voice its sweetness — a sweetness which increased when his compliments were most keenly edged with insinuations. His speech was throughout ingenious; but as a whole it was a blunder. There is an inspiration of common-sense, as well as one of genius; and crafty men often miss both forms of it.

The moment the Bishop had sunk back on his seat, Lord Brougham leaped up, and, lifting high his battle-axe with great fury and great delight, hacked to pieces the whole of the fairy creation conjured up with such skill by his right reverend friend. The Bishop sat it out well. He looked pale and tired; but he smiled through it, sometimes a little malignantly, but more often as if amused, occasionally nodding pleasantly

to his tormentor. Passing out of the House, they shook hands
with each other as cordially as two lawyers who have just been
wrangling in a court of justice. Not less animating was the
subsequent attack of Lord Normanby upon the Bishop of
Cashel. Nothing could be in worse taste than the Marquis's
attack, or more undignified than the Bishop's reply. He
plainly thought that he 'did well to be angry,' and stamped
several times on the ground as he stated that he would not
return evil for evil. A soft breeze agitated now and again the
'lenient cloud' of lawn that leaned along the episcopal bench,
but not one of the English bishops raised a snow-clothed arm
in defence of their Irish brother."

We hear much of the mere "make-believe" of which
parliamentary rhetoric consists, but there is a converse
evil, a tragic sincerity. Of this I witnessed a marvellous ·
specimen. It was a terrible and probably wholly unexpected attack made upon the late Earl Grey by Lord
Derby, grandfather of the present Earl. Lord Grey was
then Secretary to the Colonies. A "Blue Book" on some
colonial subject had recently been presented to Parliament by the Government; and Lord Derby undertook the
examination of it. His criticism was progressively more
and more insulting. The charge was neither an abstract
one, nor exclusively one relating to moral right and
wrong; it was a question also of honour, and therefore,
to such as knew Lord Grey, the idea that he could be
guilty was absurd. Lord Derby's statement was that,
however plausible the "Blue Book" might appear, so
many passages had been intentionally omitted that its
apparent testimony had become the exact opposite of
that which truth would have required. Lord Derby had

evidently got up his case with great care, and pleaded it
with the skill of a consummate advocate, and at great
length. It seemed at first as if Lord Grey could not
believe that this strange charge was seriously intended;
but as its full meaning became unquestionable, the growing indignation, and no less the suffering, of the victim
became things distressing to witness. At one moment he
was in conference with his secretary, whom he sent off in
search of papers; but of course he was not himself able
to divert his attention from what his assailant was saying
at the moment in order to ascertain what was the answer
to a preceding charge. That assailant had thus a most
unfair advantage over the assailed. The contrast between
the rigid intensity of the latter and the easy gaiety of the
former was the more painful because Lord Derby frequently called his opponent his "noble friend." Near
the close he remarked that if a gentleman gave you a false
half-crown, you supposed it was a mistake, if he gave you
another when you met next, it seemed odd; but if there
was just one person who never paid a debt except in false
money you did not know what to think.

The moment Lord Derby sat down Lord Grey bounded
forward, but Lord Lansdowne who sat next him drew him
back, and addressed the House for a few minutes, evidently to give his friend time for recollection. Then Lord
Grey rose; advanced to a conspicuous spot and stood
silent. He strove to speak; nothing was heard; again he
strove, and again and again, but in vain. The strong and
fiery soul was not duly seconded by the material organs.
Not a sound! He *did* speak, but no sound became
audible. He stood his ground; at last he made himself

heard. I still remember one sentence, broken by many pauses, "The person who has hurled against me this wholly unexpected attack has several times, while making it, designated me as his 'noble friend'; I request that, in future, he will consider that he has discharged, on this occasion, the very ultimate duty of friendship, and cease to address me by that name." The Earl of Derby bent slightly forward, lightly lifted his hat and bowed.

The Lord Derby of that day was said to have been a hard man, and if such an attack had been made on himself he would probably have felt little except a mixture of anger and amusement. Politics were said to have been to him, from first to last, more an amusement than any-thing else; and when his amusement required it, he was said not to have been above the tricks of debate. Perhaps he was afterwards the first to laugh at them. I remember that on one occasion, when an admirer of his called him "the Hotspur of debate," another person present rejoined, "The Autolycus-Hotspur, you mean." Whether the scoff was just, I know not.

Public life, however, has its comic episodes, as well as its tragedies. Here is one of them. It was in 1848, the year of the manifold revolutions; there were then, in the House of Commons, two Irish members of character, sin-gularly unlike, Mr. Sheil and Mr. Feargus O'Connor. The former was regarded as one of the chief orators in the House; he was also a celebrated wit, and memorable for having once told the House that "the Irish were a very dangerous people — to run away from," a suggestion the recollection of which might have spared us a large proportion of recent legislation. In his youth Sheil had

written a clever tragedy, and when young no more he
was said to take very common-sense views of politics
as distinguished from ultra-scrupulous views. Feargus
O'Connor was a wild enthusiast, and many people thought
him mad. He undertook the enterprise of leading a body
of 200,000 men into London, and possibly effecting a
revolution; on which occasion the London citizens
armed themselves with batons, and prevented Feargus's
army from passing over the bridges into the streets.

One night I heard a considerable noise in one of the
lobbies near the House. It was Feargus O'Connor, who
tramped up and down very vehemently near a little table
on which sat Sheil knocking his little feet together and
apparently much amused. He had just accepted office,
and had to encounter a storm of unpopularity on the part
of extreme Irish nationalists. The battle between the mad
Revolutionist and the wit was highly amusing. Feargus
began: "You were once a patriot, I believe, Mr. Sheil;
you are now in favour of a Government which is at this
moment augmenting the military establishment in Ireland." "To be sure I am," replied Sheil. "It is a
measure useful for Ireland. Its sole effect will be this.
The new English regiments will add a profit of many
thousands a year to the Irish farmers from their consump-
tion of milk and butter alone." "That's very fine, Mr.
Sheil, but I think I can recollect when you took different
views of things; if I am not far astray, when you were a
young man and addressed the mob at ———, you said
'Boys there are foolish people that talk to you about
moral force; what I tell you is this: get iron-pointed pikes
and I'll march at your head!'" "You are not the least

astray, Feargus, only that you have forgotten what the
mob answered." "What did it say, sir?" "What they
said was this, 'Lord bless you, sir, you'd no more do it
than Feargus O'Connor!'" "I would do it, Mr. Sheil,
and what's more I can tell you this; there is not a night
of my life that, before ever I go to bed, I do not kneel
down and pray Heaven to punish England for all the
wrongs she has done to Ireland." Here Sheil clashed his
small feet again together and his great dark eyes gleamed
brighter from the recess in which he sat, as he enquired,
apparently with a delighted surprise: "And tell me now,
Feargus, is it a fact that you are in the habit of saying
your prayers before going to bed?" "It is a fact, Mr.
Sheil." "Well, Feargus, I would not have suspected you
of it; but I am glad to hear it. It shows us that you have
sense enough left, after all. Follow on as you are, and
here is a little humble advice for you. Anything in the
nature of high treason that you have to transact in future,
transact the whole of it in your prayers! That is the very
safest form in which you can lodge the investment.
Otherwise, you have so often transported the House of
Commons with your eloquence that, in return, it will never
stop till it transports you to Botany Bay." So went on
the skirmishing for perhaps an hour, the spectators growing each moment more numerous; but every time the
foaming patriot renewed the attack, the little wit laid him
on his back.

In spite, however, both of London society and politics,
my thoughts were constantly reverting to Windermere. I
wrote thus to Miss Fenwick, of those she cared for
most:

"You may well call him, H. Taylor's child, 'that precious child.' He is rich in all the graces of infancy — its soft round-ness, its noble brow, cloudless eye, its luminous skin, its filmy eyelids, its coral lip, its instant and universal smile, and dimpled complacency. Those who see no beauty either in infancy or old age know little about beauty. I have been seeing, also, a good deal of your dear friend, Mrs. Edward Villiers. How winning she is — at least to those she likes. She puts me in mind of what I suppose must have been often said, namely, that a widow who is ' a widow indeed,' is only a wife whose husband is withdrawn from her eyes that he may remain more constantly in her heart. I passed several happy days in her lovely home, Grove Mill, a charming specimen of rural England, with what Beattie calls ' its pomp of groves and garniture of fields,' and Tennyson describes as —

> ' all things in order stood,
> A haunt of ancient peace.'

The union of the beautiful with the useful is very English. The squirrel here runs upon the longest branches of the elms, and runs up again gaily after an occasional fall on the road, eighty feet below; but the mill-wheel runs round and round for the bene-fit of the public, and the canal, as the barge pushes over it, ' waves all its lazy lilies and rolls on.' There are no ' minster towers ' to crown the ' three arches of a bridge.' Doubtless mon-astic towers crowned the olden forests hard by till seditious kings and ignoble nobles pulled them down. Grove Mill is an ' Elysian garden islet ' cut out of an angle at the meeting of ' Cassiobury ' and the ' Grove ' — the stately houses of Lords Essex and Claren-don. Half of it is flower-ground, and the other half a kitchen garden, full of currant and raspberry bushes; and around it winds a crystal stream, girt in some places by meadows, in some by laurel thickets, and in some by a hedge trailed over with roses and honeysuckles. The mile-long lime avenues of Cassiobury send the odour of their hidden flowers far away over the country

beyond.   The stream is populous with trout — Mrs. Edward
Villiers put her twins into it the other day, and you cannot think
how pretty they looked, with the sunbeams breaking through the
laurel boughs and sparkling, now on their hair, and now on their
smiling faces, which no one can distinguish one from another.
Alice Taylor wrote a poem describing the scene.   It contained a
line —

' Life's wasted light, and worse, its wasted shade,'

which I advised her to publish soon, as otherwise it would
become mine whenever I published next ; not mine by inheritance or purchase, but by adoption.[1]   We walked a great deal
about Cassiobury, and I offended Mrs. Edward Villiers's English
feelings very much by informing her that my Irish home was far
larger than both that place and The Grove put together.   Her
own small abode is perfect.   Those smaller English homes, belonging to persons not rich, but well-born and well-bred, who pre-
side over them with as much grace and dignity as can be found
in the noblest abodes, are the more attractive from their entire
absence of all that has a touch of the ostentatious, or of the
' comfortable ' carried to materialism."

[1] It was introduced into my poem " A Farewell to Naples."

CHAPTER VIII

TRAVELS WITH SIR HENRY TAYLOR AND HIS WIFE, CHIEFLY IN ITALY, 1843–44

IN the September of 1843, Henry Taylor, whose health had been a subject of anxiety, was ordered to pass the winter in the South, and the authorities of the Colonial Office gave him a liberal holiday in return for important services. Sir James Stephen, the Under-Secretary to the Colonies, spoke to me with sadness on the subject as we walked one day in Richmond Park. "It is a pity, to see Taylor breaking down so early." But Henry Taylor lived a much longer life than he did, though then a picture of stately strength.

I gladly became his fellow-traveller, under the impression that my earlier travels must have given me some experiences likely to be of use. On that earlier occasion a cousin of mine, a rough old soldier, just returned from an Italian tour, bade me farewell with these words: " If you are sharp you need not spend more than a hundred pounds a month; but you are not, and before you have been long in Italy you will have been carried off by robbers, married and murdered ! "

Our party consisted of four beside myself: Henry Taylor, his wife, her maid, and a delightful little boy of five or six years of age, Freddy Elliot, taken charge of by the Taylors during the absence of his father, Sir Charles Elliot, then Governor of Bermuda, one of Henry Taylor's chief friends, and the " Athulf" of his drama, " Edwin the Fair." A more amusing, vivacious, or intelligent child I have never seen, and many of his quaint sayings live on in my memory to this day. We started from London early enough to surprise our relatives and especial friends, the Calverts, in the middle of their dinner at Dover, and walk with them on the seaside later. The next day we saw that ominous memorial of the French Revolution, the tower of the ruined abbey of St. Omer, looming out like a phantom through the evening air. Out of reverence for Charlemagne, we visited the cathedral of Aix-la-Chapelle, built by him, and chosen by him as his place of sepulchre. It was night when we reached it; but we could not have seen it to more advantage than by the autumnal moonlight, — walking round it several times, and gazing on the shadowy domes that surmount its Gothic buttresses. As we walked home I repeated my father's sonnet — " The Tomb of Charlemagne."

We visited also, as in duty bound — not only to the " men of old," but to those who in our degenerate days

walk in their footsteps — the vast and glorious Cathedral of
Cologne, beneath the roof of whose chancel the towers of
Westminster Abbey might stand. There we found nearly
four hundred men employed on the works, and learned
that in eighteen years more that stupendous pile would
reach its completion, an encouragement to all builders
who build in faith. We all know that the work stood in
abeyance for centuries; but some may forget how an
apparent accident caused the renewal of the enterprise.
During those centuries a crane once used for the lifting
of stones stood on the stunted tower. The people would
not allow it to be removed, for it implied a promise. One
stormy night it fell. A small local subscription was raised
to restore it. That act renewed the great enterprise.

Our way was by the Rhine, and our progress was slow.
The weather was delightful, and the scenery not such as
one wishes to rush through rapidly. Our only trouble
was that connected with our luggage; for, as many persons
disembarked at each station, there seemed always a danger
of their carrying away our luggage with their own. To
avert such a mischance, we made a pile of all our *impedi-
menta* in a spot by itself, and on its summit the devoted
lady's-maid sat, like an old hen hatching her eggs. She
cast no glance at castle or crag. Her affections, with a
natural piety, gravitated exclusively to their legitimate
objects. There she sat, now fixing a tender eye on some
special basket; now flashing an angry glance on an equivocal stranger too near it. We admired, conversed, or
read one of the books enclosed in our netted bag, till the
boat stopped for the night. This life contented us all
except the youngest.

One night, when Alice Taylor had put little Freddy to bed, and was leaving the room, she heard a little squeaky voice from behind the curtains—"Oh, I am afraid that all the pleasant part of my life is now over; and all the sorrowful part is to come." She returned: "Six years old is young for an end of all happiness, Freddy; what makes you so sorrowful?" "Oh, Alice," he said, "every day in the steamboat I find such a nice little girl, and play with her, and love her; and every evening she is taken to a different hotel from ours; and the next day there is another nice little girl in the steamboat; and I love her and play with her, and when evening comes I see her no more; and this is the fourth day I have lost her!" Constancy was no part of his moral ideal.

What interested us far the most on or near the Rhine was the ruined castle of Heidelberg. Its position, 330 feet above the lovely river Neckar, is all that painter could desire, and in vastness and picturesque variety of outline it cannot be surpassed. Amongst all the feudal ruins which I have seen I should give the highest place to Heidelberg castle and palace — as, among monastic ruins, I should give the highest to England's Fountains, or Tintern. As we advanced, a glory streamed from it, reflected from the setting sun, which might have made us fancy that the vast pile was assailed by one more conflagration; for during the long centuries since its foundation in A.D. 1294 to A.D. 1784, when it was struck by lightning, there were few of the chances and changes of warlike times which it had escaped. We walked in the picturesque woods adjoining Heidelberg, while the autumnal sun

" Reddened the fiery hues, and shot
Transparence through the golden," [1]

and next day pursued our journey till the Rhine laid us down at Basle.

Our route included Lucerne, and I had looked forward eagerly to the pleasure of making my companions acquainted with what I have ever regarded as the grandest of the Swiss lakes, as well as the most interesting in its historical associations, from the days of William Tell to those when wives and sisters fell by hundreds beside their husbands and brothers on the battle-plain, in defence of their native land against republican France. On our arrival there, however, the weather, which had favoured us so long, began to change.

We arrived late; and Henry Taylor and I went to get our letters. To reach the post-office we had to cross one of those quaint old bridges the roofs of which are decorated with religious pictures. It was so dark that before we had advanced far upon it we fell down a flight of steps. On reaching the bottom we were grateful to find that, though a little bruised, we were still on the bridge, and not in the lake.

The next day we went to see the lake. A disappointment met me there. It had never occurred to me that the same person could look upon one class of mountains with delight and on another with dislike, and indeed with distress. When we passed on into Italy, I found that the Italian mountains were to Henry Taylor far more than they are to most people. Their long majestic summits, shaped, as Landor says, as if for the winds to run races

[1] Wordsworth — " Yarrow revisited."

on them, and the infinite grace of the curves adown which
they sank into the broad rich plains below, charmed him;
and he did not like them the less when they kept a re-
spectful distance, and thus inflicted on their inmate no
sense of imprisonment. I well remember how long he
stood beneath the ruined arch of the bridge at Narni,
looking forth on the lovely view it commands. But it
was wholly different in Switzerland. We sat upon a cliff
on the lake-side which commanded one of those views
which in my earlier travels had saddened me, because
there was then no one with whom to share my admiration.
He never raised his eyes or spoke a word. At last a
mangy old dog drew near, and upon it he fixed an attention which rubbed my sympathies the wrong way. I
concluded, however, that he was fatigued, and would
behave better the next day. The next day we took
boat, and visited the grandest portions of a lake 40
miles long, and in many parts girdled by snow-crowned
mountains from ten to twelve thousand feet high. Before
our reaching the finest of these views I brought him a
cup of hot strong coffee. All would not do; he was
grateful for the coffee, but had not a word for the
mountains!

I forgave him, however, his incivility to the Alps, when
I discovered his admiration for the Apennines; and still
more when I found that that incivility implied no indif-
ference, but was a very cordial dislike. The Alps oppressed his spirits like whispers implying painful mysteries
or threatening news. The lines of great mountains have
a mathematics of their own; they are hieroglyphics. By
those who apprehend them in part, but only in part, they

are regarded with aversion. To him they were perplexing
and distressing, as the minor key eminently was in music;
for he felt that there was a deep significance in them:
but they would neither reveal what they meant nor let
him alone. Alpine scenery was to him a sphinx that
threatened to devour those that could not guess her
riddle. They were a chaos reasserting its primeval
claims upon a world which had submitted long since to
a milder control. On our return from Southern Italy, I
took him to one more Alpine view, thinking that his
opinion of such scenes might have changed. After a long
silence he looked up and said: "I pray to Heaven I may
never see mountains *of this sort* again." I turned on my
heel and walked home; and his wife, on his return, accused
him of having insulted my mountains; to which he replied
that mountains were neither my brothers nor my sisters!

The weather gave signs of breaking; and we decided
that as the Pass of St. Gothard rose between us and the
south, it would be wise to place ourselves on its sunny
side. We hired a carriage at Hospital and set off for
Lugano.

In the first ravine on our ascent we encountered a sharp
snowstorm. Alice Taylor, being much accustomed to
her own way, was a little displeased by it, but soon passed
into a gayer mood. "Every one knows," I said, "that an
Alpine ravine is nothing without its storm, which is one
of quite a peculiar sort. A poem of mine" — I had
repeated two or three lines of it when she laid her hand
on my arm and exclaimed, "Stop! stop! I will bear the
snow!" All the other little mishaps of the way were met
in the same pleasant way, till, when pretty well advanced

on the descent, we all of us suddenly exclaimed "Italy!"
and saw the Italian sun flashing on Italian vegetation, and
knew that in another hour we should be in the land of the
vine and the maize, of the orange grove and the lemon
grove. Soon afterwards we saw the glitter of the Ticino,
and Bellinzona with its battlemented walls and its three
castles.

From Bellinzona we made our way the next day to
Lugano, passing through a country every spot of which
laughed in our faces. Just as we had sat down to luncheon, three old friends of the Taylors walked into the
room — Bingham Baring, Lady Harriet Baring, and their
friend Charles Buller, who was travelling with them, and
whose elastic step and beaming eye, as they advanced,
showed that he was glad to see us. We passed a day or
two together there. Charles Buller and I made the
ascent of the far-famed Monte Salvadore, approved by
Wordsworth, who concedes to it a view more sublime than
can be enjoyed anywhere else *from the same elevation ;*
for it does not rise above the lake higher than 2000 feet.
Charles Buller was a most agreeable converser, and he
would have become important in the political world but for

> " That blind Fury with the abhorred shears
> That slits the thin-spun life."

My chief recollection in connection with Lugano is its
church, Santa Maria degli Angioli, and its magnificent
frescoes by Luini. No one can look at his pictures without being deeply impressed by the sympathetic power
through which the genius of Leonardo da Vinci passed
into the intellect of his greatest pupil. The short time we
passed at Lugano left behind it a noble poetical memorial.

During a walk on its shore, Henry Taylor and his wife
made acquaintance with one of the peasant families living
there. He was deeply impressed by all that humble happiness, geniality, and unconscious moral elevation which
dignified that unpretending abode, and was grateful to its
inmates for their hospitality and for the thoughts which
they had left with him. The result was a poem written
at Naples.

From Lugano we went by boat to Porlezza at the
eastern end of the lake, and drove thence to Menaggio,
on the lake of Como, passing next to Cadenabbia, and
Bellagio, the loveliest spot on that lake.

About the same time when Henry Taylor was ordered
to winter in Italy, his " chief of friends," Edward Ernest
Villiers, then suffering from a pulmonary complaint, was
sent to Nice. From that place, disquieting news reached
us, and Henry Taylor determined upon seeing his friend.
We did so, taking the Lago Maggiore and Baveno on our
way in hopes of receiving there a later letter. While there
we saw the noblest views on the Italian lakes, backed, as
they seldom are, by perpetual snows, and visited of course
the Borromean Islands and the huge palace of that ancient
family, inscribed somewhat superabundantly with its
motto: " Humilitas," or as Southey calls it " The Obtru-
sive Motto's proud Humility." Among the legends
connected with the great Cardinal Borromeo this is an
amusing one. When Cardinal Giulio had shown to
Cardinal Borromeo the vast abode which he had just
completed, the latter maintained a strict silence until they
had inspected the whole. When departing, he said:
" Your Eminence, I have been reflecting that the huge

sums spent on this palace might have been given to the poor." Cardinal Giulio replied: "Your Eminence, they *have* been all given to the poor. But our notions of charity differ. I pay the poor for their labour; and your Eminence for their idleness."

On our arrival at Nice we found that Edward Villiers's health had rapidly declined since his arrival at Nice. He had exchanged his hotel for the neighbouring hill of Cimiez, and was living with his wife and their two elder children in the Maison Nicolas, among the olive woods and orange bowers. We found a very small abode within five minutes' walk of it, close to the little chapel of St. Rosalie on a narrow terrace lined by acacia trees which scented the spot with a fragrance more delicate than that of the adjoining lemon bowers. Nice had not then been changed into a French Brighton. The rest may be told in a letter written to my mother.

" Edward Villiers was still well enough, when we arrived here a week ago, to derive comfort from his friend's visit, and always spoke to him of his own approaching departure in terms cheerful and contented. During the last two days he hardly suffered, and I am full of hope that this visit, which was so much feared for Henry Taylor by his friends, will be to him no physical injury, while morally a lasting consolation. It was a deep if a sad comfort to him to have been on the spot, to have witnessed the peacefulness of his friend's last days, to have received the Sacrament with him, to have attended him to his grave, and to have assisted in helping his widow and children who would otherwise have been friendless in a foreign land. That widow had nursed her husband with an unremitting attention, hardly ever leaving his bedside night or day. The day but one before his death she read to him the burial service at his wish, and would never speak of his approaching death as other than as he regarded it, that is, as to him a blessing. It was better, she said, that she should be the bereft one than that he should. She now rides about the woods with her children. I saw her to-day, lifting up a butterfly before their eyes, and explaining to them the Greek allegory of the Soul. When they understood it, a brightness shone upon their faces, which was at once reflected on her own, worn as it had grown."

Returning over the way we had already travelled from Genoa, my friends had the leisure necessary for the enjoyment of its gladsome loveliness. The air was at once soft and bracing, and embalmed by a vegetation far richer than that which borders the Lombard lakes. Alternately we drove along a road cut like a groove along the cliffs, or dragged our wheels slowly through the sands on the shore, now gazing on the waves that indolently swayed about in masses of azure, purple or green, and now listening to their murmur, as they slid along the ledges of rock, or tossed their spray upon the myrtle bowers, or flashed from some distant promontory, reddened by the western sunset. Often we got out of the carriage to visit some church whose campanile crested a village, and in which rested the tomb of the Saint who first brought the Christian tidings to that spot, and whose feast was more honoured by torchlight processions or rural dances than would be the memory of any conqueror.

Little Freddy had, however, cause of complaint. Once he said, on rejoining us, " I have been looking for river nymphs in the streams; but I never can find one, though the gentleman who wrote that book you showed me saw them in all the streams ! "

We passed several days at Milan, and no small part of each in that wonderful cathedral, probably the grandest completed specimen of the Italian Gothic, in the creation of which, while the main design came from northern art (for its founder was a German "Freemason"), a large part was contributed by the chief Italian intellects of an early day, including Brunelleschi, Bramante, and Leonardo da Vinci, while the work was further stimulated by the saintly zeal of St. Charles Borromeo. The exterior of the building has the great merit of being *sui generis*, while several of its characteristics, including its exquisite elaboration, are rendered more effective still by the radiant marble of which its countless pinnacles are fashioned. At least I thought so, though Henry Taylor complained that a lack of massiveness was thus produced. The quasi-classical "West End" built in the revived barbarism of a later day, and under such patronage as might be expected from a Napoleon, is a sad blemish which can only be removed by the substitution for it of such a façade as was originally intended, and as is represented in an old plan of the church. As to the interior, there can be no question : it reminds one of the verse, "The Queen's daughter is all glorious within," a text more applicable to Italian churches than to those of other countries. It has not the severity or perhaps the stern spirituality of the Northern Gothic, but it has few rivals in its union of vastness with richness, and in the sacred and mysterious gloom which, notwithstanding its redundance of ornament, pervades it.

St. Peter's at Rome is of a character the extreme opposite of that which belongs to the interior of Milan: yet the gloom of the one and the glory of the other are not without a latent affinity to each other, as the radiance in the faces of Fra Angelico's saints have a remote harmony with the holy sadness in those of saints by Perugino, both classes being saintly. It was thus that the great Medieval Art sustained her great antiphonal song, "O ye Nights and Days, bless ye the Lord, praise Him and magnify Him for ever." The interior of Milan cathedral is dark, not only because nearly all the windows are of storied glass, but by reason of that multitudinous forest of pillars which shadow its double aisles. An immense additional greatness is conferred upon this church also by a sacrifice which was well worth making — the sacrifice of the usual triforium gallery, beautiful as is that feature of Gothic architecture. It is directly from the pillars that the vaulting of the roof soars aloft. Those pillars are themselves eighty feet in height. The vaulted roof of the nave hangs above the pavement at a height of more than one hundred and fifty feet. The mystic dimness is enhanced rather than diminished by the gleam that streams occasionally from the dusky marble of a pillar smitten by the light of a painted window itself unseen, or a flash from the tall reed-like tapers that stand before some distant altar. The eye loses itself in the labyrinth of that columned grove where the pillars of the transepts and chancel group with those of the nave. The vast arches which those pillars support are encrusted with sculpture; nay, the capitals of the pillars themselves, besides being enriched by a marble wreath of blended foliage and children, are surmounted by a range of niches, each with its saint, and a canopy above him. The upper portions of the high and cav-

ernous windows are embossed all over with sculpture.
Indeed the unbounded use made of the human form,
both in the interior as well as the exterior of this marvellous cathedral, the manifold details of which are all
subordinated to a single great and pervading idea, cause
it to differ in kind as well as in degree from all other
churches.   In it statues are not mere ornaments introduced into the structure. They were evidently part of
that high vision which revealed itself to the inspired imagination of its architect when brooding over his original
plan.   They constitute, rather than adorn, a great and
solid portion of the higher structure. It looks as if its
designer had been reading that chapter in Saint Paul in
which the Apostle speaks of faithful Christians as "living
stones" in the mystical church.   The architect seems
to have said, "There is no shape more noble than the
human form — that temple of a soul made in God's image — which is worthy of suggesting the antitype of a
temple reared for the worship of an ever-present God."

But those who ascend to the marble roof of the cathedral of Milan enjoy a view which no modern degen-
eracy can impair. In the midst of that army of statues
crowning its countless spires, you might think that you
stood amid the assembly of the blest. The statue of the
Blessed Virgin stands at the height of three hundred and
fifty-five feet from the ground.   In prospect beneath
spreads the whole plain of Lombardy with its rivers and
its cities. Beyond these rise several of the Apennines,
and the chief summits among the Alps — those that em-
bosom the Lombard lakes — St. Gothard, Monte Rosa,
Mont Cenis. If the morning is clear, the unrisen sun

flashes its crimson and gold successively from crest to crest.

Alas! my travelling companions were not able to ascend to that temple in the skies: but they enjoyed the cathedral of Milan more than any other Italian church.

We saw also with a deep interest, what, to all who reverence Christian antiquity, will impart no less delight than the Duomo itself, namely, the Basilica of St. Ambrogio, founded by St. Ambrose, A. D. 387. It was largely restored in the ninth century, but both then and later, the main arrangements of the original church were preserved. It has still its *atrium*, or outer court, not to be passed by Catholic penitents not yet in full communion with the Church; and it is without a transept. It boasts its magnificent baldachino, which rises above the bodies of SS. Gervasius and Protasius, to whom the original church was dedicated. At its eastern end it has still its ancient "tribune," with a grand mosaic on a gold ground, and "the chair of St. Ambrose." Its chief treasure, however, is a portion of the gates which, at the command of St. Ambrose, were barred against the Christian Emperor, Theodosius, when he approached them stained by the massacre of Thessalonica.

From Milan we made our way to Florence, where we enjoyed the warm-hearted hospitality of Roland and Lady Lucy Standish, the aunt of Alice Taylor; and certainly the most friendly of hostesses. I must reserve for another opportunity my Recollections of Italy's chief cities. In a few days we hurried on. We reached Rome in time to ascend the Pincian hill for the sunset. It was announced to us by that marvellous pealing of church

bells for which Rome has no rival. The four great ba-
silicas claimed as usual their ancient precedence. First
—the true cathedral of Rome, not St. Peter's, but St.
John Lateran. As the bells of the last rolled forth their
thunders, they seemed to put into music the words of
that proud superscription which runs round the whole
building: "To me it has been conceded by mandate both
Papal and Imperial that of all the churches on the orb
of earth, I should be the mother and the head." The
bells of St. Peter's, St. Paul's, and Santa Maria Maggiore
then made response successively in the order prescribed;
after which all the bells of Rome's greater churches joined
simultaneously in full chorus.

Within a few days more we reached the end of our journey, Naples, sleeping one night at Mola di Gaeta, one of
the loveliest spots on the seacoast, especially when seen as
I saw it first, in 1839, with the morning star suspended
over its blue waves and glimmering on its orange bowers,
still dewy from the night. My friends took up their abode
on the Chiaia and I at an hotel opposite to the public garden. I wrote thus to a friend : —

"Henry Taylor has made a sudden spring forward here in
health and spirits. At first he did not like the climate, for if the
wind blows from the sea it is hot, and if from the snow it is bit-
terly cold. He calls it 'winter, toasted at one side.' He has
taken to poetry again; and as some of it is inspired by the scenes
around us, his occupation will doubtless make him enjoy this spot
all the more, while they, in turn, will not fail to enlarge his mind
poetic, and increase its sensibilities. His old friends, Lord and
Lady Ashburton, are here. The former is a singularly active and
intelligent old gentleman, who insists upon seeing everything, as if

he were only now beginning his education. He asks every one his opinion upon every subject, without, however, much caring to communicate his own; because, as they say, his own is very apt to change, according to the point of view from which his active and versatile intellect regards a subject successively. We have been once to one of the great Accademia balls, but are not likely to go to another."

Again I wrote:

"We have, of course, been at the great Picture Gallery. The collection of pictures is one of the largest and one of the worst that I have seen anywhere; that of statues is good, and the bronzes are magnificent. The great glory of the collection is, of course, that part of it which comes from Pompeii and Hercula-neum. But Naples is a city more devoted to amusement than to art. It is dinned with a perpetual clatter of trivial dissipation. The result has been one more fatal both to thought and action than all the swamps of Holland or the snows and volcanoes of Iceland would have proved; and I believe that Naples has never produced a great man, and seldom adopted any. The house in which the Taylors live is let to them by the aide-de-camp of one of the king's brothers. He complains of the monotony of their daily life. One of the modes in which they fight against it is this. At a certain hour each day, his royal master and he strip all the beds, and rival each other in a chase after fleas!"

Among our most interesting expeditions was that which we made to Pozzuoli and its amphitheatre, where the glad-iators had to measure their strength against that of lions and tigers. Henry Taylor had always been a stern enemy to field sports. The sight of this celebrated amphitheatre stimulated that enmity to the utmost, and he wrote on our return some powerful verses threatening the present lovers of such sports that they will themselves be one day judged, as they themselves now judge those who, in pagan times, frequented the amphitheatres.

> " Pain in man
> Bears the high mission of the flail and fan ;
> In beasts 't is purely piteous."

Close to Pozzuoli is the Bay of Baiæ, the favourite retreat — owing both to its beauty and its luxurious climate — of the most dissolute among the Roman nobles.

Pompeii is, of course, the chief marvel near Naples. To walk there, from street to street, and see not only the frescoes still fresh on the walls, but all the details of daily life — the wheel-ruts, the hinges of the vanished doors, the signs over the shops, the ovens with their rolls of bread baked before the day of destruction, the lamps and the snuffers, the pipes for the baths, and the advertisement of shops to be sold, and, amongst these trifles, the image, impressed upon the lava, of a woman arrested in her flight, and still clasping her babe to her breast — to see these things is to shake hands with antiquity, and not to stare at it alone. The past lives again, and the illusion is aided by the resemblance between the men gone by and those here at the present day, who in their characters and their manners are thorough Greeks still, though without a touch of the Greek genius, while in many places they retain much of the Greek costume. To enter into the spirit of the region it is necessary to forget Italy, and to remember that Southern Italy is still Magna Græcia. There are there hardly any remains of the middle ages, and none of the Roman Empire, except what may be found in the ruined villas.

Another of the characteristics of this region is its marvellous fertility. Half the way up Vesuvius the country
people plant vines in a soil which seems to consist of
nothing but lava and *tufo*. As you ascend you look down
on a scene well entitled to its name, the Campagna Felice.
—a tract of mulberries, oranges, and almonds, glowing
with flowers at almost all times of the year; gardens
divided by hedges of aloe, and occasional cornfields that
triple the produce of less fortunate lands. With the
single exception of Capri, which is a rock of limestone,
the whole region is volcanic. In past ages Ischia was
what Vesuvius is now; while the summit of Vesuvius, then
not half its present height, was covered with vineyards.
In many places are the craters of extinct volcanoes. In
not a few is a small lake like that of Avernus, with a ruin
reflected in its gloomy pool, and a ridge of flat-headed
pines hanging like a cloud beneath the yellow green of
the evening sky. Boiling streams, issuing through fis-
sures in the rock, are so common that you hardly remark
them. On the coast of Baiæ there is an island which rose
in the course of a week about two hundred years ago,
while near Pompeii spreads a league of rich pasture over
which boats sailed in days of old. Vesuvius is a different
mountain every year both in size and shape, and the quantity of matter flung up by it is said to have been sufficient
to form four mountains of its present size. Again and
again all becomes ruin, but the fugitive inhabitants always
return.

The last time I made the ascent of Vesuvius it was from
Terra dell' Annunziata. I was alone, and after climbing
about half-way up the mountain, I found myself in a black

wilderness of embers, such as we might imagine to be ruins of a planet after its conflagration. Appalling as the region was in colour, nothing could exceed it in its beauty of shape. The waves of the sea after a subsiding storm could not be more graceful than the hills and hollows into which the mountain was moulded by the gradual drifting of its sands. At last I found myself on the edge of the crater, and started back. The abyss below me was two thousand feet in depth. Round it clouds of sulphureous smoke eddied like tormented spirits beating against the walls of their prison. I heard the sound as of distant seas. Suddenly an immense column of smoke leaped up out of the depth, and reached, as in a moment, a vast height above it, distending itself as it rose, and then — caught by the storm it had itself raised — drifted away over the remoter side of the crater. As that column grew thinner I saw within it showers of stone and burning metal, which fell along the slopes of the crater in red-hot masses. The same thing recurred at brief intervals — the respirations of the mountain. The scene was a very awful one; but I remembered that I stood on the windward side of the mountain.

I must not allow my recollections of Nature's great things to make me forget the little boy whose lively ways helped us to bear the inevitable crosses of the pleasantest travel, while his misfortunes were all his own. On one occasion he had felt the touch of what he called " a very dangerous whip "; and on another he had been sentenced to go to bed without his supper. On this last occasion his remonstrances took the form of a skilful rhetoric.

" It is not for myself I am unhappy, Alice," he said,

still clasping the handle of the open door. " It is all for
you! Oh, how can you ever send the story to my poor
mother at Bermuda? You will have to write — ' How can
I tell you the dreadful news? Your darling little Freddy
is dead! He died last night of starvation. He was put
to bed without a morsel of supper, and in the course of
the night he died from hunger! Oh, what a sight it was
in the morning when there he lay dead before me.' It is
not for myself I am unhappy, Alice. I am only thinking
of you ! "

The next morning he was as bright as ever. It was
suggested to him that as he was now such a traveller, he
should learn geography. He answered, " How much I
should like that if I had but time! But no sooner am I
dressed in the morning than I have to eat my breakfast;
then I have to play with my little paper cocks; then I
have to see how many boys are in the garden," and so on,
recounting the amusements of each half-hour, and ending:
" I have not one hour to myself in the whole course of
the day ! "

But it was not to Freddy alone that we owed many a
laugh. The ways of the people were always amusing.
One day I dined at Torre del Greco alone. The cook,
when all his work in the kitchen was over, came upstairs
in a white paper cap, and stood behind my chair for half
an hour, expatiating on the special merits of every dish,
and on the mode in which a wide experience had made
him understand how they should be dressed. When this
grand official had disappeared, the son of mine host, a
youth of about twenty, took his place, and told me stories
in some Neapolitan *patois*. Suddenly a thought occurred

to him, which denoted something of great importance had
to be shown to me. The passages about the house were
long and dark, but he beckoned me to follow him. When
my patience was nearly exhausted, he opened a door,
and brought me into a large room, with a large table, on
which lay a small infant, apparently of a month old. He
snatched it up, danced all about the room with it, and then
affirmed that neither Italy nor Sicily could show another
child to equal it in beauty. While his raptures were at
their height, a horn was heard in the street; and he hurried me to a circus just under the windows, in which a girl
rode round and round standing on a horse. The crowd
were contented with clapping their hands; but he leaped
up on his seat and exclaimed, at the highest pitch of his
voice: "How much I should wish to have that girl for
my wife!"

While my friends remained at Naples I made solitary
expeditions. One of the most interesting of them was
that to Capri, at which I had intended to pass but a night,
but where I was detained for a week by a rough sea. The
twelve palaces built on that island by the Emperor Tiberius in his old age commanded its twelve finest views, and
suggest the fancy that among the divine attributes
claimed for themselves by the Roman emperors, that of
omnipresence was one. In each palace he dwelt for one
month in the year. Hardly a vestige of them remains,
except of that one near the "Azure Grotto," a thing more
curious than beautiful. Anacapri lifts up its precipices to
the height of 1,800 feet. Five hundred steps carved — no
one knows when — out of those precipices, lead toward
this unwarlike acropolis, itself surrounded by meadows

and pastures that breathe a cooler climate, than the lands below.

On my way to this spot I passed through the village o Capri. Its population gathered around, and put many questions to me. On learning that I was on my way to Anacapri, they loudly expressed their surprise.

"What can take you there?" they enquired. "The people up there are a savage race. They will probably murder you! You will never be heard of again."

"How often have you been there?" I asked.

"Never since we were born," was their answer. "We are civilised folk down here!"

I soon reached the five hundred steps, and, though I had to sit down more than once, reached Anacapri within an hour. The villagers drew round me in surprise more than curiosity, and we conversed half by words and half by signs.

"How long had I been at Capri?" "A week." "A week! How could you live so long among such rogues and thieves?" "Do you see much of them?" I asked. "We! We never went down into that dirty hole in our lives. We should grow as corrupt a set as they are if we did! We have all we want up here. We spin our own wool, and make our own clothes, and drink out of our own well, and milk our own cows, and go to our little church twice a day. The old padre is quite perplexed to find a single mortal sin to absolve us from, unless he has the luck to light on some mad youth who has gone down into Capri out of curiosity. There was such a youth sixty years ago. He went a second time, and soon afterwards he died; and a holy nun had a vision,

and saw Satanasso fling the reprobate down the abyss
of Vesuvius."

"What can make the men and women of Capri so
wicked?"

"What else could they be? We pity them very much.
They are always living in the world, running out on the
shore to cheat foreigners, or getting on board ships from
every nation under the sun, and learning the vices of all.
You had better let them alone, and live up here with us
for the rest of your life."

Old Lord Ashburton laughed long when I told him
the tale, and affirmed that Capri and Anacapri were an
epitome of the world.

When the storm ceased I landed at Sorrento, and
thought it the loveliest spot upon that coast. To hold
one's nose over the ridge that overhangs its *piano*, and
see at once, and smell, its multitudinous thickets of orange
and lemon, while the sea-breeze blows over them, is an
enjoyment to be equalled by few. When you approach
the town, a mystic character is imparted to it by a ravine
two hundred feet in depth with which nature has protected
it on three sides, the fourth being girt by the sea. The
woody walls of that ravine create a gloom out of which
glitter lamps from many oratories, themselves unseen, scat-
tered about it at various heights. I enjoyed all the walks
and drives in the neighbourhood, and the numberless fragments of antiquity adjoining them, especially along the
seacoast road to Massa, and thence on to the southern
extremity of the Bay — a promontory on which, as the
classic authorities affirmed, Ulysses built a temple to his
guardian goddess, Minerva. I made my way next to

Amalfi, with its wonderful cliffs and its views of the Bay of Salerno; and afterwards to Castellamare, where night after night I took my walk, beside its bay, over which the evening star cast a pathway of silver as bright as that which, in the north, is cast by the moon. That line of glory seemed to be a bond connecting the Tomb of Virgil at the northern side of the bay with the birthplace of Tasso at the southern — Tasso, the only epic poet who chose an entirely Christian theme.

The noblest spot in the immediate neighbourhood of Naples, and the view which I enjoyed most, is that occupied by the monastery of the Camalaoli. The prospect from it includes the bays of Naples and Gaeta, as well as the mountains that girdle and the islands that stud them. Next in beauty to that view I thought the prospects from Capodemonte and the Certosa of St. Martino, near the castle of St. Elmo. This Carthusian church, besides being rich in really fine pictures, commands far the finest view to be enjoyed from within the city.

The northern side of the Bay of Naples, if inferior in beauty to the southern, is the richer in associations connected with the saddest and the most critical periods of the Roman Republic. If Baiæ was the abode of Rome's vilest sons, near it were spots made touching by their connection with her greatest, and that in their most memorable days. In the little island of Nisida, the son of Lucullus possessed a villa. Brutus had retired to it after the assassination of Cæsar; Cicero joined him there; and there the two conversed on the fortunes and fates of that country which both loved so well, and upon which both were so soon to close their eyes for ever. What

manner of discourse was held is probably known by those
who have read the "Imaginary Conversation between
Cicero and his Brother," by Walter Savage Landor. It
was in this villa that Brutus and Portia parted. But
another and not distant spot had witnessed, not for a few
days, but for many silent years, the silent sorrows of a
man greater than either of these — the Roman to whom
Rome had owed most, and to whom the world had owed
that her greatest empire was Roman, and not Cartha-
ginian — Scipio Africanus. Disowned by the country he
had saved, he retired into voluntary exile at his villa on
the seacoast, not many miles from Parthenope, where
those who hated his greatness dared not molest him.

The spot in which he passed those solitary years is
known by the single word " Patria," taken from the inscrip-
tion placed on his tomb by his command — " Ingrata
patria, nec ossa quidem mea habes." Perhaps the inscrip-
tion became all the nobler when it consisted of the single
word " Patria," which expressed a surviving affection, and
did not condescend to reproach.

Pliny records that near that spot he had seen an olive
tree, and a myrtle, both of them said to have been planted
by the hand of Scipio Africanus two hundred and fifty
years before. His daughter, the mother of the Gracchi,
retired to a spot, once the residence of Marius, about ten
miles to the south of her father's tomb. After the death
of her husband, the King of Egypt sued her to share his
throne, but in vain. Of those twelve children whom she,
had shown to the Campanian lady, all died in childhood
except a girl and those two illustrious sons, Caius and
Tiberius. It was to her that those sons owed their

Greek learning, their heroic characters, and those patriotic labours their devotion to which cost them their lives. She named the spots their blood had dyed "consecrated places." The Gracchi were no enemies to the noble order. They had warred but against their vices, and in defence of the ancient right of the Poor. If they had not warred in vain, slavery might never have superseded honest Roman labour, nor the vices engendered by slavery corrupted her domestic life, nor the Roman armies in her decay given place to the mercenaries that betrayed her. Seventeen centuries later, the widowed Vittoria Colonna must often have looked down from her castle cresting the heights of Ischia upon the ruins of Cornelia's house on the promontory of Misenum. One of these women had lost her great father and her noble sons; the other her husband; yet neither was crushed beneath the blow.

Henry Taylor wrote several poems at Naples. Of these the most important is the one entitled "Lago Lugano." It recorded a day spent beside that lake, the preceding October, and with a rare union of philosophy and eloquence it embodied the reflections that day had bequeathed to him on a momentous theme, namely, " Civil and Moral Liberty." There may be any amount of civil freedom where yet there exists no freedom of the heart, because it is ruled by pride or by worldliness. Such its theme.

> " From pride plebeian and from pride high-born,
> From pride of knowledge no less vain and weak,
> From overstrained activities that seek
> Ends worthiest of indifference or scorn;
> From pride of intellect that uplifts its horn
> In contumely above the wise and meek,

> Exulting in coarse cruelties of the pen ;
> From pride of drudging souls to Mammon sworn
> Where shall we flee and when ? "

The stanza employed in this poem, in some respects
the converse of the Spenserian stanza, was the invention
of the poet. The poem was almost wholly written within
one day, though Henry Taylor was generally a slow writer.
During my rambles I too had written a poem, entitled
" A Farewell to Naples." Three-fourths of it celebrated
the praise of the bay; and the remaining fourth is a farewell to the city. I subjoin the last.

" A FAREWELL TO NAPLES.

> From her whom genius never yet inspired,
> Nor virtue raised, nor pulse heroic fired ;
> From her who, in the grand historic page,
> Mountains one barren blank from age to age ;
> From her, with insect life and insect buzz,
> Who, evermore unresting, nothing does ;
> From her who, with the future and the past,
> No commerce holds, no structure rears to last ;
> From streets where spies and jesters, side by side,
> Range the rank markets, and their gains divide ;
> Where Faith in Art, and Art in sense is lost,
> And toys and gewgaws form a nation's boast ;
> Where passion, from affection's bond cut loose,
> Revels in orgies of its own abuse ;
> And appetite, from passion's portals thrust,
> Creeps on its belly to its grave of dust ;
> Where Vice her mask disdains, where Fraud is loud,
> And naught but Wisdom dumb and Justice cowed ; —
> Lastly, from her who, planted here unawed,
> 'Mid heaven-topped hills, and waters bright and broad,
> From these but nerves more swift to err hath gained,
> And the dread stamp of sanctities profaned,

And, girt not less with ruin, lives to show
That worse than wasted weal is wasted woe, — [1]
We part, forth issuing through her closing gate
With unreverting faces, not ingrate. "

We did not remain in Naples long after the weather had become reliable. Every day we heard stories that quaintly illustrated the ways of the people. Many of them were connected with the marvellous proficiency which its inhabitants had attained in the art of thieving. On the day of my arrival there I lost my pocket-handkerchief, though fully on my guard, within five minutes after leaving my hotel. On complaining, the answer I received was — "Why did you not keep it in your hat?" I once heard this warning given: "Do you chance to have a hollow tooth stuffed with gold? If so, do not yawn in the street! Some one will whip the gold out of it, and be off before you have time to close your mouth!" The fault, however, was not always on one side. Such must be our inference if we are to give credence to the following story.

In a hotel much frequented by the English, there abode a burly and hot-tempered man who never ceased from denouncing the two chief objects of his aversions, namely, the pickpockets and the Jesuits. Against the former he had a new story every day. He alone was secure against them. They were no match for him. He knew their ways! One day he came to dinner somewhat late, but flushed and triumphant. "They would let him alone for the future!" He told his tale. In the best street in Naples, the Toledo, and when it was still nearly broad

---

[1] In substance Alice Taylor's line quoted in page 144.

daylight, an attempt had been made on him by a villain —
who had evidently many confederates. He was passing
through a crowd. It pressed upon him — always a bad
sign. Suddenly he felt distinctly a hand pressing his
waistcoat pocket: the next moment a man pushed past
him and fled. He felt for his watch: it was gone! He
pursued the robber, shouting to the crowd, and commanding them to stop him. On the contrary, they plainly
facilitated his escape. The villain rushed through a by-
street to the left. He pursued him — next through a
by-street to the right; there he closed upon him, and
knocked him down with a single blow of his fist. "The
coward prayed me to spare his life; and I in turn
demanded my watch back. The villain surrendered it
to me. I pushed it down to the bottom of my pocket,
and dismissed the rogue with a parting kick!"

The moment he had crammed his dinner, he exclaimed,
"I must dress for the ball at the Accademia. My story
will make some of those Neapolitan grandees a little
ashamed of their Naples!" He ran upstairs and rushed
to his toilet table. What was his amazement at finding
there his watch! At last there came to him a horrid
recollection. Before going out, he had left his watch on
his table to keep it safe from the pickpockets. He had
to return to the *salle à manger*, and confess the latter half
of the story. He ended with: "I shall return the watch
at once to its owner." "Do not trouble yourself about
that," drily replied an Italian nobleman. "The watch is
a gold watch, and its owner must be a gentleman. He
will neither claim the watch, nor accept it back, for that
would be to confess that he had run away, thinking that

his assailant was mad, as all Englishmen are supposed to be by our ignorant common people here."

We were not sorry to leave Naples. One gets tired of seeing ecstatic groups cheering mountebanks on the quays; crowds surrounding a single actor whirling himself about with mad gesticulations on the top of a tub; dozens of boys galloping their crazy little carriages right at the luckless stranger; scores of strong men lying asleep in the sun with fleas on their faces. This is the undelightful side of Naples. Did such things exist when those most majestic of structures first stood side by side between the neighbouring desert and the sea? Three thousand years ago, did the temples of Pestum share their reign with Punchinello?

In a few days more we were at rest; for we were at Rome, and Rome is rest to those who understand it; and, to make our visit there perfect, we were at Rome during the Holy Week. But my recollections connected with Rome on this and other occasions would need many chapters. I may record them elsewhere, but not now.

Here I need hardly add that our regrets when obliged later to leave Rome were of a very different sort from what they had been when leaving the Bay of Naples. Henry Taylor had very greatly enjoyed Rome, especially its music during the Holy Week, and its pictures, for of pictures he had acquired a great knowledge and a fine appreciation in Italy. He admired most the Florentine school, which most represents strength, action, and passion, as I admired most the Roman school. He enjoyed also very much his daily drives in the Campagna, of which I remember Edwin Lear, the painter, affirmed that in its simple majesty it resembled, more than any other region that he knew, the noblest and most characteristic scenery of the Holy Land.

I must tell one story more of little Freddy Elliot, though it seems to imply that, even before his sixth year had taken its departure, the more worldly motives of action had begun to assail him. When we first reached Italy, his attention had been often drawn to the grave-eyed Franciscan monks, whom he met walking along the road in their brown cloaks and wooden sandals. To his enquiries Alice Taylor replied that they were holy men called monks, who renounced the world and all thought of themselves, that they might devote themselves entirely to prayer, to the service of others, and the mortification of the body. There were also holy women, she said, who lived the same life, and were called nuns. He was delighted. There was nothing, he said, he would enjoy so much as living wholly for others, and keeping his body under. When he was a man he would become a monk. Alas, before we left Italy, his scheme had undergone a serious modification. One day he came to her and said: " Alice, I have made a little change in my plan of life. I have been thinking that it might be better still if, instead of becoming a monk, I were to marry a nun! She would then have to be always practising prayer and mortification; and as she would never think about herself, she would be always thinking about me, and finding new ways of making me happy."

We returned to England by Florence, where we passed several more delightful days with Lady Lucy Standish and her family. Next we visited Bologna, Venice, the

Tyrol, and Germany. We travelled at our ease, and were able to spend a day or two at each place of importance. The weather was delightful, and Henry Taylor's health had improved far beyond what we had hoped when we started on our nine months' travels. All things had gone well with us, and we had cause for nothing but gratitude. Henry Taylor and I left Alice Taylor and Freddy at a German wateringplace, and returned to England in time for him to keep his appointment to the hour at the Colonial Office.

I may be allowed to add a few words respecting the great poet, and the great man with whom I travelled.

When poets were first given the title of the " irritable race," the term must have been intended to apply, I think, rather to the Latin poets than to the Greek. At least, it is difficult to suppose that one so large-hearted as Homer or so high-hearted as Sophocles, could have had about him anything so petty as habitual irritability when in health ; still less can we attribute it to the " myriad-minded man " — Shakespeare. In the England of our own day the poet most entirely free from it was probably Sir Henry Taylor. This could not have been otherwise, for his most marked characteristic was " magnanimity. After an intimacy with him extending much over forty years, I never saw him once out of temper or once made anxious about trifles. He lived in a large world, built up by justice and truth, and in him there was no small world. In this he was unlike another great man once described to me by an ardent admirer, yet one whose description ended — " And yet I can tell you that inside that great man there sits a little man ! " He had no small ambitions, and needed none as a stimulus.

Without it he could work hard for a friend, for any task of duty, for his country; but for personal success he cared little, and failure gave him little or no annoyance. Immediately after the failure of his first drama he devoted seven years to the composition of " Philip Van Artevelde," and if that had failed also, it would not have cost him an hour's serious distress. He was not only free from morbidness, but without a touch of sensitiveness. No criticism pained him, and no friend feared to speak to him with entire frankness. In his young days he was said to be a severe censor; but as life advanced, his judgments became more indulgent without becoming less just. He judged deeds as before; but not always those who did them.

He was a man of extraordinary moral strength, though of a temperament far from strong. He had no fear of public opinion, and was always not only foremost to defend an absent friend when unjustly assailed — witness his poem designated " Greatness in the Shade," written when Sir Charles Elliot was the object of attack — but fearless in resisting all false judgments, especially when opposed to justice and to the public weal.   In this respect he resembled his friend and mine, James Spedding, one of the few who did not side with the South during the American War.

As a character such as I have described is sometimes more tempted than others to the vice of pride, it may be well to add that by no virtue was he more signally marked than by humility. Of that no one could have doubted who had ever heard him read morning or evening prayers, or seen him learn lessons in science from his son, when, at

the age of twelve years, the boy — already marked by
extraordinary abilities — strove not to smile at his father's
occasional mistakes. I should have wished to have written more at large of a character so rich in noble qualities,
but this is needless, as the true greatness of a character
depends less upon the number of its great qualities than
on the genuine greatness of those few qualities which
suffice for true greatness.

His life, like his character, was a great one — too
inwardly and too simply great, and also too unconsciously
great to allow of its greatness being appreciated except
by the few. It was much enriched by his many friendships; for what was said, I think, of Southey, might
have been said of him, namely, that he had a " genius for
friendship." His home was pre-eminently a happy home;
although in the death of his eldest son the same shadow
had crept across it which darkened the home of
Southey.

Above all, that house was gladdened to the end by the
brightness of that devoted wife, whom, when he married
her, he introduced to his old friends as his " wife and
child." She suited him in all respects, delighting him
with an entire sympathy, and ministering to him with
equal success when he was in sickness and when in health.
The sparkling wit, the bright intelligence, and the generous affections, which from her youth had attracted so
many to her, never diminished as the years went by;
while by herself they were valued chiefly because they
enabled her to cheer him more effectually in the more
languid moods of advancing years. She kept his eye as
bright in his eighty-seventh year as it had been on his

marriage-day. Well might that have been said of her which he said of Edward Villiers's wife, in an elegy alike pathetic and true:

> "For one was with him, ready at all hours
>   His griefs, his joys, his inmost thoughts to share,
>   Who buoyantly his burthens help'd to bear,
>   And decked his altar daily with fresh flowers."

CHAPTER IX

A SHORT TOUR IN SCOTLAND IN 1845

IN the November of 1845 I made an expedition into
Scotland. As I left Miss Fenwick's house beside
Windermere she put a small volume of Burns's poems into
my hand, and said, "You know nothing about Burns's
poetry: read that book in Burns's country, and tell me
what you think of him when you return." I made my
way to Glasgow. Its stone streets were cleaner and state-
lier than most of the commercial cities in England, and
the Clyde, down which I steamed as far as Bute, com-
bines majesty and loveliness in a very remarkable degree. Next I went to Edinburgh, the most picturesque
metropolis I know to the north of the Alps. Few cities
boast an Acropolis. Edinburgh boasts two — the Castle
Hill, lacking nothing but a building worthy to crown it,
and the Calton Hill, lacking nothing but the completion
of its Parthenon and the removal of Nelson's monument,
the size of which dwarfs many a better one not far off.
The Salisbury Crags and Arthur's Seat, though I believe
only eight hundred feet high, are far more mountainous
in character, owing to the grandeur of their outlines and
the solidity of their cliffs, than many a spongy mountain

that lifts its pig's back to the height of three or four thousand feet elsewhere.

Few cities have such an historical character as Edinburgh. No one can pass by Holyrood Palace without recalling the day when

" To the Lords of Convention, 't was Claverhouse spoke :
    ' Ere the King's crown goes down there are crowns to be broke,' "

and a hundred incidents recorded by the heroic man who strode down that street, humming his own ballad, to announce to the meeting of his printers and creditors that the wand of Prospero was broken, and that he stood before them a ruined man; but that he would work on for the discharge of debts only nominally his own, as long as God continued his life. He redoubled his labours; and within a very few years one of the Abbeys of his native land received him to her rest.

I was too short a time in Edinburgh to see much of its society; but two of its celebrated men of letters were very kind to me — Lord Jeffrey and John Wilson. In the house of the former I had the good fortune to make acquaintance with a delightful person, afterwards well known as Lady Eastlake. Wilson I had long known as a poet, and as the "Christopher North" of "Blackwood's Magazine," in his contributions to which he always wrote with the full "courage of his opinions" about Wordsworth till he taught the world to put aside the patronizing as well as the contemptuous tone, and to recognise in him the chief poet of the age.

I did not see Wilson in his own house in which his daughter then lay lamentably ill; but I met him in

Messrs. Blackwood's reading room and elsewhere, and was much struck by him. The lofty stature and massive frame seemed types of a nature high and strong. He told me that when a young man he had walked all round Ireland with a blackthorn stick in his hand and a knapsack on his shoulder. The younger Mr. Blackwood took me one day to the University to hear him lecture. He was very eloquent.

I was much pleased with the neighbourhood of Edinburgh, and well remember how much struck I was by the happy effect of the white evening mists, which, separating ridge from ridge in the landscape, changed large stretches of it from a hilly to what seemed a mountainous land. I was deeply touched both by Melrose and by Roslin Abbey, the former of which I saw by moonlight, obedient to the command of "The Last Minstrel — not the last." Those ruins have spoken their penultimate word in the language of poetry. Possibly their ultimate word may be spoken in the language of religion, the older of the two powers.

After a reluctant adieu to Edinburgh, I saw a considerable part of the Highlands, and though I lost much by the lateness of the season, I gained perhaps more by escaping the crowd of travellers. I had had more than enough of London crowds and hurry; and I went to the far north in search of space and time. I found both in the Scotch Highlands. Loch Katrine delighted me, perhaps all the more because I reached it just as the dusk of the evening was descending and mingling with the steely gleam of its mirror.

I was pleased to find that the poor people spoke of

Ellen Douglas and other characters of the "Lady of the Lake" as if they had been as real as the scenes described. The Trosachs deserve all the praise they have received, nor can I ever hear them named without a fair vision rising up before me of rocks, and birch-trees with their silver stems, and the tangle of their golden broideries waving amid branches that would not let the autumn wholly go, — though the Highlands have many scenes that exceed it, some in grandeur and some in loveliness.

I was not then able to visit Glencoe, but I have seen it in a recent delightful visit to the Scotch Highlands, beginning with the glorious scenery of Inveraray and ending with the sacred island of Iona — two spots so closely connected, both with the later political destinies of Great Britain and her earlier Christian memories. Glencoe, even independently of its terrible associations, has a character so awful about it, as well as so sublime, that no one who has ever seen it can forget it. The same thing may well be said of Loch Etive, its winding waters and the crowding mountains that overshadow them. Loch Etive assisted me several years ago in writing a poem taken from an ancient Irish epic, said by high authorities, such as Eugene O'Curry, to have descended by oral transmission from times earlier than the Christian era. This fragment, one of Ireland's "Three Sorrows of Song," is named "The Sons of Usnach,"[1] who, when exiled from Ireland, passed over to "Alba," and effected large conquests, chiefly in the neighbourhood of Loch Etive, records of which are amply supplied in a work

[1] Macmillan and Co.

published in 1879[1] and attested largely by local traditions and by the Irish names of many spots.

Of all the Scotch lakes, few are so fine as Loch Etive. I was delighted also by Loch Awe, especially as seen from a point which commands, from a hill at the opposite side of the water, a view of Kilchurn Castle, asserted by Edmund Burke to be the finest view in the Highlands.

Wordsworth, during his Scotch tour with his sister, was greatly struck by Kilchurn Castle, and addressed a solemn and impressive poem to it. When still but a boy, I was asked by two lady friends (two of the party of ladies who had visited O'Connell at Derrinane) to read to them some of Wordsworth's poems. The volume opened at his "Address to the Ruins of Kilchurn Castle," and I began to read in a tone which I intended to be solemn: "Skeleton of unfleshed Humanity!" One of the two ladies (she was certainly as thin as a skeleton) leaped up indignantly, and exclaimed, "Well, I *am* the *thinnest* woman in Ireland; but I cannot approve of *personal remarks.*" She thought I was addressing her.

I found, on arriving at the village late in the evening, a large hotel with lights and fires in all the rooms. It was with difficulty that I got a small one at the back of the house. They told me that the house belonged to Lord Breadalbane; that they expected him that evening; that, whenever he came, the whole of the house was prepared for him, and that when he took his departure he made them a present, but was never presented with a bill.

I was unfortunate in the weather at Loch Lomond, but

---

[1] "Loch Etive and the sons of Usnach," by R. Angus Smith (Macmillan).

was fully compensated at one spot on it — Inversneyd. It is the glory of that lake. I tarried there, and read Wordsworth's poem, "The Highland Girl," at the foot of the waterfall, and close to the trees which, "like a veil just half withdrawn," enhanced the beauty it in part concealed. The Highland Girl was gracious to me, emerging out of the mist with no grace impaired, and not a month added to her "twice seven consenting· years," the loveliest object in a scene all loveliness. She was still as free as ever from the "embarrassed look of shy distress," though her endeavours to speak to the stranger in English were still as imperfect as when her poet gave us that tenderest of all metaphors : —

> "So have I, not unmoved in mind,
> Seen birds of tempest-loving kind
> Thus straining up against the wind."

Many years later Wordsworth added to the girl two companions, the Italian "Votaress" at Lugano, and the "Helvetian Shepherdess," but of her alone he then said :—

> "Time cannot thin thy flowing hair
> Nor take one ray of light from thee."

The mill, alas! was gone; an inn had taken its place; and the "household lawn" had been changed into a garden. The Highland Girl had not lacked her little local fame; and they told me that she had long since been living beside another lake. I took up my knapsack and struggled on for a whole day, pushing against a storm. I arrived to find that she had left the spot a few days before.

The immediate neighbourhood of Inversneyd is so

exquisite that, had I not known Wordsworth's severe veracity, I should have supposed that he had placed the girl there as the only spot worthy of her. Coleridge would not have scrupled to do so. He would have pronounced the statement "subjectively true."

Higher up on Loch Lomond I remember seeing a lovely island on which stood a few yew trees, remnants of the ancient forests. There, too, remained the ruins of a solitary tower; and there dwelt for upwards of forty years a lonely man, the last descendant of the ancient house of Macfarlane, though no longer its heir. Can that have been Wordsworth's Brownie's Cell? The recluse had died nine years before the poet had looked upon the spot and asked in vain "How disappeared he?" All that is recorded of him is that he never spoke, and that he perseveringly pulled up all the larch trees planted from year to year on that island. In Ireland how many a chief, Gael or Norman, may have died in such a retreat! How many may yet so die!

Of course I did not leave Scotland without visiting the Vale of Yarrow, the classic river of Scottish song, one probably as well sung as either the Ilyssus or the Cephysus. But I could only succeed in seeing St. Mary's Loch by climbing a hill. Wordsworth visited the Yarrow a third time with Sir Walter Scott and wrote a third poem on it. It was sent in MS. by Dora Wordsworth to Mrs. Hemans, who read it to Sir William Rowan Hamilton and me in Dublin with much sweetness and pathos. In a very short time she too was "one of the departed," and found her place in that noble dirge breathed by Wordsworth over Scott, Coleridge and the other English poets who

had so swiftly followed each other "from sunlight to
the sunless land." I passed on to Abbotsford. Everything there was touching, not the least so the bust of
Shakespeare which must have been looked on so often
with reverence and tenderness by the Shakespeare of
prose. There too I saw the ponderous shoes in which
Scott pushed his way through his plantations, and the
knife with which he hacked at them.

During the days of his dying, he repeated at times the
old Latin hymns of the Catholic Church. I visited that
great and good man's grave at Dryburgh Abbey. There
he lies in one among the loveliest ruins which conse-
crate still the land of Wallace and Bruce, and of those
earlier Scotch kings who repose with the Norwegian
kings in Iona. I was not then able to visit that sacred
island, to whose Irish monks two-thirds of Saxon England, and more, as Montalembert affirms, owed its conversion to Christianity; but I passed a night and part of two
days there last year. The best book I have seen on that
island is the Duke of Argyll's. He has also done much
to preserve its ruins — a real boon to his country.

Among the most striking objects in Scotland I should
place the city of Stirling and the prospect commanded by
its castle which looks down upon the "mazy Forth un-
ravelled." I visited there what had been one of Scotland's
stateliest cathedrals. The interior was then divided into
three churches, wholly separated, and in which three sermons were often preached at the same time. A verger
led me around the building. Standing before what had
once been the high altar, I observed one surviving piece
of ancient sculpture, apparently the emblematic Lamb.

" The Lamb ? " I said, pointing to it. " Na, na," replied the verger; " that's na a Lamb! that's just the wolf, the arms of the gude city of Stirling! "

The Cathedral of Glasgow, however, when I saw it in 1845, was in as bad a condition as that of Stirling; and it has since then been splendidly restored: perhaps that of Stirling may be restored by this time, or is destined to be so.

The Highlands of Scotland, if less " well finished," seemed to me to possess two advantages over those of England; their colouring is richer and the region is vaster. They comprise two-thirds of the kingdom; and the imagination if not the eye, gains by one's consciousness that one may travel for many days without reaching their limit. I was also greatly pleased by the southern Lowlands of Scotland, by its far-famed " Border-land," and by its rivers with their steep and wooded banks. I soon discovered also that we owe but to a false tradition the notion so common that the Highland race — that is, the descendants of the early Irish race in Scotland — have an exclusive possession of imagination, the Lowland having on the other hand monopolized all its prudence, industry and thrift. The Lowlanders too cherish their legends, reverence antiquity, enjoy song, and fully appreciate the pathos of human life. An Edinburgh Scotsman, evidently belonging to the mercantile class, was highly offended because I had chanced to name a certain duke of unbounded wealth as " one of Scotland's great men." He answered, " He is not one of Scotland's great men, for he is not a real chief."

But I soon discovered that, both in the Lowlands and

the Highlands, the real chief was not dependent either on
wealth or on heraldry.

That real chief was the chief of Scotland's peasant
bards — Burns. On the plains, on the hillsides, and on
the lakes they all sang his songs. I do not know that
any other country now possesses a national poet in as
full a sense as Scotland possesses one in Burns. She
honours him, and therefore deserves to have had him. I
stood by his grave before leaving Scotland, and remembered
Wordsworth's lines to him:

> " He shewed my youth
> How verse may build a princely throne
> On simple Truth."

I was his convert, and owed him a loyalty. The book
had been my guide book in Scotland. It did not guide
me to the best hotels, or to the best views; but it guided
me to the heart of a " never-vanquished nation " and him
who sat there enthroned. I read his book on mountain
and moor, by the fruitful slope and the torrent's fall, by
the woodland red with the embers of the dying year, and
by the cottage hearth. It had interpreted for me everything that I came across, whether of character or of
manners, whether of mirthful or of sad. I saw all things
with Burns's eyes: and Scotland became in turn the interpreter of Burns. During my farewell visit to Edinburgh
I wrote a poem in token of gratitude to Burns. Parts
of that theme were a painful record. But Burns's " Highland Mary " stretched forth to me a fresh young hand, still
white though it had done a day's work in this lower
world. The poem, intended to be a tribute to one alone,

turned out to be addressed to three — to the one great Lowland bard, to his Highland love, and to Scotland, doubtless well loved by both. Burns's "Highland Mary" was published by "Christopher North" in "Blackwood's Magazine," I believe in 1846.

CHAPTER X

1844-45.

It was my Father's Illness that stimulated him to write "Mary Tudor" —
Our Expedition in 1845 to Paris, and next to Cumberland — His Love
for Windermere — Our Visit to Miss Fenwick there — Derwentwater —
Rydal and Ulleswater — Southey's house — Sara Coleridge — Her
Genius and noble Character — Our Correspondence on Wordsworth —
My Reply to her Letter, and to her Remarks on the Comparative Merits
of Milton and Dante.

EARLY in the year 1844 my father had been attacked
by a painful and dangerous malady. It was to him
a summons to action. He had often affirmed that in the
great gallery of royal portraits bequeathed to England by
her dramatic poets, there was one serious omission, —
that of Queen Mary Tudor and that if none worthier
undertook the theme he would himself do so. The
character of that sovereign he aid frequently, had been
misconceived, and it had also been designedly misrepresented even in her lifetime, as Dr. Maitland had
abundantly proved, by political enemies bent on her
destruction. These men took no account of all that was
highest in her character while they exaggerated all that
was worst in it, till a false tradition had taken possession
of the nation's mind. What we lacked was an impartial
representation of her. When his life became precarious
he considered that to leave a just representation of her
behind was on his part a debt of honour. He began his

task on the 10th of April, 1844, and finished it on the 14th of September, 1844, that task consisting of two dramas, completed within five months of suffering and anxiety, and published without the author's final corrections. On its completion he went to London and placed himself in the hands of Sir Benjamin Brodie. The immediate prospect of a series of painful operations did not daunt him. He was a man of strong courage; and the hour before the arrival of his surgeon was spent in reading aloud an account of a picture gallery filled with paintings by old masters, accompanied with occasional remarks of his own respecting the mode in which the different subjects were probably treated by their respective painters.

In the summer of 1845 he had to submit himself again to the same severe discipline. When released, the first use to which he put his renewed strength was a visit to Paris, with my mother and me. There he was never tired of inspecting the Louvre and the many magnificent churches. On our return to London my parents became acquainted with my dear and honoured friend, Mrs. Henry Nelson Coleridge, daughter of a poet for whom he had a great admiration. That year also they became friends with one who had long wished to know them, Miss Fenwick. From London we had gone to the lake-land of the north, passing a week or ten days at Halsteads with Mrs. Marshall, then a widow.

After we had visited once more all our favourite spots on Ulleswater, we crossed the Pass of Kirkstone and descended into the valley of Windermere. The Pass was grander still than it is now, for the mountain road had

then no walls and the mountains no fences: there was
indeed " no hint of man," no

> " Wages of folly, baits of crime,
>   Of Life's uneasy game the stake,
>   Playthings that keep the eyes awake
>   Of drowsy, dotard Time."

And Wordsworth had then a full right to say that " he
loved a country in which Almighty God kept a good
deal of the land in his own hands." We passed about
a week with Miss Fenwick, who was then in health for
her unusually good, and we enjoyed our visit as much
as she enjoyed the society of her new friends. Brief as
was the acquaintance, the friendship into which it turned
at once seemed as if it were an old one; for sometimes
people fall into friendship at first sight, as others fall in
love. My father spent there, I am convinced, the happiest
week of his later life. His childhood was with him again;
for his mother, it will be remembered, had sent her child
at ten years old to a tutor at Ambleside. He seemed
to have forgotten nothing in that neighbourhood. He
had been accustomed to climb its precipices and track
the course of its streams, and he never forgot anything
beautiful there that he had once seen. Walking with
me beside the Rothay near the spot where it joins the
Brathay, he pointed with a grave delight to the rock from
which he had first cast his line into the water forty-eight
years previously, when a boy of eleven years old. He
used to speak with such minute detail of Windermere
in my boyhood that when I first visited it I seemed but
to return to something long loved. It was his favourite
among the English lakes. Derwentwater might be more

exquisite in details, and Ulleswater grander, because closer to the mountains, but he had a fuller satisfaction in the placid amplitude of Windermere, and the grace of those winding bays, with curves as sinuous as those of a sea-shell. His favourite points of view had always been those from the hill of Elleray and those from the grassy slopes above Low Wood Hotel, with the Langdale Pikes leaning forth their bulls' heads from the distance towards the lake. We have a picture of him as a boy from a spot close to Low Wood Hotel. It may have been from that spot that, as a boy, he swam across the lake where it is three miles across. Just before reaching the opposite shore he was seized with a cramp and was with difficulty saved.

On leaving Miss Fenwick I revisited Derwentwater where my father had in 1833 made the acquaintance of Southey, whom he had long admired as a poet and as a man. The lake must have interested him profoundly, not only from its beauty but from its associations with the heroic Lord Derwentwater and his not less heroic wife, of whose perilous night escape with her infant child, Walna Crag remains the memorial. To me that lake has another and very special interest in connection with many remembered friends and especially with Sara Coleridge, who was brought up in the house of her uncle Southey and who had spoken to me often of the scenes among which she had wandered as a child. She wrote of it thus when she was a child no more: " Keswick and Rydal and Grasmere are my Eden — watered with my tears as they were — but how truly says the poet:

> ' Dew-drops are the gems of Morning
> But the tears of mournful Eve.' "

I cannot better describe Sara Coleridge than by repub-
lishing here the substance of a letter which I wrote to her
daughter, when, in 1873, she published that delightful book
" The Memoir and Letters of Sara Coleridge." [1]

" In their memories she will ever possess a place apart from
all others. With all her high literary powers she was utterly
unlike the mass of those who are called literary persons. Few
have possessed such learning and when one calls to mind the
arduous character of those studies, which seemed but a refreshment to her clear intellect, like a walk in mountain air, it seems
a marvel how a woman's faculties could have grappled with
those Greek philosophers and Greek Fathers, just as no doubt
it seemed a marvel when her father at the age of fourteen 'woke
the echoes' of that famous old cloister with declamations from
Plato and Plotinus. But in the daughter, as in the father, the
real marvel was neither in the accumulated knowledge nor in the
literary power. It was the spiritual mind.

'The rapt-one of the God-like forehead,
    The Heaven-eyed creature,'

was Wordsworth's description of Coleridge, the most spiritual
perhaps of English poets — certainly of her modern poets. Of
her some one had said : 'Her father had looked down into her
eyes, and left in them the light of his own.'
" Her great characteristic was the radiant spirituality of her
intellectual and imaginative being. This it was that looked
forth from her countenance. When Henry Taylor saw Sara
Coleridge first as she entered Southey's study at Keswick, she
seemed to him, as he told me, a form of compacted light, not
of flesh and blood, so radiant was her hair, so slender her form,
so buoyant her step and heaven-like her eyes.

[1] " Memoir and Letters of Sara Coleridge." Edited by her daughter.
(Henry King & Co.)

"Great and varied as were your mother's talents, it was not from them that she derived what was special to her. It was from the degree in which she had inherited the feminine portion of genius. She had a keener appreciation of what was highest and most original in thought than of subjects nearer the range of ordinary intellects. She moved with the lightest step when she ranged over the highest ground. Her 'feet were beautiful on the mountains' of ideal thought. They were her native-land; for her they were not barren; 'honey came up from the stony rock.' In this respect I should suppose that she must have differed from almost all women whom we associate with literature. I remember hearing her say that she hardly con-sidered herself to be a woman of letters. She felt herself more at ease when musing on the mysteries of the soul, or discussing the most arduous speculations of philosophy and theology, than when dealing with the humbler themes of literature.

"As might have been expected, the department of literature which interested her most was that of poetry — that is poetry of the loftiest and most spiritual order, for to much of what is now popular she would have refused the name. How well I remem-ber our discussions about Wordsworth! ' She was jealous of my admiration for his poems because it extended to too many of them! No one could be a true Wordsworthian, she maintained, who admired so much as I did some of his later 'poems of "accomplishment,"' such as 'The Triad.' It implied a disparagement of his earlier poems, such as 'Resolution and Independence,' in which alone, she said, the Wordsworthian inspiration uttered itself. I suspect, however, that she must have taken a yet more vivid delight in some of her father's poems. Besides their music and their spirituality, they possess another quality in which they stand almost without a rival, their subtle sweetness. I remember Leigh Hunt once remarking to me on this characteristic of them, and observing that, in this respect, they were unapproached. He was right. It is like distant music when the tone comes to us pure and without any coarser sound of wood or wire; or like the odour on the air when we smell the flower without detecting in it that of the stalk or of the earth. To this characteristic of her father's genius a certain quality of her own bore a resemblance; and one is reminded of it by the fairy-like music of some of the songs in her ' Phantasmion.'

" There is a certain gentleness and modesty which belong to real genius, and which are in striking contrast with the self-confidence so often found in persons possessed of vigorous talents, but to whom literature is but a rough sport. It was these qualities that gave to her manners their charm of feminine grace, self-possession, and sweetness. She was one of those whose thoughts are growing while they are in the act of speaking, and who never speak to surprise. Her intellectual fervour was not that which runs over in excitement; a quietude belonged to it, and it was ever modulated by a womanly instinct of reserve and dignity. She never thought for effect, as many do. She never found it difficult to conceive how others should differ from her in their conclusions. She was more a woman than those who had not a tenth part of her intellectual energy. The seriousness and softness of her nature raised her far above vanity, its coldness and its contortions. Her mind could move at once and be at rest.

" I fear the type of character and intellect alike to which your mother belonged must grow rarer in these days of ' fast ' thinking. Talent rushes to the market, the theatre, or the arena, and genius itself grows vulgarised for want of that ' hermit heart' which ought to belong to it whether it be genius of the masculine and creative order, or of the feminine and susceptive. There will always, however, be those whose discernment can trace in your mother's correspondence, and in her works, the impress of what was once so fair; yet, alas, how little will be known of her even by such persons ! Something they will guess of her mind; but it is only a more fortunate few who will appreciate her yet higher gifts, those that belong to the moral being. Yet if these have a loss which is theirs only, they have also remembrances which none can share with them. They remember the wide sympathies and the high aspirations, the courageous love of knowledge, and the devout submission to Revealed Truth ; the domestic affections so tender, so dutiful, and so self-sacrificing ; the friendships so faithful and so unexacting. For her, great things and little lived on together, through the fidelity of a heart that seemed never to forget. I seldom walk beside the Greta or the Derwent without hearing her describe the flowers she had gathered on their margin in her early girlhood. For her they seemed to preserve their fragrance and their freshness amid the din and the smoke of the great metropolis."

A little before we left Gate House, Miss Fenwick's residence, I wrote thus to Sara Coleridge :

" A thousand thanks to you, my dear friend, for that lock of your father's hair. I could hardly have valued more a tress from a saint's head, than I value one which may once have touched that ' God-like forehead ' seen so often in my youthful fancies, but never, alas, in the light of day. I shall never again feel that veneration for any other man which my sister and I used to feel for your father, when we read him together, and thought, on laying down the book, that we could gather amaranths from every meadow. I am not now quite so much a believer in heroes as once ere a certain ' Idoloclastes Satyrane ' taught me to shun idols, or later, ere that wicked and unfeeling thing, Experience, had bullied me into believing that every man has his infirmities. This new philosophy does not yet, however, wholly tyrannise over my old habits. I threw off Byron early, as a vicious young horse throws off a bad rider, and I have outgrown Shelley, though not at all my admiration for his wonderful genius ; but there remains one unsubverted throne occupied by an aged man with dreamy eyes, and lips once brightened by Parnassian springs, and still breathing Elysian airs. I believe his name is S. T. C. I have been lately reading a letter from my great scientific friend, Sir William Rowan Hamilton, Astronomer Royal of Ireland, of whom Wordsworth told me that he was the only man of genius to whom he would apply the title of 'wonderful' except your father. Hamilton used to tell me that the shallow views of almost all the scientific men whom he met at the British Association made him melancholy; and that nearly the only Englishman of our time whom he regarded as a *philosopher* was Coleridge.

"On Wednesday last I accompanied my father and mother to Keswick. We arrived after dark at the Royal Oak; but, led by "the spirit in my feet," I groped my way to the spot where the boats are moored. The lake stretched before me, not with a silver gleam, but a steely gleam, so that the shadow of the mountains could hardly make it darker. After ten o'clock I went out again; but moon there was none, and I looked in vain for the mountain ridge at the opposite side of the lake, whose fresh and gladdening brightness had exhilarated me the last night I spent here, several years ago, and made me fancy that the whole hillside must be one bed of primroses. I next went in search of the house of your Uncle Southey, that true poet whose poetry never preached, though before its face all the vices and all the furies fled, while all the human affections flowered, and changed into virtues without knowing it! In earlier days that spot had a great interest for me on his account only; on that night for your sake also. I came to the bridge on the Greta, and only discovered that it was a bridge from the light of the water which dashed itself obliquely in a white line under and against the arch. I felt sure that his house must be near, and heard next morning on enquiry that it was, though the night had hidden it.

"The next morning we went out boating. First we landed on Derwent Island, that surviving fragment of Eden, where a cousin of mine, the wife of Henry Marshall, now reigns as queen. We passed next by St. Herbert's Island, and rejoiced to learn that the dwellers in that region still remember how dearly St. Herbert and St. Cuthbert loved each other; how the anchoret of Derwent bade the bishop at Holy Island to pray that they might die on the self-same day, and how that prayer was granted, the friends expiring at the same hour, St. Herbert with the whispers of Greta and Derwent in his ears, St. Cuthbert with the sea-dirge that murmurs round Lindisfarne. We passed the dusky vale of Borrodale, landed at Lodore, and tracked the waterfall far up its rocky bed. Later in the day I returned alone to the little bridge near Southey's dwelling, turned up a narrow walk to the right, and soon found myself opposite the small square house which had been so long the abode of so much genius, so much learning, so much industry, so much unpretending piety, and so much happiness. You at least will remember 'The Poet's Pilgrimage.' It does not rank as high as Southey's greatest poems, such as Thalaba, Kehama, and Roderick, or as the finest of his short pieces, such as the 'Funeral Song on the death of the Princess Charlotte,' and the 'Ode' written 'during the negotiations for peace with Buonaparte in 1815,' but we owe to that poem the touching description of the poet's house; and as I stood beside that honoured door a vivid picture rose up before my eyes. I seemed to have shared Henry Taylor's privilege, and looked in upon that beautiful household when its circle was yet unbroken, and its brightness undimmed.

> "' My gentle Kate, and my sweet Isabel,
>   My dark-eyed Bertha, timid as a dove,'

and he, the 'only and the studious boy,' seemed again reunited, as I trust that they and another, though not named in that poem, will one day be united, a family in Heaven. I remembered your mother telling me what a beautiful sight it was to watch her daughter and her cousins, then not quite little girls, from an upper window, as they played in a field behind the house. I found the field at last; but there were no fair and happy girls in it. I passed into the garden; and found there but a single flower, a rose-bud, which I brought home with me. The little kitchen garden was sad and forlorn, and the gate in the corner would not open; and I had to retrace my way along the weedy walks. I had intended to have entered the house, but did not do so; it seemed like intruding. Southey's library ought to have remained at Keswick, together with his house, preserved as his monument."

A short time before, while at Paris, I received a most remarkable letter from Sara Coleridge, one that cannot but interest all who appreciate the higher criticism, and especially all admirers of Wordsworth. They will find it in the " Memoir and Letters of Sara Coleridge." Vol. II. (Henry King and Co. 1873.) My answer to it may interest some readers. We agreed entirely in our admiration of that great poet; but differed much in our comparative estimate of his earlier and later works.

PARIS, September 28th, 1845.

I have been reading again your "Scale of Wordsworth's poetry." I shall profit by it much, though we shall not always agree on the subject. I read as far as I could with your eyes, and hope I have thus improved the clear-sightedness of my own. In the volume which you allowed me to take to this loud and vainglorious city, I had already marked, but only in " pencil-touches easily effaced " (I quote a line of John Auster's), in the table of contents, the poems which had hitherto been my favourites, and also the few for which I have no liking, the latter by a different mark. We agreed much more often than we differed. To this, however, there are exceptions. You have given two marks of approbation to " The Brothers." I am ashamed to say that I had not given that poem one. I see no fault in it.

And the omission was solely some strange lack of appreciation. I have often, though such a strong Wordsworthian, thus been surprised at the amount of beauty which I have eventually found in poetry of his which had yet remained long undetected by me. The late Lord Chancellor Cranworth used to laugh at me for my enthusiasm about Wordsworth, "though," he once added, "I must admit that he wrote two very good sonnets. One of them begins, 'Pure element of waters;' and the other, 'Hail, Twilight, sovereign of one peaceful hour.'" "He never wrote any such sonnets!" I replied; "I have read all his sonnets twenty times over, and know a large proportion of them by heart; I am *certain* that no sonnet of his contains those lines." He took down the volume, and there they were! Again and again I had read them; but some mysterious veil had always hidden wholly their beauty. It may prove thus with me again. Those sonnets *are* beautiful.

However, I am not going to assume that in all cases where we differ I am to end by adopting your opinion, least of all where mine is the positive opinion and yours only the negative one. For instance, how could you have given one mark alone to "The Happy Warrior?" Again, you can spare two only to the most *majestic* poem in the language — "Laodamia"; while "The old Cumberland Beggar" has extorted three from your liberality. You will reply that the latter is a true Wordsworthian poem. I admit that. His early poems have doubtless most of what you call his 'idiosyncrasy'; but then, some of his later poems have enough of it, and are richer in other high qualities than any, except quite the first class of his early poems. Remember that the decline in the great Roman school in painting was chiefly caused by such a devotion to Raffael's idiosyncrasy that the invariable question became not whether a new picture was good, but whether it was like Raffael. My admiration of Wordsworth is composed of two different elements, namely, my admiration of what is peculiar to his genius, and my admiration of what he has

in common with other first-class poets; I must therefore adjust
the balance between these two admirations; and therefore I
cannot agree with those who admire even the inferior poems of
his earlier and most characteristic manner more than the best
poems written in his later style, such as his magnificent
"Stanzas on the Power of Sound," or his exquisite "Triad."
On the contrary, I prefer several poems which belong to the
better, but not to the best, poems of his second manner, such as
"The Armenian Lady's Love," "A Flower Garden at Coleor-
ton," "The Poet and the Caged Turtle-Dove," "Ode to Lycoris,"
to many poems of his earlier style, though not to the best among
them. The earlier, it will be said, are always strong. True, but
they are often greatly inferior in grace, sweetness, and refinement, both of thought and expression. Without what is absolutely peculiar to his genius, and to it alone, Wordsworth would
not have been a very great, that is, an original poet; but if this,
his special merit, had been his only merit, he would have lacked
several of those perfections which, in their aggregate alone, make
up a first-class poet, as well as an original poet.

Some will say that this amounts to a concession that you are a
more thorough Wordsworthian than I am. In one sense it does;
you are a greater admirer of the special Wordsworthian genius —
I of Wordsworth's poetry taken as a whole. You could spare a
large proportion of it. I could spare at most one volume out of
his six.

Why do you give "Michael" but one mark of approval?
Why have you nothing to say for "Yarrow Revisited," and the
exquisite sonnets in the volume which bears that name — sonnets
which have a mellowness made up of wisdom, love, and rest
about them that amply atones for any slight diminution of strength
with which some few may be charged, when compared with his
"Sonnets Dedicated to Liberty," which constitute a single great
poem in themselves, and his noblest save one. It is hard to say
which of the three poems named after the Yarrow is the most

beautiful; and to me it seems that his "Vernal Ode," his ode beginning "Who rises on the banks of Seine" (a palinode like your father's "France"), the "Stanzas on the Power of Sound," and his "Dion," are quite equal in depth of thought and moral elevation to anything except the "Great Ode," which last, doubt-less, he regarded as the high altar of his cathedral of song, and to which he always assigned the highest place in all his editions.

To this letter on Wordsworth I may be permitted to add another in reply to one from Sara Coleridge, and discussing with her the comparative merits of Milton and Dante.[1]

"It seems to me strange that you should prefer Milton to Dante, and that on the ground that he possesses more of sweetness and pathos. Only turn to the passages in the 'Paradiso,' beginning in Canto III., lines 93 and 104; Canto VI., line 14; Canto XVII., line 56; Canto XXV., line 1; Canto XII., line 31; Canto XII., line 3; Canto XIV.; Canto XXII., line 41. The sweetness of Dante's genius, in spite of its severity, is illustrated in countless ways, as, for instance, by his frequent and exquisite allusions to birds and to children. Among these he is ever at home, and they would no more have fled from him than from St. Francis. What can unite more of tenderness and pathos with a noble severity than the passage in which Beatrice reproaches Dante because he had loved her less faithfully when ennobled by death than while still begirt with the imperfections of earth? His poetry, I grant, has not as much majesty as Milton's, but there belongs to it, on the other hand, a far more pervading sense of the infinite, and also —a converse merit— far more of the beautiful *in detail*. He is also much more consistently philosophical. Dante could never have built up for himself such an utterly false and incoherent an ideal as Milton's 'Satan.' No one can admire what is so splen-

---

[1] (1896.) The most interesting works on Dante with which I am acquainted are those by Dean Church and by Dr. Hettinger, translated by Father Sebastian Bowden of the Oratory.

didly great as Milton's higher poetry than I admire it: but that is the very reason that I find it difficult to forgive him for not doing more justice to such greatness. Without going so far as Dr. Johnson, who affirmed that Satan is the hero of 'Paradise Lost,' we cannot deny that Milton invested him with a high poetic interest, and that he did so by (notwithstanding passages which seem disclaimers of this), representing him, even after his revolt, as still remaining 'not less than Archangel fallen,' heroic, at least in comparison with those who shared his fall, but dared not further share his fortunes. Compared with them, he alone retains magnanimity. Surely such a conception was an absolute misconception, whether measured by a philosophical or by a poetical standard, not to speak of one higher than these. He lived in an age indulgent to revolt, but I will not say that this had anything to do with the choice of his subject or with his treatment of it. It may be referred to causes solely within the limit of letters. His studies had been chiefly classical and Biblical; and by a singular error of art he resolved to treat a spiritual subject after the model of a classical epic, though his first intention had been to make it a tragedy, beginning with Satan's address to the sun. His second plan was one which Dante could never have adopted. A classical epic might have been written by a Greek on the subject of the Giant War; for the giants and the Olympian divinities were alike finite powers. It was far otherwise with the subject chosen by Milton; and ought not the treatment of it to have been equally different? A rebel against earthly potentates may yet possess many high qualities. A rebel against infinite Goodness and Sanctity must be the enemy of all that is high and pure — all that is worthy of reverence and love. He cannot be represented as retaining any one high quality without a proportionate degradation of the being against whom he rebels. I remember that Archbishop Whateley once remarked to me on the dulness of those who did not know that Milton had become an Arian, until the publication of his 'Latin Treatise,' avowedly such; and he asserted that 'Paradise Lost' was unequivocally Arian no less, referring especially to one particular passage. That passage could never have been written when he wrote his beautiful early poems, which in their spirit leaned far more to the Catholic than to the Puritan side; especially if we take note of 'The Pilot of the Galilean Lake,' who bore the sacred keys and the word "hæmony' as interpreted by your father, in a sacramental and mystical sense. Remember, too, the sonnet to a 'Virgin wise and pure,' and the exquisite 'Praise of Chastity' in 'Comus,' which is written wholly in the spirit of the medieval ascetics and not of the later moralists. At that time Milton would have shown something of that sacred reserve which Dante never discarded when dealing with holy things; he would never have made the Almighty discuss predestination, like a school-divine, or made spiritual angels hurl material mountains on their foes — spiritual not less. Yet Dante was himself a great master of the scholastic philosophy — a man deeply read in Scotus, Aquinas, and Buonaventura. He knew well what Platonism had done for Christianity, and yet with what dangers it had threatened Christianity when used by those who did not know that there was a yet higher truth to which Platonism owed allegiance. I cannot doubt that Dante would have immeasurably preferred transcendentalism like that of your father to Locke's philosophy or that of his more materialistic successors. It seems to me not a little likely that in his musings the great poet-prophet of Italy may have seen that later birth from a German soil — the transcendentalism of recent times. I allude to certain philosophers, not of the materialistic but of the 'subjective' school, who at once recognise and disparage several great revealed truths, affirming that though they are to be held in honour because they are derived from 'pure reason' and represent great ideas, yet it does not follow that that ideal truth corresponds with any external and objective truth. Such a philosophy sees whatever it sees upside down. The Christian creed confesses that God made man in his image. If he had not done this, obviously man could never have known God. A revelation would have been impossible. That subjective philosophy, which separates ideas from external realities, replies with its counter creed, ' No, it is the human Mind which creates to itself a, God in its own image ! ' Theism itself it brands as an anthropomorphic religion. May English transcendentalism long resist what is said to have so deeply infected that of Germany !

" Against this error Dante protests in many places — amongst others in the Paradiso, Canto III. There he represents himself as beguiled by a singular form of delusion. A glorious vision is presented to him. He is tempted to turn away from it, and why? That temptation comes from the assumption that the vision is not a reality but a reflection — a reflection from something behind himself. Later, when corrected by Beatrice, the type of Catholic theology, he speaks of this form of error as :

> " ' Delusion opposite to that which raised
> Between the man and fountain amorous flame.

This form of error comes from a diseased individualism. The Church, which is historical and universal, seems to me our protection against it.

" Dante's most special merits often hide a greatness higher still. The vividness of his imagery makes many of his readers — nay, of his loudest admirers — insensible comparatively to a nobler characteristic of his poetry, namely, its spirituality, which is quite as remarkable as its strength ; and his mastery over details blinds them to his sense of the Infinite. Almost all the long poems of the world, except Homer's, fall off towards the end. On the contrary, it is at the close of Dante's ' Paradiso ' that his unrivalled sense of the infinite asserts itself most strongly. The poet has advanced through Heaven from sphere to sphere of glory. At the end of the poem a glimpse of the supreme of wonders is vouchsafed to him. But it is only for a single moment. That vision is the ineffable mystery of the Trinity in

Unity and the Incarnation — the Beatific Vision upon which the eyes of the blessed are fixed in everlasting trance. It is only for a moment that a mortal, clad in man's flesh, can endure it. God, brought infinitely near, remains not less infinitely remote; the intellect sinks in stupor, for it is finite. But still the will rushes forward toward the vision; still love holds its own! This is indeed to grapple in song with the infinite. I quote again from Cary's translation :

> " ' Here vigour failed the tow'ring phantasy ;
> But yet the will rolled onward like a wheel
> In even motion, by the love impell'd,
> That moves the sun in heaven and all the stars.'

" All the great faculties and qualities needful to inspire the highest poetry are found in Dante — originality, invention, imagination, beauty, passion, suggestiveness, conciseness, thought, pathos, self-possession. The last of these is, as Shelley affirmed, possessed by Dante in such a marvellous degree that when he compared, in connection with that characteristic, Dante's poetry with his own, it made him despair. The concentration of all those qualities upon one great poem, and that a poem devoted to the theme most worthy of song, made Kenelm Digby affirm that, though Shakespeare was the greatest of all poets, yet Dante had given to the world the greatest of all poems. I cannot but concur with that judgment. I do not think that with it the ' Paradise Lost ' can compare."

CHAPTER XI

MY FATHER'S DEATH IN 1846. MY MOTHER'S IN 1856

My Father's Death, preceded by but a Week's Illness — It took place in
1846 — He had never had any Fear of Death; and when it came he
met it without Alarm, and with a most humble Confession of his
entire Belief in the Christian Religion, a Belief strongly expressed
in his Poetry — The Year after his Death, I published his Two Dramas
on "Mary Tudor" — Total Neglect of them during Twenty-eight
Years — After that Time a growing Recognition of their Merits — The
Death of my Mother, nearly Ten Years after that of my Father.

THE year 1846 was a year of deep calamity to me
and mine. In it my father died. I had passed
the spring at Curragh Chase, and his health had seemed
to be good. In June I went to London. Late in July
I received a letter informing me that he had been taken
suddenly ill, and that his life was in great danger. I
reached home a few hours before his death. His
strength was rapidly failing. That morning he had frequently asked whether I had arrived. As I entered the
room he saw me, and exclaimed: "I am so happy!"
All his family were around him except his two younger
sons, then on professional duty. He knew that he was
dying, but he uttered no complaint. At the end there
was no struggle. When the last breath had been drawn,
his wife rose, and slowly and silently closed his eyes —
the last sad office with which she had ministered to him
during forty years, and more, of a happy married life.

He passed way at about two P. M. of the 28th of July, 1846, in the fifty-eighth year of his age. The reverence and affection with which he was regarded by the poor was attested by the crowds in which they followed him to his grave.

I may here quote a few sentences from a letter written by a friend, at our house an ever-welcome guest, one remarkable alike for learning, piety, and high principle — the Reverend Dr. John Jebb.

"I had ample opportunities of knowing him intimately, and it is my conviction that every sentiment of his heart was based upon the purest principles of a sound, deeply seated, and influential religion. How unostentatious was his religious faith! This to me was one of the great charms of his character. Intellectually, no one of common feeling and information but must have admired him; I am thankful that so many opportunities were given me of knowing how entirely subservient he made his highly gifted intellect to the best purposes of morality and Christianity; and this pious inclination strengthened ever with his years. His surely was a happy life, in the best sense of the word. I rejoice also to know that he had at the last so fully the comforts of religion administered to him; and above all that he had that within, the answer of a good conscience towards God."

I often regretted that one so eminently patriotic as my father was in the highest sense of that often-abused word (for to the real interests, and to the honour both of England and Ireland he was ever devoted) had not had an opportunity of serving his country in Parliament. For a parliamentary career he had special qualifications, though whether the gift of eloquence was among them I

do not know.   His was a singularly well-balanced mind;
he no more thought than spoke after a rhetorical fashion;
and his absolute conscientiousness of intellect would
have caused the strife of parties to present to him many
painful dilemmas.   He would probably if in Parliament,
have admitted with Burke that parties were *there* inevitable; but to join any of them would to him have been
difficult, for with none was he in more than partial
accord.   He was with the Liberals as regards all laws
that imposed civil penalties on religious convictions, and
from the first had ardently supported Catholic Emancipation.   He was also in favour of Free Trade so far as
duties on corn were concerned.   But on the other hand
he was opposed to whatever disturbed, in the democratic
interest, the balance which it had long been the boast of
the English Constitution to sustain between the monarch-
ical, the aristocratic, and the democratic powers.   He
used to call himself a Liberal Tory, or a Canningite,
except on the question of Parliamentary Reform, a moderate measure in favour of which he regarded as our
only defence against a revolutionary one at a later time.
If he had entered the House of Commons he would have
exerted his influence to prevent parties from degenerating into factions whether by exaggerated violence, by
unfaithfulness to their respective principles, or by taking
tricky advantages over the opposite party.   If he had
been in the House of Lords his position would have been
less trying to him than in the House of Commons.   On
one occasion a member of the government wrote to inform
him that he would probably be offered a peerage; but he
was not in sympathy with that government, and stated as

much, thus declining a title, as his father had done before him.

That the conservative elements in my father's political convictions were in harmony with a love of liberty equally strong, is shown in many of his sonnets, such as those entitled "Liberty of the Press" and "The True Basis of Power." The latter I will here quote.

THE TRUE BASIS OF POWER.

" Power's footstool is opinion, and his throne
The human heart: thus only kings maintain
Prerogatives God-sanctioned.   The coarse chain
Tyrants would bind around us may be blown
Aside like foam that with a breath is gone.
For there's a tide within the popular vein
That despots in their pride may not restrain,
Swollen with a vigour that is all its own.
Ye who would steer along those doubtful seas,
Lifting your proud sails to high heaven, beware!
Rocks throng the waves, and tempests load the breeze;—
Go, search the shores of history — mark there
The oppressor's lot — the tyrant's destinies.
Behold the wrecks of ages, and despair!"

With him the claims of liberty and those of authority rested upon the same basis, and that was a moral one. He believed that liberty could not exist long where reverence and obedience to lawful authority were not exercised too.   He believed that where a supremacy at once of popular power and physical force was erected, the educated minority would soon be practically disfranchised.   On the other hand he believed that while the chief *initiative* power ought to belong to the educated class the majority ought to possess a substantial *restraining* influence sufficient to prevent a selfish class-legisla-

tion.   While the Reform Bill of 1832 was being discussed,
I remember his walking up and down the library and saying: "I never agreed with Canning in his opposition to
reform in Parliament.   I was always in favour of cancel-
ling rotten boroughs and representing large towns; but
this bill is not a reform, but a revolution."

A person then present replied, "That is a hard saying!"   He answered, "I do not mean that it is a revolution at this moment, nor in ten years, nor in twenty
years."   He stopped and thought, and after a few minutes
proceeded, "It will be a revolution in fifty years."   He
spoke in 1832.   The recent revolutionary legislation
began in 1881, *i.e.*, within a year of the time he had predicted.   My father, of all the men I have known, was the
most long-sighted.   People used to say of him, "He saw
distant things as through a telescope," and his predictions almost always turned out correct.   This was because
he combined a great imagination with a great reasoning
power, and because many of the passions which obscure
other men's vision did not for him exist.   He had no
resentments.

A short time after my father's death I wrote thus to
Sara Coleridge:

"Your prayers for my mother have been heard.   She thinks
only of him, not of self.   It is said that maternal love is the
most unselfish of the affections.   I am disposed now to think
that a wife's affection is more unselfish still.   A mother sometimes seems to regard her child as in some sort her own property,
and when it is snatched away, to feel amerced of her own.   My
mother always felt as if she belonged entirely to her husband.
The expression of her countenance is changed: much that

belonged to it is gone, and something new has come into it.
It was otherwise on the death of her two young daughters.
She has settled an annuity upon every widow in this place,
dating it from his death.   Her faith is probably strengthened
by that which supported him, when first informed that his malady was fatal.   He answered: 'I am a Christian, a humble
Christian, saved by the mercy of God, through the merits and
death of our Saviour.'   One of the last things we heard him
murmur was: 'All is peace and quietness here,' laying his hand
on his breast."

"He was saved by his unexpected death from the intense suffering which must otherwise have been inflicted
on him during the next three years by the great Irish
famine."

I published his "Mary Tudor" during the next year
(1847).   There was a "conspiracy of silence" about it.
On the other hand, even then a few of our most distinguished men of letters greeted it with an ardour such as
is seldom bestowed on a drama.   Cardinal Manning
wrote to me thus in 1847: "Perhaps my feeling as to
the work may be tinged by sympathy with the 'Idola
Ecclesiastica'; but Gladstone's is not; and we agreed in
placing 'Mary Tudor' next to Shakespeare"; and Sir
Henry Taylor, Lord Blackford, Lord Coleridge, and
many others wrote of it in terms hardly less strong.   My
judgment would hardly be accepted as impartial.   What
they especially remarked upon in the work was its manli-
ness, its dramatic insight, its pathos, its grace as regards
diction and metre, and, above all, its absolute impar-
tiality.   As I have said in the latest edition of the work,[1]

[1] George Bell and Sons. 1884.

"The author was an Anglican, and could have had no bias in favour of Mary, neither had he any against her. His mind knew no partisanship, and in the subject he recognised a theme too high for one-sided zeal. The interest which he took in the chief characters of that age was a human and historical, not a controversial interest."

After lying neglected for twenty-eight years, it was called out of obscurity. Lord Tennyson had written his "Queen Mary" without knowing that the subject had been treated before, though of course that need have been no reason for his rejecting it.

In some critique on "Queen Mary" there happened to be a reference to "Mary Tudor." All the copies except about a hundred had been lost long before at the printers'. These copies were then speedily sold off. It has since been republished by George Bell and Sons.

It is not my purpose to write here in detail of my father's character; but I may quote the conclusion of a brief memoir of him, prefixed to the latest edition of his "Mary Tudor."

"His was a nature more common in past days than at present; a character obedient to high laws, and a disposition affluent in affections; an intellect large, proportioned, and judicious; a soaring spirit, and a temper ardent, but also magnanimous and urbane; and I remember that one who bent above him after his death said: 'In that brow I see three things — imagination, reverence, and honour.'"

I.

"At times I lift mine eyes unto 'the Hills
Whence my salvation cometh' — aye and higher —
And, the mind kindling with the heart's desire,
Mount to that realm nor blight nor shadow chills:

With concourse of bright forms that region thrills:
I see the Lost One midmost in the choir:
From heaven to heaven, on wings that ne'er can tire,
I soar; and God Himself my spirit fills.
If that high rapture lasted need were none
For aid beside, nor any meaner light,
Nothing henceforth to seek, and nought to shun:—
But my soul staggers at its noonday height
And stretching forth blind hands, a shape undone,
Drops back into the gulfs of mortal night.

August 6, 1846.

II.

" To-night upon thy roof the snows are lying;
The Christmas snows lie heavy on thy trees:
A dying dirge that soothes the year in dying
Swells from thy woodlands on the midnight breeze.
Our loss is ancient: many a heart is sighing
This night, a late one, or by slow degrees
Heals some old wound, to God's high grace replying:
A time there was when thou wast like to these.
Where art thou?   In what unimagined sphere
Liv'st thou, sojourner, or no transient guest?
By whom companioned?   Access hath she near,
In life thy nearest, and beloved the best?
What memory hast thou of thy loved ones here?
Hangs the great vision o'er thy place of rest?"

Christmas, 1860.

After the death of my father, my mother continued to live in Curragh Chase, the beloved home of her married life, though darkened by the death of two lovely girls, one at the age of eleven years, the other at that of fifteen. My eldest brother, Sir Vere de Vere, and his wife took the same tender care of her, as in the preceding generation had been taken by both my parents of their widowed mother.   Very soon after my father's death those dread-

ful years of the great Irish famine succeeded, years during which it was hardly possible for a mourner to lift her
head again. At last, however, they were over, and a
spring came that felt like a spring, and helped to restore
their light to eyes long dimmed, and their old tones to
voices long changed. It was thus with my mother. The
words of Artevelde when speaking of Adriana would have
applied to her:

> "She was one made up
> Of feminine affections, and her life
> Was one full stream of love from fount to sea."

As much of gladness as was needed for the peace of
others returned to her; not more. Again she enjoyed
the wild flowers of May, and again in the evenings she
and my eldest brother played together the music of
Mozart and Beethoven. Occasionally in the summer she
passed a few weeks at Derwent Island and on the shores
of Coniston Lake with her nieces, who regarded her
almost as a mother. Nearly ten years passed thus away,
and many more might thus have passed. She took a
renewed interest in things new and old. Now she
passed a week with her surviving daughter and her children. At another time her eldest son read her the last
page he had written of a translation on which he was
engaged. The original was a work on political philosophy by Donoso Cortes, Marquis of Valdegames, the
friend of Montalembert, a work not less needed by the
present time than by that for which it was written. But
to all these things an end was brought by the Russian
War. She had two younger sons, a soldier and a sailor,

who fought in the Crimea. The anxieties of that war were too much for her. A few months of horrors such as we read of in all the newspapers during that winter of unprecedented severity developed a heart complaint; and she died, but not until she had seen both those sons again after their return. How often the mortality among soldiers may be exceeded by that among their wives and mothers!

The following sonnet was written by my sister. I sent it to Cardinal Newman, who was deeply moved by it.

TO HER MOTHER'S BIBLE.

She read thee to the last, beloved book!
Her wasted fingers 'mid thy pages stray'd;
Upon thy promises her heart was stay'd;
Upon thy letters linger'd her last look
Ere life and love those gentlest eyes forsook:
Upon thy gracious words she daily fed;
And by thy light her faltering feet were led
When loneliness her inmost being shook.
O Friend, O Saviour, O sustaining Word,
Whose conquering feet the Spirit-land have trod,
Be near her where she is, Incarnate Lord!
In the mysterious silence of the tomb
Where righteous spirits wait their final doom,
Forsake her not, O Omnipresent God!

ELLEN O'BRIEN.

Her youngest son, the soldier, was the first to follow his mother. He married the daughter of an ancient Norman stock which had come to Ireland in the days of Strongbow, and become known as that of the Burkes of St. Clerans. Two of her brothers died heroic deaths, one of them being the celebrated Australian explorer. My youngest brother's two names were Francis and Horace, bestowed in memory of the two "Fighting Veres" of Queen Elizabeth's time. His married life was a happy one, and he left behind him three daughters. But it was a short life, and its end was strange. As an engineer he was charged with the execution of certain military works at Woolwich. One of the soldiers employed on them misconducted himself repeatedly, and my brother had to reprove him severely. The offender watched his opportunity, and soon afterwards fired at him from one of the windows of the barrack as he stood in the court beneath. The bullet pierced his lungs, and after a few weeks he died. He bore his sufferings during that period not only with perfect fortitude, but with cheerfulness and often with gaiety. He entirely forgave his murderer; and a little before his death said, "Take me out into the Barrack court, and lay me there on the ground. A soldier should die in the open air."

CHAPTER XII

THE GREAT IRISH FAMINE 1846–1850

The first remedial Measure — Great Meeting of Irish Proprietors, in January, 1846 — The Temporary Relief Act — Depôts of Food formed — Relief Committees — Indian Meal distributed widely and gratuit-ously — The private Charity of England immense — Letters from emi-nent Irishmen — Lord George Bentinck's Proposal — Unjust Charges brought against Irish Proprietors — Labours of many Irish Ladies — The terrible Sufferings of the Irish Poor, chiefly in the Latter Part of the Visitation and from the Diseases generated by Famine — The large Proportion who died of Fever in the Emigrant Ships or after landing.

THE county of Limerick, in which I resided during the famine, was not one of those with the densest population or the most dependent on the potato crop. It therefore suffered less than many other portions of Ireland from the Great Famine, which has often been spoken of as if it lasted but for one year, whereas it lasted for large portions of four, namely, 1846, 1847, 1848, and 1849, while for several years later, the enormous emigration proved that the Terror, "though baffled, still retired with strife." During those successive years the calamity assumed different characteristics, and was met by different reme-dies, all of them well-intended, and carried out with great energy, but, unhappily, not selected with equal judgment, or attended by equal success.

The first remedy applied was that of public works; but those works were professedly introduced almost wholly as a test of destitution. This was to copy from a very questionable original. In England, before the Poor Law Reform of 1835, paupers were often employed in alternately digging gravel pits and filling them up again; but that test seemed to have originated rather with the wiseacres of the time than with its wise men, for it did not check such pauperism as brought the country which had vanquished Napoleon from approaching the brink of destruction. That the problem of Ireland when the ordinary food of a whole people melted away before their eyes, was one of extreme difficulty we are bound to confess. If the State resorts to great public works, such as railways, it must prevent companies from undertaking them; and if it spends large sums on local drainage, it must interfere with the ordinary rate of wages, and check the ordinary agricultural efforts both of proprietors and farmers. Many other difficulties stood in the way; and among them a wrong method of relief was the first adopted, that of works being nearly valueless. Presentment sessions were held everywhere, roads were half made and left unfinished; but the old English test of destitution was at that time neither needful nor safe.

It was not wise to assemble thousands of men on works that seemed but a mockery. Labour has its moral relations as well as its material. It has its dignity, and it retains that dignity so long as the employer and the employed alike gain an honest livelihood out of it, and the land is thus made to support its children. In the absence of such mutual aid and mutual respect, labour acquires a bitterness which nature never intended. No doubt the labourers were often unreasonable; but that was exactly what many of the wisest men in Ireland had reminded Parliament and the Government of before the experiment had been tried, insisting on it that measures of a different sort were necessary in the first instance, especially the formation in nearly all parts of the country of depôts at which food might be given gratuitously to those obviously destitute. Important public bodies reiterated the statement that charity should bear the name of charity, and that the works on which, in the second place, the people were employed, should be works either directly tending to increase the produce of the land, or else works that indirectly enriched the country.

In the middle of September, 1845, a committee of landlords was formed in Dublin. On the 14th of January, 1846, a great meeting of peers and members of Parliament took place, in the Rotunda, a meeting almost unexampled in the number and the high position of those who attended it, and who belonged to all parties alike. Among their chief resolutions were these: "We deem it our solemn duty — the present system having failed — to call upon the Government in the most imperative terms to take such measures as will secure local supplies of food sufficient to keep the people alive, and to sacrifice any quantity of money that may be necessary to attain that object. That we regret that the means hitherto adopted . . . have on the one hand proved incommensurate with the evil, and, on the other hand, have induced the expenditure of vast sums of money upon useless or pernicious works. That this most wasteful expenditure, tending, as it does, to diminish our resources, and increase the probability of future famines, has not been the result of neglect on the part of the resident proprietors of Ireland, but of an impolitic and pernicious law, which they were compelled to carry into effect, notwithstanding repeated protests to the contrary. . . . That any system of relief to the able-bodied that does not lead to the production of food, or articles that may be exchanged for food, will diminish the capital of the country, and that in proportion as capital decreases, poverty will increase." Many other resolutions were passed, especially recommending assisted emigration, the reclamation of waste lands, loans to farmers, as well as proprietors, for the improvement of their lands, with a right to compensation on their part in case of their removal.

This great meeting in Dublin was attended by more than fourteen peers, twenty-six members of Parliament, and six hundred landed proprietors. Its resolutions were marked by public spirit and practical wisdom. Its one great fault was that it was not held very much earlier. Parliament met a few days afterwards. The Irish Secretary made a deeply significant statement. He quoted from the report of the Commission of Poor Law in 1835. This was its statement, namely, that Ireland then contained 1,131,000 agricultural labourers whose average earnings did not exceed from two shillings to two shillings and sixpence a week; and that of these one-half were destitute during thirty weeks of every year. There had been many Parliaments and many Governments, and they had created many commissions which had prescribed many remedies; but it was the prescriptions not the remedies which had been swallowed, and the disease had not been removed. No doubt many an eminent statesman and many a great proprietor had to share a great blame between them, one belonging both to a remote and to a proximate past. Alas, there is no sleep so profound as that of habit! The Irish people itself had long slept that sleep, and hardly knew that aught was amiss! Except during the rude awakening times of recurrent lesser famines they were merrier than they are now; and their cheerfulness proved a snare to their rulers.

The treatment of the great Irish Famine passed through three periods. The first was that of unproductive public works used as a test of destitution. That system soon detected itself. It was demoralising. The destitute believed that as these test works were a sham, the payment would prove a sham too; and they saw no reason why their labour should not be a third sham. To their amazement, when their work came to be measured in some places, their payment turned out to be more than double that given for good work on farms. It was a competition between the official measurers and the agitators, a rehearsal, as some affirm, of an analogous competition in subsequent times between the "Land League" and the "Land Court." The agitators were beaten. Soon afterward, the labourers professed at least to give some work, though I remember that an old man complained, when dying of a chill, that "the boys had not allowed him to work enough to keep himself warm."

The second period was far better managed. It soon became apparent that relief through a system of false labour was twice as costly as a system of relief by supplying the destitute with Indian meal. Moreover, it left wholly without relief many who from age or infirmity could neither work nor pretend to work, and lastly it

produced an ever-increasing animosity among all classes
in Ireland who knew that one-half of the cost of these
imaginary works was legally charged upon Irish land,
while the money that might have helped to develop its
vast resources was almost wholly thrown away.   These
things spoke for themselves.   Several momentous changes
took place in rapid succession.   The first of these was a
permission by the Lord Lieutenant, on his own authority,
through what was called "Mr. Labouchere's letter," to
include various reproductive works among those on which
the destitute population were employed.   The letter
authorizing this expenditure was issued on the 5th of
October, 1846; and the amount actually expended under
it was about £239,476.   This change was a frank confession of error and a very salutary improvement.   But
the evil continued to be immense.   Destitution was still
at best but imperfectly relieved, while the number of
labourers employed rose in three months from 20,000 to
400,000.   A new system of relief was introduced under
the name of the "Temporary Relief Act," by which Relief
Committees were formed in nearly all parts of the
country and established depôts from which food was distributed to the destitute.   The relief thus given in
Indian meal cost less than half what the unproductive
works had cost, and gave relief far more effectually, and
with far less suffering to the aged and infirm.

The measure passed on the 26th of February, 1847.
But, most unfortunately, its operation did not extend
beyond the 1st of November, 1847.   No serious provision
for future "State aid" was then enacted, and the destitute were left to such aid as could be afforded by a poor

rate raised locally from land the chief produce of which had failed. Beyond this, private charity was nearly the only remaining resource. I have already stated that the private contributions from England, from America, and from the few in Ireland who (rents having nearly ceased) still had resources, were truly magnificent; but long after the autumn of 1847 there remained in Ireland a destitution such as large aid from the State can alone cope with. A Poor Law was never intended to deal with vast and prolonged famine except partially. To do more is beyond its competence, and can but drive out of cultivation the land which has already refused to yield its increase. Private charity has also its limits. The State must do the rest, for she alone has the power of anticipating her future resources. The whole nation, when its total forces are drawn upon at once in its two spheres, of space and of time, can on such occasions adequately assist the suffering part; which, however, when it recovers itself, is bound both to repay its own debt and assist the other parts when the trial successively falls upon them.

It was during and after the autumn of 1847 that the chief suffering connected with the famine prevailed; but, for the reasons already assigned, the harrowing scenes associated with it in too many parts of Ireland were comparatively rare in our neighbourhood. There was much suffering; but not that prostration which for a time causes a nation to change its character. The extraordinary elasticity, which has always imparted to Ireland a strength such as robustness imparts to other countries remained. There was a perpetual excitement; the alternation of the tragic and the comic remained; the change-

ful humours held their own.   Many scenes that illustrate
them recur to my memory as I muse on past time, and
others find a place in my correspondence, a few passages
of which I will record, leaving sadder themes for a later
time.

I will copy here some portions of my letters to my
kinsman, Stephen Spring Rice, early in 1847.   He was
at once a devoted lover of Ireland and an admirable man
of business, as well as one of boundless energy, and with
his great friend, Mr. William Prescott, both of whom
had a large acquaintance with the wealthy men of "the
City," contributed largely to the formation of the chief
among the charitable societies of that time, namely, "The
British Association for Relief of extreme distress in
England, Ireland, and Scotland."   He was a practical
man.   Once, I remember, after there had been much
discussion as to whether rations of Indian meal would
suffice to keep up a man's physical strength, he said,
"Nothing like trying the experiment; I will eat nothing
else for a week."   He kept his word, but failed to con-
vince his opponents, who told him, when the week was
over, that his strength had been sustained by his *previous*
good dinners.   At another time I remember his saying,
"We should not blame our poor people for being riotous
when they see their families in danger of starvation.   If
they give me a good beating on some occasion you will
see how little grudge I shall bear them on that account."
I wrote to him thus on the 14th of February, 1847: "I
rode to Shanagolden last Tuesday, having heard that
'Shanid' was in insurrection from that place to Glin,"
and that on Tuesday a meeting of a very singular kind

was about to take place. It was not one of the ordinary
"presentment sessions." It was a committee put on its
trial on a charge of maladministration, a committee over
which a singularly respectable and conscientious country
gentleman presided, and on which there sat a number
of farmers, and one or more of the parochial Catholic
priests, the three judges consisting of three other priests
belonging to a distant parish; while a mob of angry
peasants surrounded the place of meeting. Fortunately
the military mustered strong. The mob would have
been larger still, and probably hotter also, but for the
inclemency of the weather. During my ride I had sometimes difficulty in preventing myself from being blown
off my horse.

I did what I could to keep the people quiet. They
assented to what I said, but reiterated the same statement, namely, that a certain dreadful engineer, who was
"after starving the people at Skibbereen," had been sent
to them in place of a predecessor who had won their
confidence, and for that reason had incurred the dislike
of their committee. The resident magistrate informed
me that he had nearly evidence sufficient to justify him
in sending certain conspirators to prison for setting the
mob against the newly appointed engineer, and also for
an attempt to coerce the committee into signing a memorial in favour of retaining the engineer removed by the
Government. The inferior members of the committee
acted after a very equivocal fashion. The chairman
stood his ground gallantly. He declared that he would
rather be torn in pieces than sign such a memorial; and,
throughout a day of very considerable danger to him,

acted with sense and spirit, notwithstanding the evident intention of some among the intimidated farmers on the committee to leave him a mark for popular indignation as soon as the military had taken their departure. This capitulation was averted, however, or else the committee must have lost its influence for ever. The moral of my tale is this: place as few as possible of the farmer class upon a committee; or jobbing will not turn out its sole defect. I shall not soon forget the alarmed surprise exhibited on that occasion by some among the members of the committee, when one of their number started up and denounced the inhumanity of the rest. His eye flashed, the cheek flushed, the whole burly frame shook, the lifted arm trembled with emotion. It was not altogether hypocrisy, it was also the temporary, sympathetic sincerity of a good actor who merges himself wholly in his part. He was for the moment the convert of his own eloquence. The courses he denounced so unexpectedly were right courses; he had been one of their advocates; and every one in the mob who cheered him knew that well.

The local knowledge of the farmer class on those occasions did not atone for their lack of independence. They thought what they had to think, and changed their thoughts as well as their language when the occasion changed.

The meeting broke up; nothing having been done, and the whole matter ended in what Father T. calls a "bottle of smoke." The military took their departure. The chairman was in no hurry to depart. He was right. For about an hour we walked up and down the street,

which became every moment more crowded and tumult-
uous. At last a window was thrown open. A bulky
man, the parish priest, leaned out of it, and exclaimed
in a loud voice, "What are you all doing there, making
such a confusion in the street that I cannot walk down
it as far as Sullivan's the butcher's to order a leg of
mutton for my dinner?" The next moment the window
closed with a slam. The appeal was irresistible, and the
crowd dispersed. The chairman remained a chairman
as long as it was his duty to do so. He then went to
another county, and the neighbourhood lost its most
sensible resident magistrate.

About this time, the proprietors took great pains to
replace the potato with a more advanced agricultural
industry, and established a large number of agricultural
societies. Their intention was ultimately to affiliate all
those lesser societies to the Royal Agricultural Society,
and to enlist the services of a skilled agriculturist for
each barony. They intended next to give prizes, distribute tracts, provide good seed for the farmers, and
urge upon the Government a large scheme for the founding of agricultural schools, with model farms attached
to them. These excellent efforts came to nothing.
The trouble of the time was too great for their success.
Another great endeavour was made — Lord George
Bentinck's measure for the expenditure of sixteen millions on the construction of Irish railways. Lord George
was intensely in earnest on the subject, and maintained
that the measure would give employment to 108,000
labourers, out of the 500,000 then employed on unproductive works, affirming also, on elaborate calculations,

that the State could not eventually lose a farthing by the
enterprise. The scheme was opposed not only by the
then Government, but by Sir Robert Peel, and rejected.
I can well remember the intense excitement in Ireland
on that occasion. Of course it would, though so costly
a scheme, have required supplementary aid for the relief
of multitudes remote from the proposed railways; and
the plan adopted by the Government when it substituted
the "Temporary Relief Act" for the "Labour Rate Act,"
if it had but continued long enough in operation, would
have effected all that was absolutely necessary at that
time. If, however, Lord George's proposal had been
adopted in conjunction with another proposal then strongly
urged in Ireland, for the reclamation of improvable waste
lands, or lands but half drained, the cost of such enterprises being chargeable upon the lands improved, it may
reasonably be believed that, after the cessation of the
famine, Ireland might have made a great and rapid
advance in prosperity. But, alas —

> "These are imperial works and worthy kings."

The age does not favour them, neither does the ignoble
strife of parties; and, though political economy does not
by any means rebuke them, political economists commonly
disparage them.

Here is a fragment of a letter to an English critic : —

"All measures of relief must depend for success on the
machinery through which they are worked. Our machinery
is complicated, and therefore not easily extemporised. It consists chiefly in 'Relief Committees!' Do you know what that

means too often? Here are the dramatis personae of one. 1st, a man of high principles, but so modest that he can seldom get in a word: 2nd, a man who seconds every motion: 3rd, a wrong-headed man who contradicts every one, and does not know what he himself wants: 4th, a quiet, dry official, who, when questioned, answers that he is there to execute orders, and, when threatened, replies that if his career should be suddenly closed by assassination, he supposes that some other official gentleman will receive orders and execute them: 5th, (outside) a gloomy-looking crowd staring in through the windows with sharp, wolfish eyes, a clasped fist, and the other hand clutching a neighbour's shoulder: 6th, a few little boys waiting for the 'scrimmage:' 7th, a frantic old woman screaming like a Banshee: 8th, a big man who lives on whisky and snuff, with great staring eyes, a gaping mouth wide open, and dilated nostrils as black as if the jackdaws had built their nests in them: 9th, a smiling young girl pushing through the crowd to sell her cakes, and civilly requesting a policeman to stand out of her way: and, 10th, an angry multitude blowing horns in the distance. Perhaps, however, you will say that we must not pity ourselves (and self-pity is certainly one especial source of Irish weakness), merely because gentlemen who choose to boat on Bantry Bay, and measure their strength against the Atlantic waves, do not find the water as smooth as the Thames just above Twickenham.

"All this will not read much to the credit of my poor fellow-countrymen; but the marvel is, that, considering their sufferings, and the dangers before them, their deeds should be so much better than their words. The legislation of this century has been generally benevolent. If it had also been sagacious, and sympathetic; if it had not been tardy; if, when the sins of commission ceased, there had been no serious sins of omission on the part of statesmen who made Ireland the battlefield of parties, the Irish difficulty would long since have ceased; and the Irish character would have been better understood, both in what it possesses of noble, and in its weaknesses. The child-like would have remained; the childish would have put on manhood; but the two qualities have a common root."

A fragment.   To an Irish friend, S. E. S. R.:

"Since 'prayer and provender hinder no man,' here is a story to make you laugh amid your labours. Do you know old D. O'G.?   He is the agent of Lord G. the most amusing man of his day, who tells me that 'a Revolution comes up his approach every day, and goes down again without doing any harm,' and that, though assured by his agent that he has the finest estate in Ireland, he could not have a dish of beef or mutton on his table but for the aid of a single rich field in his domain.   The fierce ways of his agent, at a time when nearly all proprietors abstain from claiming rents, are enough to set the whole country in a blaze.   A letter from this unceremonious old fellow was shown to me the other day.   It was addressed to a bailiff who had shirked the 'serving' of certain 'notices,' intimidated by a wild flock of anonymous missives, decorated with 'cross-bones,' and warning him, the bailiff, to prepare his coffin.   The agent's answer to the bailiff ran thus:—'Paddy Madigan!   What bloody jackasses those fellows at Askealon must be to think they could vex me by shooting you!   Sure you know well that if they shot ten like you I could get twenty more to do my bidding!   Serve those notices forthwith!'   Some days later D. O'G. went to serve the 'notices' himself, accompanied by police.   A few of the non-paying tenants had come to meet him, while the main body of them waited in the distant region called 'mountainous,' because wild and wet, though flat.   They accompanied him on his way.   He did not conceal the contempt in which he held them; but a Gael pardons a good deal to a member of a surviving and important family belonging to that ancient race. Their faces darkened as they listened, but they made no reply. The police suggested a retreat. He, most likely, told them that they might 'go to Hell or Connaught,' but that he would go where he intended to go. They returned home. He pursued his way through a thunderstorm, as swiftly as an immense greatcoat saturated with rain permitted. The tenants gathered round him in dark masses as he advanced. At last it seemed to him time to tell them a bit of his mind. The sky had suddenly cleared; he stripped off the greatcoat, and gave it to one of the tenants to hold, placing his dripping umbrella in the hand of another. He then made them a brief harangue, which ended thus: 'I'll exterminate the whole of you.'

"He then turned round and pursued his homeward way, bending a little forward, and with his clasped hands behind him, but never looking back — the two men with the wet greatcoat and the umbrella trudging next to him, and a huge crowd behind whispering in low tones. It was his absolute absence of fear that saved him. Six days later he had a greater escape. He went to Rathneale, and mounted a flight of steps leading into a house where some of the tenants had promised to meet him with a portion of their rents. The steps, as well as the street below them, were thronged; he stood on the highest step, with his bailiff beside him. Through the crowd a man pushed his way, and up the steps, drew a pistol, placed its barrel close to the breast of his intended victim, and fired. The pistol flashed in the pan. The crowd divided; and the stranger escaped. The intended victim turned and clutched his bailiff round the shoulders, exclaiming, 'This is your doing! It was you that set him on!' The bailiff replied, 'Sure it was not I! Your Honour well knows I would be the last man to do anything of the kind.' The fearless old man buttoned up his greatcoat, and strode down the steps, red with wrath, and exclaiming, 'I never was more insulted in my life!'"

I add the postscript of a letter from a poor man to his landlord:

" POSTSCRIPT, — Well, Honoured Sir, is it not a long time you are staying away from your devoted people, among your friends in Manchester?   I am told that the English are a mighty wild people."

Another fragment:

May 9, 1847.

MY DEAR S. — It was a trying day when the experiment of relieving distress through unprofitable works was initiated, and we shall have another formidable day when the second and wiser experiment takes its turn, that of distributing Indian meal gratis.   The change is unpopular; for half labour at a double rate of payment grows to have its attractions; moreover, the people are assured that the rations distributed will be unwholesome food and insufficient.   To make a new system overlap upon an old one is a difficult matter.   A poor man, when reproved the other day for the violence threatened, made me an answer full of pathos: " Ah, Sir, what we are in dread of is this, that while the gentlemen are doing their best, and the Government is doing its best, ourselves and our little families will die of the hunger, unknown to God and the world.   But we cannot die unknown to the great God ! "

Riding to Rathneale, where, as you are aware, nearly the whole of the work is transacted by my eldest brother, I met lately a large crowd rushing out of the town like men flying from an invading foe.   The sight was a tragic one.   It was impossible to make them stop, or give me any further information than that they were speeding somewhere to kill cattle.   I got a man to hold my horse, clambered to the top of a wall and addressed them.   Those near stopped, and some of those far ahead came back.   Observing that the gathering seemed a quiet one, the military and police, who had followed them, returned to the town; and not long afterward a priest took his place beside me, and when I had finished, addressed them much more effectively. He told them that if they plundered the carts of meal, no more would be sent, that the gentlemen on the Relief Committees would have to "rise out of them," and that the destitution would soon be such that not a priest would be able to get his breakfast! After about half-an-hour, they gave us three cheers, and we led them back into the town. The next day another crowd went to the residence of the Protestant clergyman, and told him that they had come to kill his sheep. He answered that in that case they would do him a great service. "I have a better living in England," he said, "and if you kill my sheep, I shall have a fair excuse for residing on it in future."

Another fragment:

"We had lately a curious instance of mother-wit on the part of an Irish engineer, who had received orders to remove ten per cent. of the labourers from the Famine works, the system of relief by food depôts being gradually substituted for them. It placed him in great danger. Neither the inspecting officer nor the Relief Committee dared to give him any list of the labourers to be displaced. He had to face an angry crowd, and no police force could have protected him except for the moment. He named a spot on which he engaged to meet the malcontents, rode up to it alone, and ostentatiously unarmed. and smilingly informed them that, though the Government was disbanding its labourers elsewhere, he had won leave to retain eighty per cent. of them for an indefinite time, that number being of course to be selected *by themselves* as the best judges; but that his opinion was that the labourers retained should be exclusively of the poorest class. The next morning the walls, gateposts, etc., were covered with warnings to all persons who had land, to leave the works, or prepare their coffins. This engineer is now the most popular of his class."

Another fragment:

"My dear S. — Lest you should be disquieted by some news-paper paragraph, I write to tell you that we are nothing the worse here for having been visited by an ugly armed party, not even the ladies taking it as anything ominous. Almost close to the house I met six men, armed with guns, who informed me that they had not come in order to insult any one in the house-hold; on the contrary, they held our whole family in the highest respect; but only to shoot Coghlan, the steward — who had gone away only two minutes before. They demanded that I should get him dismissed, which I refused to do. They were perfectly civil with one exception, namely, that as often as I advanced towards them they raised their guns, and pointed them at me, thus giving me to understand that they did not choose that I should have a chance of recognising them. After a little time they made a second apology, discharged one gun and walked off. William Monsell says that they would not let me near them, because they could bear anything except a long speech from me; and certainly it is neither every orator nor every singer who has sufficient command of voice to stop when he likes it.

Coghlan was the head of two factions which had been at war for many years, plotting against each other day and night. Both he and his rival died; but that rival's wife lived on for many years, cherishing an immortal hatred against her husband's enemy. When old and dying, she declared that she forgave all her enemies except Coghlan. Her priest refused to give her absolution unless she forgave him also. Again and again he implored her to have pity on herself; and all her neighbours adjured her to 'be said by his Reverence.' Months passed, but she remained implacable. The last night came, and the neigh-bours sat round her bed, some affirming that she still breathed, others, that she had already passed away. Suddenly, she raised herself to a sitting position, and said, 'Coghlan, I forgive you

now; and the Almighty God may forgive you if he chooses' —
sank back and died. It will be observed that those last words
are susceptible of two different interpretations. . . ."

Another fragment:

"My dear S. — It was a very trying day; but it is over.
During most of it wild mobs marched about in all directions,
blowing horns. An immense meeting was held on Newtown
hill; but the wind there was very cold, and they descended
towards evening without having reached any conclusion; but
eventually most of those placed on the Relief lists came in and
claimed their portion. In Pallas the people refused to accept
the rations, declaring that they were too small to support a
family, and threatened to kill the clerk who distributed them.
It was a tragic thing to see the white face of his wife, who
watched everything and every one in silence. I found it was
the best plan to ask the ringleaders of each group a number
of questions about himself and his own circumstances. As
those circumstances often differed much from those of his
neighbours, the spokesman by degrees lost his representative
character, a thing fatal to his influence; and it became more
easy to raise a laugh against him.

"The poor people made strong complaints as regards many
of the Relief rules; but as we had a printed copy of the Instructions it was easy to make the poor fellows understand that we
must either obey those Instructions or cease to be members of
the Committee.

"I had a singular illustration of the transient nature of political considerations compared with those of a personal character.
The day that news arrived of O'Connell's death, I informed a
huge crowd of the event. There was a minute's silence; and,
after that, nothing more except an enquiry respecting the next
meeting of the Relief Committee. The priests are doing their
utmost to keep the people quiet, and never tell them, what some

theologians, I believe, hold — namely, that in cases of absolute necessity, men have a right to kill their neighbours' herds, in order to save their own families from starvation, provided that this be done with the full intention of repairing the loss whenever it is possible to do so. The people are much more in a panic than in a bad temper. Many of them say that after the Relief System by rations has been tried for a time, it will be abandoned. *What if this prophecy should prove true ? "*

The relief depôts were established within two or three miles of each other, under the management of local members of the Relief Committees, who had to decide among the several claimants for food, which was given in proportion to the numbers in their respective families. I was in charge of the depôt nearest to our residence, with the parish priest as my coadjutor, Father T., a man friendly to all and devotedly attached to his flock. He was a practical man, always looking to the useful, and caring nothing either for the sentimental or the popular. That part of his character I had learned when the potato failure was still but a rumour. I met him walking in a high state of excitement. "Have you heard the news?" he exclaimed, "What is this new Government about? Is this a time to allow arms to all the people in Ireland? The Irish Secretary is after making a great harangue in Parliament, saying that the Irish are ' fine spirited fellows, and would be proud to have arms,' and the ' Freeman's Journal ' says he is a great statesman! Arms, indeed! Arms! What to do with them?" After a minute's meditation, he proceeded, "The Government is calculating that, when they have all got arms, one-half of the Irish people will shoot the other half; and then the Govern-

ment will step in and hang the first half." Again he
paused, meditated, and resumed, "I had rather than a
good shoulder of mutton have the breaking of that great
statesman's nose."

Father T. was as much incensed as he had been when
the eight ruffians who had terrorised the parish for years,
but against whom none would inform, carried off a young
girl from her father's house by night, thus to force her
into a marriage with one of them; but who, in defiance
of all traditional usage in Ireland on such occasions,
neither brought a horse for her, nor a "side-car," nor a
"highly respectable woman," to prevent the girl from
"feeling in dread!" All else the old priest could forgive; but not this lack of respect to a girl. She felt
with him; informed against the men, and got them all
transported except one, who had lifted her on his shoulders
as they were crossing a bog.

When the day for distributing the Indian meal had
arrived, Father T. furnished me with my instructions.
"Do you see that big crowd there surrounding the house?
There are twice as many far away with a greater right to
relief than half of these have; and if we give all the meal
to these, there will be none left for the starving creatures! I'll begin by telling that crowd that we can only
admit one man into the room at a time, for fear some
argument might arise between them. Each man is to
take his turn and show the way that he is in, how much
land he has, and what family he has. We will work on
as long as there is light, putting all their names down
into a list; and then we'll give the quickest relief to the
worst cases. Now observe! When a man has told his

story, I never will contradict him, for if I did you would not get through five cases in an hour. If I consider the case is one for relief, I 'll say little or nothing to the man; but if I know that it 's only tricking us the man is, I 'll say what is fitting to say; and the last word you 'll hear from me is the word *transeat.*"

The first to enter was Pat Molony, best described in the very language of Gerald Griffin's peasant as "a mighty intricate little cratur." "Well, Pat," I asked, "how much land have you?" "Indeed," was the answer, "I believe, your Honour, it was up to thirteen acres they counted it; but what good is that when it is not land at all, but a corner of a bog, which no one knows better than the Reverend Father T."

"It would not give a breakfast to a jack-snipe in August," replied Father T., taking a long and resonant pinch of snuff, and adding in a lower voice the word *transeat.*

"Long life to your Reverence," rejoined Pat.

"Send in the next," said his Reverence, "and lose no time about it," remarking to me in a whisper; "his land's bad, but he has £75 lodged in bank."

We had to deal with about forty men before the evening darkened about us. Many of these got a good place in the list; but the fatal word *transeat* stretched like a bar before the expectations of many more — persons who had no real claims.

As we walked home through the wood I remarked, "But, Father T., some of those poor fellows will be disappointed when they see the lists; and it is you they will cross-question, for they regard me as a mere 'innocent' that gets his information from you."

"Well, sir," he answered, "if I answered all the questions they ask, I should have enough to do. I am not bound to answer questions that might do them mischief. They know this well — that it is for them and their interests I am at work day and night. Those that want the relief will get it; but in that big crowd there was many a man that in five minutes would tell you lies enough to thatch a gallows."

He desired his people to keep the peace at all times, and knew how to bring his teaching home to them. On one occasion it was thus described to me. Said Father T.: "The Government has you entirely in their hands, and if you do anything out-of-the-way, they can put you into a hobble at any moment. I'll make it plain to you." Providentially he had a string in his pocket. He took it out and placed one end of it in his left hand. Next he said, "The potatoes are gone, and there's no food except what Government gives you at the depôts. If you refuse to accept it, they will force it on no one; but when you come for it next there will be none for you. It will be just like this." Then he made a loop on the string, and dropped it down the forefinger of his right hand, and next looked round and said, "See that! there they have. you caught! They need not spend a penny more; and whom will you have to thank but yourselves?"

"When we saw the thing with our eyes we could not but believe him," they said to me.

In other parts of the country, matters sometimes went less quietly. At F— there was a large attendance of the Relief Committee, but a small police force for their protection, though on that committee sat gentlemen of high

influence, besides the burly parish priest and a small
Protestant clergyman.   After hours spent in profitless
debate, a mob came up from a distant part of the county.
The court house was sacked and the ejected committee
took up its stand on a sheltered spot near.   It was not
sheltered, however, from those warlike strangers, half
of whom occupied a hill in the vicinity, and in a few
minutes the sky was darkened by a flight of stones,
which fortunately whizzed above the heads of the committee, most of whom expressed their sentiments briefly
but characteristically enough.

" I charge this upon the Government," exclaimed a very
ruddy-faced gentleman.

" Where are the police? " demanded his next neighbour.

" It 's likely they went for a lark to the races at W. ;
they have had no sport lately," said another.

" If I had known we should have had such a shower as
that, I should have brought my Scotch plaid," remarked
a fourth, "and left at home this cloak with its velvet
cape. "

" It 's likely that that English military force called
' the police ' stopped a bit on the top of the hill just to
' make their meditation,' " remarked the schoolmaster;
"they are a mighty devout lot. "

In a few minutes more the crowd on the hill reap-
peared, after having made a collection of all the stones
to be found.   It was plain that they were in earnest.
The wisest member of the committee, a dry old man,
very deliberately took off his spectacles, pushed them
far down a well-worn spectacle case, with the remark,
" I 'm sorry this minute that I refused Sir George R.

last Wednesday, when he offered me thirty-nine pounds ten for my brown mare! My son Tom never was able to drive her and never will."

The Catholic priest, looking at his watch, summed up thus: "I'll tell you what it is, gentlemen, if you do not see a troop of cavalry riding down that road within three minutes from this time nothing will remain for you but to put your trust in the Lord," to which the little Protestant pastor softly made response, "The Lord forbid."

Within three minutes the troop was in sight. Earlier still it had come in sight of the crowd on the hill. One among that crowd exclaimed, "The army entirely," and another, "It would be fitter to give a taste of the stones to them than to our own gentlemen."

The finale was thus described to me by a lady:

"Mr. G. F. came up to me yesterday afternoon, with his usual scared look, and exclaimed, 'Oh, Lady D., did you hear of the accident that happened to her Majesty's Regiment, the ——, this day? They were riding smartly along to save the lives of the Relief Committee at F. The people got sight of them and rushed down and gave battle to them with stones. It was a long road, and the walls were so high that the soldiers could not get at the villains, and her Majesty's army was badly hurt, and many were knocked from their horses; and, what is worse than all, one of them lost his helmet, and a smart boy jumped the wall, and ran off with it. They hid it at first in a bog-hole close by; but now they have sent it to a poet who lives in a parish twelve miles off, and he has engaged to write a song on it in time for the great horse-fair at Rathneale; and he is to get 10s. 6d. for it; and that song will be sung at every fair, and all the races, and wakes, and other places of entertainment in the south of Ireland for the next fifty years!'"

It must seem strange that in the midst of that most deplorable of all things — a famine — the tragic and the comic should be thus inextricably interwoven. All who know Ireland, however, are aware that this intermixture is with her an almost invariable characteristic, and, far from mitigating the tragedy, often increases it by contrast.

The quainter scenes were hardly remarked by us at the time. Here is a sketch of an Irish country gentleman's life, written by Stephen Spring Rice, in a pamphlet not published, and commenting on one written by an English statesman, who had himself worked hard and with high ability in connection with the famine, but who laboured under the delusion that Irish proprietors were reposing on a bed of roses.

"What was the life led by an Irish squire at that time? You might have seen him leaving home before daylight, that sunrise may find him within his relief district, into the destitution of which he has to enquire. Till sunset makes it impossible for him to continue his work, he has to pass ceaselessly from house to house, making every possible enquiry, and exerting all his ingenuity to detect the frauds attempted by those who wish to job. . . . Being well known, the people troop down from the hill tops to meet him, in their tens or twenties, threatening or imploring; and he has to use his best eloquence for soothing, cheering, or for checking and reproving them. Wearied at last, he returns in the twilight to his home, doubting whether he is not carrying to it the seeds of disease caught in the hovels he has visited. But he does not go home to rest. His whole night, and far into the next morning, is occupied in reducing into an available form the rough memoranda of each case which he has collected in the daytime. The next day, perhaps, he has to attend presentment sessions. Amidst roars of anger and cries of suffering he has to attempt to work out a novel and complicated system; sick at heart with seeing the gradual realisation of his worst fears — the famine, fever, and gradual demoralisation of the lower classes, the ruin of the higher. Throughout the day little notes are showered in scores on the table; these are the petitions of the poor, materials for his work by night; for when he at last goes home they must be all deciphered, classified, considered, and prepared for the next meeting of the Relief Committee. . . . And what rest does he get by night? Every half-hour he starts up from an uneasy sleep, haunted by one idea that still recurs. He dreams that he has lost a little scrap of paper on which he had recorded the name of one that required immediate relief, and that from his carelessness a family is starving."

What was the reward for all this suffering? The most unbounded misrepresentation, both in England and in Ireland, and in the latter country frequent violence. The letter from which I have quoted records a case in which several members of a Relief Committee were carried off and imprisoned, and another in which four members of one, including the chairman, barely escaped with their lives. And the district described, far from being among the most afflicted portion of Ireland, was at that time one of the least suffering, one in which a single proprietor was at his own cost executing an industrial work valued at £8,000, to provide support for the labourers employed on it.[1]

The same letter (S. E. Spring Rice's), one memorable alike for its ability, its energy, and its moderation in tone, refutes the charges brought against the Irish proprietors for not having, in response to "Mr. Labouchere's

[1] Foynes.

letter," availed themselves more largely of the government loans for drainages, etc., the sum spent on those
works amounting to £200,000. The answer was briefly
this. The proprietors had from the first demanded that,
while the charity distributed by the State should be
given under the name of charity, the relief works should
be of a reproductive, not an unproductive character. But
on this subject the concession was not made until the
labouring population had become profoundly demoralised.

The writer says, "I rejoice that the efforts which were
made for taking advantage of it were not more successful, knowing at what ruinous expense the works were
conducted under it by the officers of the Government
who had the exclusive control in the matter" (p. 19).
Again he shows that the practical abandonment of *task
work* had raised the rate of wages so high that the works
became ruinously costly. "The gentry had no authority
for checking it; and in many cases where they pronounced an opinion against it, their lives were placed
in imminent danger . . . For raising stone in a quarry,
the workmen asked a price that in ordinary years would
have raised the stone and built the house into the bargain" (p. 27). Under those circumstances the money
to be borrowed from the Government could not possibly
have been repaid.

Everywhere, and in all classes, there was then a reign
of helpless suffering. The worst part of that suffering
was the part endured by the humbler class; but that
suffering was not confined to it, or to men only. Ladies
laboured hard in aid of the poor, and especially among
those of them who struggled to emigrate. Many ladies

succumbed under the labours of those years, or under the privations which they endured in silence. Over others there came a change which did not pass away for years. The eyes which had witnessed what theirs had witnessed never wholly lost that look which then came into them; and youth had gone by before their voices had recovered their earlier tone.

I refer to these things because most unworthy misrepresentations have been made, both long since, and in late years, sometimes in ignorance, sometimes with a political aim, respecting the general conduct of the Irish upper classes during the famine years. As long ago as 1878, an eloquent writer as well as an ardent politician on the popular side, and, I believe, a "Home Ruler," Mr. Alexander M. Sullivan, distinctly contradicted those charges in a well-known work entitled "New Ireland." He does not spare the absentees, cowardly and selfish deserters of a brave and faithful people, nor deny that there were bad landlords, as well as good; but he affirms that the overwhelming balance is the other way " (p. 63). Cases might be named by the score in which such men scorned to avert by pressure on their suffering tenantry the fate they saw impending over themselves. "They went down with the ship" (p. 64). Mr. Sullivan did justice not less to the magnificent *private* charities sent to Ireland from England and from America, and to the labours and vast contributions of the Quakers; while of the terrible sufferings of the Irish poor, especially in the later and direr period of the famine, and of the patience with which those sufferings were borne, when the dreadful reality was felt in its fulness, he writes with the pathos of an absolute sincerity and without exaggeration. From his work and that of an Irish Catholic priest ("The History of the Great Irish Famine," by the Rev. John O'Rourke), I shall have to make many quotations when dealing later with the sadder part of the subject.[1]

Father O'Rourke refers often to the exertions made by many of the gentlemen of Ireland on behalf of their fellow-countrymen, whether in the way of active labours, or labours of the brain. In many cases I was a witness of these efforts. Among those who worked hardest was Mr. Monsell, later Lord Emly. I accompanied him and Lord Arundel and Surrey (the late Duke of Norfolk) to Kilkee, and we passed the next day in roaming over famine-stricken moors and bogs in its neighbourhood, then among the most severely tried districts of Ireland. I shall not soon forget one visit, which, accompanied by the local inspector, we paid to a deserted cabin among the morasses. Its only inmate was a little infant, whose mother was most likely seeking milk for it. On slightly moving the tattered coverlet of the cradle, a shiver ran over the whole body of the infant, and the next moment the dark, emaciated little face relapsed again into stillness. Probably the mother returned to find her child dead. Mr. Monsell burst into a flood of tears. Nothing was said; but a few days later, on Lord Arundel's return to England, the inspector at Kilkee received a letter from him enclosing a cheque for two hundred pounds, to be added to the local relief fund. Mr. Monsell addressed an admirable letter to the then Irish Secretary. He

---

[1] I hope to write a second chapter at a later time.

insisted on it that the labours upon which the starving
people were employed should be productive labours, and
that charity should bear the name of charity. "If you
use your opportunities well, if you develop Ireland's
resources, if you increase its capital, if you improve its
agriculture, if you distribute its wealth as it ought to be
distributed, its progress in the next two or three years
will be greater than the progress ever made by any country within the same time." This appeal no doubt tended
largely to elicit "Labouchere's letter," including agricultural improvements among the destitution works.

Another friend of mine to whom Ireland was deeply
indebted was Mr. John Godley, a man highly honoured
by all that knew him, not for his great abilities only, but
still more for the noble energy and the exalted practical
purposes to which they were ever applied. He had made
colonisation a subject of deep philosophical study, and
had found in Ireland (his country, though his character
was, as often happens in Ireland, especially an English
one) a field on which it was possible to realise his loftiest
ideal of colonisation, its old Greek ideal, namely, the creation of a new colony retaining the civilisation of the
parent one, and as far as possible, reproducing its image
on a new soil. To effect this, and at the same time to
find a remedy for a calamity almost unexampled, was a
work worthy of aspirations and energies like his. He
wrote a pamphlet expounding his scheme, and drew up a
memorial in its favour, signed by eighty persons, many
of them men of known abilities, and including numerous
members of both houses of Parliament, and Irish propri-
tors in large numbers. (1) A million and a half of Irish

emigrants were to be located in a settlement to be made in Canada, with the assistance of the State. (2) A religious provision was to be made for them and their pastors from the first. (3) To help the emigrants to settle on the land, "aids to location" were to be provided. (4) The enterprise was to be under the management of a "joint-stock company," entitled "The Irish Canadian Company." (5) The Government was to lend nine millions in aid of this scheme. Unfortunately it was opposed both by the Government and by Sir Robert Peel, then in opposition, and rejected by Parliament. Mr. Godley founded the settlement of Canterbury in New Zealand; but Ireland lost the benefit of his services.

Another Irishman who laboured in a special manner for his suffering fellow-countrymen at that time, and did so with entire success, was my brother, Sir Stephen E. de Vere. Emigration had then assumed enormous proportions. In 1845 the emigrants were 74,000; in 1846, above 108,000; in 1847, they had reached 215,444. It was attended by extraordinary sufferings and an immense mortality. The emigrant ships were then sailing vessels; the voyage to the United States and Canada occupied about six weeks and often many more. The accommodations had from the first been insufficient, and by the sudden increase in the number of emigrants had become incomparably worse. Remonstrances were in vain. The grievances were denied by interested parties; the emigrants were flying for their lives, and had to accept whatever was offered to them. My brother was resolved that at least an accurate knowledge of the facts, a knowledge derived from personal experience, should be supplied to the public and to Parliament. On the sudden cessation of the public works, he took passage for Canada with a considerable number of those who had been employed on them under his supervision, and conducted them to Quebec, sharing with them all the sufferings and perils which then belonged to a crowded steerage passage. Those who escaped fever on their sea-passage frequently caught it on landing, the dormant seeds of disease becoming rapidly developed by the stimulus of better air and food, and by infection. It was so on this occasion. They reached Quebec in the June of 1847, and in a short time nearly all of those whom he had taken with him and lodged in a large, healthy house were stricken down in succession, during a period covering about eight months, and received from him personally all the ministrations which they could have had from a hospital nurse. After their recovery, they found work in Canada, and settled later chiefly in the United States. He returned to Europe in the autumn of 1848, bringing home with him a few for whom the American climate was unfit. But the aim for which he had toiled was accomplished. His letter describing the sufferings of emigrants was read aloud in the House of Lords by Earl Grey, then Secretary for the Colonies, and the "Passengers Act" was amended, due accommodations of all sorts being provided in the emigrant vessels. Most of those emigrants who on reaching Quebec went into the crowded and infected hospitals died there. It is impossible to guess how many thousands of emigrants may have been saved by this enterprise, for the enormous Irish emigration continued and increased for several years after the famine. In 1850 the emigrants were above 209,000; in 1851, they exceeded 257,000. The deaths on the voyage to Canada had at one time risen from five in the thousand to sixty in the thousand; and the deaths while the ships were in quarantine, from one to forty in the thousand. Still larger numbers died at Quebec, Montreal, and the interior, according to Sir Charles Trevelyan's official record. Large numbers of the Catholic clergy who had ministered to the sick caught the infection and died, amongst others the good Catholic Bishop of Montreal. The loss of life among the ministering nuns was frightful.

A second detachment of emigrants, sent out wholly at the expense of my brother, followed during the next autumn those who had first gone, and were also received and provided for in his house, until the natural fear of infection had abated, and it became possible to procure employment for an Irish emigrant restored to health.

CHAPTER XIII

CARDINAL NEWMAN

WHEN first I made acquaintance with Newman I was young and impressionable, and for that reason all the more able to appreciate at least a portion of what was most remarkable about him. It was late in 1838, and Oxford, apart from its illustrious inmate, would have well repaid me for my journey from Ireland, not then a short one. The sun was setting as I approached it, and its last light shone brightly from the towers, spires, and domes of England's holy city. Such a city I had never seen before, and the more I saw of it the more deeply was I touched. Its monastic stillness is not confined to its colleges; much of the city besides, in spite of modern innovations, wore then an aspect of antiquity, and the staid courtesy of those whom I met in the streets, contrasted delightfully with the bustle, the roughness, and the surly self-assertion encountered in the thoroughfares of our industrial centres. I had often to ask my way; and the reply was generally an offer to accompany me on my way. It reminded me of what I had heard respecting Spain — namely, that every peasant there is a gentleman. As I walked I recited to myself Wordsworth's sonnet on Bruges, and wondered why the most patriotic of poets had not rather addressed it to Oxford. There seemed a rest about that city, bequeathed to it by the strength of old traditions, which I have nowhere else enjoyed so much, except at Rome.

"While these courts remain," I said to myself, "and nothing worse is heard than the chiming of these clocks and bells, the best of all that England boasts will remain also." " Nothing come to thee new or strange " is written upon every stone in those old towers, which seem to have drunk up the sunsets of so many centuries and to be quietly breathing them back into modern England's more troubled air.   How well those caps and gowns harmonise with them !   Certainly Oxford and Cambridge, with all the clustered colleges, are England's two anchors, let down into the past.   May they keep her long from drifting from the regions dedicated to piety and learning into those devoted but to business or pleasure.

> " The ancient spirit is not dead :
> Old times, I said, are breathing here."

In Oxford there then abode a man, himself a lover of old times, and yet one who in fighting his way back to them had in the first instance to create an order of things relatively new — John Henry Newman.   I had left for him a letter of introduction from an eminent Fellow of Trinity College, Dublin, the Rev. J. H. Todd, to whose learning, liberality, and patriotism, Ireland has owed much.   Early in the evening a singularly graceful figure in cap and gown glided into the room.   The slight form and gracious address might have belonged either to a youthful ascetic of the middle ages or a graceful and high-bred lady of our own days.   He was pale and thin almost to emaciation, swift of pace, but, when not walking, intensely still, with a voice sweet and pathetic both, but so distinct that you could count each vowel and consonant in every word. When touching upon subjects which interested him much, he used gestures rapid and decisive, though not vehement; and while in the expression of thoughts on important subjects there was often a restrained ardour about him; yet if individuals were in question he spoke severely of none, however widely their opinions might differ from his. As we parted, I asked him why the cathedral bells rang so loud at so late an hour. "Only some young men keeping themselves warm," he answered. "Here," I thought, "even amusements have an ecclesiastical character." He had asked me to break-fast with him the next morning and meet his young friend, Frederick Rogers, afterwards Lord Blachford, a man later as remarkable for high ability as high principle, and especially for what Sir Henry Taylor called his marvellous gift of "sure-footed rapidity" in the despatch of business. After breakfast he placed me in the hands of Mr. Mozley, who became my guide among the objects of especial interest at Oxford, an office not less kindly discharged the next day by Mr. Palmer, afterwards Sir William Palmer, well known from his theological works. I shall never forget the kindness which I received at that time and later from distinguished men, several of whom reminded me that my family name had old associations with Oxford, while others gave me letters to eminent persons in Rome.

I did not see Newman again till after the lapse of three or four years. Many things had occurred in the interval. He had read much, he had thought much, and he had

written much. His fame had grown; so had the devotion of his friends, the animosity of his enemies, and
the alarms of many admirers. Those alarms had been
much increased by one of the recent "Tracts for the
Times," the celebrated Tract No. 90. The wits were
contented with averring that No. 90 only meant " No Go."
Several of the University authorities, however, thought
that the tract was no laughing matter, and instituted
proceedings against its author, Newman, probably with
regret, but in the conviction that it was injurious to the
Thirty-nine Articles — which Mr. O'Connell had called
the " forty stripes save one " inflicted by Queen Elizabeth
on the Church of England; but the High Church reply
was that if the Thirty-nine Articles felt aggrieved, so
much the worse for them, since in that case they must be
opposed to " patristic antiquity," by which the Church
of England professed to stand. Many pamphlets were
written on the subject, one of them by a layman, my old
friend, R. M. Milnes, afterwards Lord Houghton. I remember Wordsworth reading it and giving it high praise;
and I remember also Dr. Whewell's reply to some one
who expressed surprise at Milnes holding any opinion
upon such a subject. "Oh, he holds none; but he took
a fancy to write a philosophic essay on the subject of
the day; so he wrote what he thought a philosophic
mind like Thirlwall's might think." It was a very brilliant
essay.

The stir made by Tract 90 gave it an immense circulation, with the proceeds of which Newman bought a
library, now included in that at the Edgbaston Oratory;
but though he bore with a dignified self-control what his

friends regarded as a persecution, yet a tract generally regarded as one that explained the Thirty-nine Articles by explaining them away could not but increase the distrust with which he had long been regarded both by the Evangelical and the Establishment party in the Church of England. Several recent occurrences, on the other hand, had impaired Newman's confidence in her position, especially the "Jerusalem bishopric," which he regarded as a fraternisation of that church with a German non-episcopal community, and also as a hostile intrusion into the diocese of an Eastern bishop possessing the "apostolical succession and primitive doctrine." Against that measure he and Dr. Pusey had solemnly protested, but in vain. Their interference had given great offence in high ecclesiastical quarters; and not a few made themselves merry at the war between the bishops and their chief supporters, while a story went round that the wife of some dignitary had openly stated that she could not approve of the *indiscriminate* study of "the Fathers" among the clergy, because it tended to "put thoughts into the heads of young curates." Newman was then *quadraginta annos natus*, yet even he apparently had not escaped this danger; for though his mastery of "the Fathers" was almost as much an acknowledged fact as his mastery of Holy Scripture, their teaching no longer, as once, seemed to him much to resemble that of the Established Church. He wished to be at liberty, and he resigned his Oxford preferment and retired to Littlemore. That voice of which the "solemn sweetness," as Mr. Gladstone described it, had pierced all hearts at St. Mary's, was heard there no more except in sad memory and sadder anticipation. Men remembered that pathos

so much more powerful than any vehemence could have
been, that insight which made his gentleness so formidable
a thing, those dagger-points of light flashed in upon the
stricken conscience, and, most of all, that intense reality
which sent a spiritual vibration over the land, with the
warning, " words have a meaning, whether we mean that
meaning or not." These things men remembered, perhaps the more because they saw the man no more.

Littlemore was but three miles from Oxford. He had
retired there to a hermitage stiller even than Oxford, that
Oxford described by " Wulfstan the Wise" as serener than
the summit of Olympus, the Olympus which he thus
describes:

> " So tranquil were the elements there, 'tis said
>   That letters by the fingers of the priest
>   Writ in the ashes of the sacrifice
>   Remained throughout the seasons uneffaced." [1]

To Littlemore I walked alone through the fields from
Oxford. The little hermitage had been changed to a little monastery by the addition of some small rooms which
sheltered a few young men who, like those that accompanied Plato in the garden of Academe, walked with him
that they might learn from him. One of these youths was
afterwards well-known as Father Ambrose St. John, who,
but for his premature death, would have been Newman's
biographer. Another was Father Dalgairns. I asked one
of them whether they recited the " canonical hours" of
the breviary, and understood that they did so. I was
deeply interested that day by my interview with Newman,
though he seemed to me more reserved than when I had

[1] " Edwin the Fair," by Sir Henry Taylor.

first made his acquaintance, and very grave, if not actually depressed. The final casting-up of an account is a more difficult process than the preliminary ranging of the figures one beneath another. Newman's long and arduous studies had collected a vast mass of philosophical and theological materials; and the details were doubtless arranging themselves in his mind and pointing towards the sum total. That sum total, perhaps, looked daily less like what he had contemplated in his youthful anticipations — a Church of England triumphant here below, pure as the earliest day-dawn of the faith, venerable as the sagest antiquity, cleansed from medieval accretions, enriched by modern science, daily rising up out of the confusions of the sixteenth century, and delivering itself from secular bonds at no loss but that of diminished revenues; a gradually increased colonial extension, making her the inheritor of a second *orbis terrarum* — and ultimately a reunion with the earlier one.

Such, ever since my boyhood, had been my aspiration: how much more must it have been his! Yet that day as we walked together — for he was good enough to accompany me most of the way to Oxford — those aspirations did not seem to smile upon him amid the summer field flowers as they had smiled four years previously that night when the cold Christmas winds blew the cathedral chimes over us. Newman's mind, however, was not like Mr. Ward's, which always saw with a diamond clearness what it saw at all; it included a large crepuscular region through which his intelligence had to pass before its dawn broadened into day. No one could appreciate better than he the subtlety of illusions or their dangerous consequences; no one could feel more profoundly the pain of severing old ties; but he has told us that he could never see why any number of difficulties need produce a single doubt as regards matters of faith; and perhaps he might have added that he could never see why any amount of suffering need paralyse action in matters of duty, when at last certainty had emerged from the region of doubt. Daily I heard reports, which he met neither with encouragement nor denial, but with reserve. Some of his followers began to whisper, " Our great admiral will transfer his flag to another ship." Others said: " The Church of England will be the better for losing a formidable guest. The acorn blown by a chance gust into a china vase if it continued to grow there would break it up."

In 1845, Newman's secession was not attended by that of as many others as had been expected, though it included one a great power in himself— the poet Faber— who renounced poetry for a higher work; but it left profound misgivings in the breasts of others, who continued their researches, carried their principles out in their parochial labours, and watched the signs of the times. They had not to wait long. The "Gorham judgment" was pronounced, and within a few years about three hundred of the Anglican clergy— some say four hundred— had followed his example, many of them, like Mr. Allies, to their worldly ruin and that of their families, together with a far larger number of highly educated laymen. Newman's lectures were believed to have assisted many persons in doubt at that crisis. Mr. R. H. Hutton, whose work on Newman appears to me far the best thing on the subject which I have seen, wrote in it as follows:

"When Newman at last made up his mind to join the Church of Rome, his genius bloomed out with a force and freedom such as he never displayed in the Anglican communion";

and elsewhere he thus illustrates that remark:

"The 'Lectures on Anglican Difficulties' was the first book generally read, amongst Protestants, in which the measure of his literary power could be adequately taken. . . . Here was a great subject with which Newman was perfectly intimate, giving the fullest scope to his powers of orderly and beautiful exposition, and opening a far greater range to his singular genius for gentle and delicate irony than anything which he had hitherto written. Never did a voice seem better adapted to persuade without irritating."

I was among the many present at those lectures in 1850, and to me nothing, with the exception of the "Divina Commedia" and Kenelm Digby's wholly uncontroversial "Mores Catholici," had been so impressive, suggestive, and spiritually helpful. I was also struck by their impassioned eloquence, which brought to me the belief that if this man had chosen for himself a Parliamentary career he must have carried all before him. The extreme subtlety which belonged to his intelligence was then shown to be but one of many faculties, and opposed no hindrance to his equal power of exciting vehement emotion; though he did so apparently unconsciously, on this occasion, perhaps, restrained by the solemnity of the subject discussed, and the circumstance that the lectures were delivered in a church. Many passages might

be cited in illustration of this remark, such as the last
half-dozen pages of the tenth lecture, contrasting the
calamitous condition of the Church in the days of Jan-
senism, the French Revolution, and Napoleon, when the
Pope was a prisoner, and when many among the Church's
enemies boasted that the papacy was at an end, with
the sudden change when her chief enemies had vanished,
and there had returned to her an energy and health not
hers for a very long preceding time.   Nothing about
those lectures was more remarkable than the celerity
with which they were composed.   They were written as
they were read — once or twice a week, I think — a rapidity as great as that with which the successive chapters
of his "Apologia" followed each other many years later.
His genius was always stimulated by a sudden pressure.

I had become a Catholic more than five years later
than Newman.   The time when I saw most of him was
in 1856.   Soon after the Catholic University had been
opened by him in Dublin at the command of Pope Pius
IX., he requested me to deliver at it a series of lectures on literature.   I considered myself incompetent
for such a task; but I could not refuse compliance with
a wish of his, and, although not a professor, I delivered
about a dozen lectures, the substance of two among
which was long afterwards (A. D. 1889) published in a
volume of essays.[1]   When the day for the delivery of the
first lecture arrived, Newman invited me to take up my
abode in the larger of the two University houses, over
which he presided personally, surrounded by a considerable number of Irish students, together with a few

---

[1] Essays Literary and Ethical (Macmillan).

foreign youths of distinguished families attracted by his name.

The arduous character of Newman's enterprise in Dublin became the more striking from the contrast presented by the humble houses which bore the name of the "Catholic University," to the monumental buildings of Trinity College, Dublin, not to speak of the magnificent homes provided for learning and religion at Oxford and Cambridge by the piety of Catholic ages. The difficulties connected with the creation of a new university are great under the most favourable circumstances; here they were immeasurably increased by the determined opposition of successive governments and Parliaments, which steadily refused to concede to the Catholic University a charter, a public endowment, or University buildings. The opposition was stimulated by a vehement doctrinaire enthusiasm in favour of the "Queen's Colleges," long since admitted (excepting that at Belfast) to be a comparative failure. The purely secular character of those colleges was solemnly protested against by the larger part of Ireland, both Catholic and Protestant, on the double ground that they violated the "rights of parents," nearly all of whom preferred "religious education," and also because in them, though not in Ireland's popular education, religion was banished from those higher studies with which it is so vitally connected, and banished at a time when youths are deprived of the safeguards of home. The error was a grievous one, and both England and Ireland feel its consequences to this day. It added a new secular ascendency to the sectarian one.

The poverty to which religious education was thus condemned, besides its more serious consequences, had others with a touch of the ludicrous about them; but, as some one remarked, "no one who laughs with consideration would laugh at such a jest." I confess I was pained by the very humble labours to which Newman seemed so willingly to subject himself. It appeared strange that he should carve for thirty hungry youths, or sit listening for hours in succession to the eloquent visitors who came to recommend a new organist and would accept no refusal from him. Such work should have fallen on subordinates; but their salaries it was impossible to provide. The patience with which he bore such trials was marvellous, but he encountered others severer still. I cannot think that he received from Ireland aids proportioned to what ought to have been his. The poor, who had no direct interest in the University, paid for it in large annual contributions, but the middle and higher classes were proportionately less liberal; and there were, perhaps, jealousies besides, to which it is now needless to advert. In Ireland, however, Newman found many private friends who honoured him aright and were greatly valued by him. Among these were Dr. Moriarty, long the head of All Hallows College, and later Bishop of Kerry; Dr. Russell, Principal of Maynooth, the learned, the accomplished, and the kind; Dr. O'Reilly, S. J.; the late Judge O'Hagan, and others. He worked on, cheered by the grateful sympathy of men like these, including that great Irish scholar, Eugene O'Curry, to whom he had given the Irish professorship, and whose lectures — a most valuable store-house of Irish archæology — he attended.

He was cheered by the great interests of religion which he believed to be at stake, and by the aid which Irish genius and Irish aspirations, if true to their noblest mission, must largely, as he also believed, have ministered to them. In that hope he gave Ireland three of his noblest volumes and seven of the best years of his life. Newman was one of those who could work and wait. I remember his saying to me once, when things were looking dark:

"We must not be impatient. Time is necessary for all things. If we fail at present to create a Catholic University there remains another great benefit which we may confer on Ireland. We can in that case fall back upon a second college in the Dublin University, one on as dignified a scale as Trinity College, and in all respects its equal; one doing for Catholics what Trinity College does for Protestants. Such a college would tide over the bad time, and eventually develop into a Catholic University."

Many years have passed since he spoke, but neither a Catholic University nor a Catholic college, founded at once on the two principles of "religious education" and of educational equality, has yet been provided. A Newman was given to Ireland, one longing to make of her what she was named in early Christian times, namely, "the School of the West," and apparently she knew nearly as little what to do with the gift as England had known. The opportunity was lost. A foundation stone was laid. On that occasion I wrote an ode, not worthy of its theme, but one aspiration of which may yet be fulfilled. It was that the statue of Newman might one day stand in the chief court of an Irish Catholic University.

When I had been but a few days in Newman's house I fell ill of scarlatina, and the first of my lectures had to be read aloud by another person. I wished to be taken out of the house, lest the infection should spread, but for some time that course was interdicted; and every day, in spite of countless other engagements, Newman found time to sit by my bedside occasionally, and delight me by his conversation. When advancing towards convalescence I went to Bray for sea air, and he drove out to see me. I remember urging him to make an expedition with me, when I was well enough, amid the beautiful scenery of Wicklow, and his answering with a smile that life was full of work more important than the enjoyment of mountains and lakes — a remark which Wordsworth would have thought highly irreverent. I remember also saying to myself, The ecclesiastical imagination and the mountain-worshipping imagination are two very different things: Wordsworth's famous "Tintern Abbey" describes the river Wye, its woods and waters, its fields and farms, as they could only have been described by one whose eye saw things visible and things invisible both. The one thing which it did not see was the great monastic ruin, for of it that poem says not one word; and now here is this great theologian, who, when within a few miles of Glendalough Lake, will not visit it, though St. Kevin consecrated it by flinging the beautiful Kathleen from the cliffs into its sullen waves.

I had to pass many a day at Bray, for my scarlatina was followed by other maladies, and so exhausted my strength that my poor attempts at exercise often ended by my having to lie down at full length on the road. A

little later I went to Wicklow, and thence to Killarney,
in hopes that the mountain air might restore me. That
hope was long unfulfilled. I used to look at Mangerton
and say, " Is it possible that I ever climbed a mountain? "
But I am degenerating into " inferior matter." At Killarney I met my honoured friend Dr. Moriarty, with whom
I had first made acquaintance when he was the head of
that admirable missionary college, All Hallows, which
the Irish Church owes to a priest of lowly degree and of
no high ability, but rich in charity and faith — a man to
whom far lands have owed many of their best pastors.
The Bishop was making a visitation of his diocese, and
offered me a place in his carriage. I gladly accepted it;
and rejoiced the more when I found that our road passed
through some of the most beautiful scenery in Europe,
that combination of mountain and seacoast which has
ever to me appeared to surpass in spirit-stirring beauty
every other kind of scenery. As we drove along by cliff
and bay our discourse was chiefly of Newman. One
night we slept at Derrynane, O'Connell's home. He
would have liked Newman better than Newman would
have liked him.

It was one of Fortune's strangest freaks that brought
two of Oxford's most eminent sons to Dublin — Dr.
Whately, Protestant Archbishop there, and Newman.
For seven years they dwelt nearly opposite to each other,
at the northern and southern sides of St. Stephen's Green;
but, I believe, never met once. Newman considered that
it was not for him to pay the first visit; and the Archbishop perhaps thought that a renewed intimacy with his
old friend might excite polemical jealousies in Dublin. I

was present, however, at a meeting, the first since their
Oxford days, between Newman and Gladstone. It was
at the hospitable board of my dear friend Sir John
Simeon. They sat next each other after the ladies had
left the dining-room, but their conversation was confined
to the topics of the day. Newman, however, at a later
time, when in London, was the guest occasionally of
Dean Church and of Lord Blachford.

Newman and Sir Henry Taylor had also a singular
sympathy for each other, though they had never met, and
though there was so much antagonistic in their opinions
and dissimilar in their characters and pursuits. If they
had met early they would probably have been friends.
They had in common a fearless sincerity and a serene
strength; but one of them had found his training in the
schools and the other in the world and in official duties.
Another man of letters for whom Newman had a great
love was Walter Scott. He delighted not only in the
"Waverley Novels," but, like Mr. Ruskin, in Scott's
chivalrous poetry. His own great poem, "The Dream
of Gerontius," Sir Henry Taylor used to say, resembled
Dante more than any poetry written since the great
Tuscan's time. Sir Henry could not have failed to admire also some of his short poems, such as his beautiful "Lead Thou me on," so strangely called a hymn,
and another poem not less admirable, though little known,
respecting that painless knowledge of earthly things possessed by the happy departed. The last stanza of it
expresses the theological teaching that it is neither with
merely human feelings, nor with eyes turned towards the
earth, that the souls of the blest regard the shapes of

this lower earth. On the contrary, their eyes are fastened on the Beatific Vision; and it is in the mirror of the Divine knowledge that they contemplate so much of earthly things as is needed, in that region where charity is perfected, for the exercise of intercessory prayer. The mode in which they possess a serene knowledge of earthly things is thus illustrated in connection with a well-known passage in the Apocalypse.

> " A sea before
> The throne is spread. Its still, pure glass
> Pictures all earth-scenes as they pass ;
> We, on its shore,
> Share, in the bosom of our rest,
> God's knowledge, and are blest."

"The Dream of Gerontius," as Newman informed me, owed its preservation to an accident. He had written it on a sudden impulse, put it aside, and forgotten it. The editor of a magazine wrote to him asking for a contribution. He looked into all his "pigeon-holes," and found nothing theological; but, in answering his correspondent, he added that he had come upon some verses which, if, as editor, he cared to have, were at his command. The wise editor did care, and they were published at once. I well remember the delight with which many of them were read aloud by the Bishop of Gibraltar, Dr. Charles Harris, who was then on a visit with us, and the ardour with which we all shared his enjoyment.

Newman's tale of "Callista" is a book singularly different from his "Loss and Gain," one being a vivid picture of a certain section of modern English life and the other a not less vivid picture of life in the days of the old

Roman Empire. The last was written, as he informed
me, chiefly with a pencil in railway carriages, during a
Continental tour. No one who has read that work can
doubt that it was no less within the power of its author
to have become a master of prose fiction than to have
become a great poet or a first-class parliamentary orator.
Such versatility would to most men have proved a serious
peril, and we have probably lost much of the best poetry
we might otherwise have inherited from Scott, Coleridge,
Southey, and Landor, owing to the circumstance that
they had equal gifts for other things as for poetic tasks;
but Newman was saved from such snares by his fidelity
to a single and supreme vocation. He was eminently
fitted, as I believe, to be a great historian, and a history
of the early Church by him, as his " Historical Essays "
prove, even if it had descended only to the time of
Charlemagne, must have proved among the most valuable
of historical works from the absorbing interest of the
theme and the many years which Newman had given to
the study of early Christian times. His other avocations
prevented us from having such a book from his hand.
In the meantime, we possess in the work of a great friend
as well as ardent admirer of Newman (I allude to Mr.
Allies' work, "The Formation of Christendom") a
treatise on the philosophy of early ecclesiastical history,
at once so profound and so eloquent that it may largely
console us for the loss of one work more by Newman.

At one time the Pope had given Newman a commission
to make a new English translation of the Holy Scriptures
from the Vulgate. He told me that he had heartily desired to undertake the task, but that unexpected difficul-

ties, connected in part with vested interests, had presented themselves, in addition to those inherent in such a work; and thus another frustration was added to the many which beset his life — frustrations of which I never heard him complain. Certainly self-pity was no weakness of his.

If he had translated the New Testament and the Psalms alone into English such as his would have been, it would have imparted to countless readers "the freedom of no mean city," opening out worthily to them those treasure-houses of manly and spiritual devotion — the Breviary and other office-books of the Church.

After Newman had ceased to be connected with the Catholic University of Ireland — which I trust may yet reward his labours, even if it does not wholly fulfil his ideal — I saw him chiefly through my annual visits on my way to the Cumberland Mountains and to Wordsworth's grave. I never stood beside that grave without a renewed wish that those two great men — surely England's greatest men of thought in her latter day — had known each other. In many of their opinions they would have differed; but the intensely English character of both, and the profound affection cherished for his country by each, would have been a bond between them.

There often exists between very different men a latent resemblance — sometimes even a physical resemblance — which long escapes observation. I was interested by hearing that after Wordsworth's death, several friends, permitted to take a last look at one whom they had long loved and honoured, as he lay on his bed of death, were deeply impressed by the resemblance which his face then bore to that of Dante — as preserved in the best portraits — a resemblance which they had never noted before.

One of my most interesting visits to Newman was paid when I was on my way to Rome, early in 1870, the year of the General Council. Of course we spoke of the definition of the Papal Infallibility then regarded as probable. I well remember the vehemence with which he exclaimed, " People are talking about the definition of the Papal Infallibility as if there were and could be but one such definition. Twenty definitions of the doctrine might be made, and of these several might be perfectly correct, and several others might be *exaggerated* and incorrect." Every one acquainted with Newman's teaching was aware that he fully believed the doctrine — nay, that he had expressed that conviction in nearly every volume published by him subsequently to his conversion. Consequently, when a letter of his, written to a private friend in Rome and published without his knowledge, had been misunderstood, and had consequently produced a considerable though transient excitement, all such persons knew at once that what that letter contested was not the doctrine of the Papal Infallibility, but the expediency of defining it at that particular moment. When, some months later, the definition was made, it proved to be a most moderate one, and therefore much disappointed the so-called " Ultramontanes." Several years later, Newman, in his " Letter to the Duke of Norfolk," replying to Mr. Gladstone's " Vatican Pamphlets," distinctly stated that the definition made by the Council, so far from being an extreme one, was a strictly moderate one. It therefore belonged to that class of definitions which, six months before it was put forth,

Newman had spoken of to me as being perfectly correct. As he has been much misrepresented on this subject, I deem it a duty to him to record that conversation.

To men who were acquainted with Newman only through his books it was rather as a mind than as a man that he presented himself; but the converse was the case with those who enjoyed his intimacy. To them his great attraction lay in what belonged to his personal being — the strange force of which often made itself felt almost at once, so entirely free was he from conventionality. Amid the society of those with whom he was not in sympathy it is true that the shyness of his nature bred a sort of isolation; but, notwithstanding, with that reserve there was mixed a frankness. You might be left with a restricted knowledge, but not with an erroneous impression.

W. S. Landor makes some one say that the thoughts of a true man should stand as naked as the statues of the God of Light; but he might have added a converse assertion, namely, that a man's most sacred feelings should be often shrouded in a dimness like that of the same god's Delphic laurel grove. There was much in Newman which could only be made known to those deeply in sympathy with him, and the disclosure of which to others might easily have led them into error.

What men felt most in him was his extreme, though not self-engrossed, personality. It was a very human personality, one that imposed upon him a large share of human sensibilities, and, perhaps by necessary consequence, of sorrows, cares, and anxieties. He had also, it is true, a strong sense of humour; but in all serious matters seriousness was exigent, and nothing came to him lightly, although he had, notwithstanding, a strength that raised him up under its weight. Silence and stillness but kindled more the interior fires, and a narrow limit increased their force. His nature, one —

> " Built on a surging, subterranean fire,
>   That stirred and lifted him to high attempts," [1]

was far more likely to be stimulated than kept down by pressure of any sort. He had vehement impulses, and moods which in his " Apologia " he calls " fierce; " and these were stung into activity in him, as in Edmund Burke, by the sight of oppression or injustice. But his temper was also one that abounded in sympathy. He was full of veneration. It was thus that, as he tells us, the lightest word of his bishop in his Anglican days was a conclusive challenge to his obedience; and that when some one pointed out Mr. Keble to him for the first time, he looked on that good and gracious man with awe, and " when Mr. Keble took his hand he seemed sinking into the ground." He tells us also that the " Christian Year " had largely helped to teach him two great truths, to which he had always clung closely, and that he had ever considered and kept the day on which Mr. Keble preached the Assize sermon in the University pulpit as the start of the religious movement of 1833.

In others also he greatly valued veneration, and thought that, even when astray, it was still a thing entitled to sympathy. He told me that Mr. Keble possessed that quality in an extreme and even unfortunate degree; that it had always been directed especially to his father; and

---

[1] Philip van Artevelde.

that the thought that in becoming a Roman Catholic he would place a gulf of separation between him and his father, must have rendered it difficult for him seriously even to ask himself the question whether such a step had become a duty. With Dr. Pusey — "dear Pusey" he almost always called him — the obstacle to conversion was, he thought, of another sort. He remarked to me that with many great gifts, intellectual as well as spiritual, Dr. Pusey had this peculiarity, "he never knew when he burned," the allusion being to a sport among children, when they have hidden something away and encourage the blindfolded searcher by exclaiming as he gropes his way nearer and nearer to it, "Warm," "Hot," "You burn." Dr. Pusey, he said, might see a doctrine with clear insight, yet take no cognisance of another proximate to it — indeed, presupposed by it. "For years," he said, "many thought Pusey on the brink of Rome. He was never near it." Thus, strange as it seems, the two old friends co-operated even in separation; they stood at two ends of the same bridge, and the one at the Anglican end of it passed the wayfarer on towards the Roman end, though he always strove to hold him back when half-way across.

The intense personality of Newman is curiously illustrated by a remark made by Mr. Woolner, the sculptor, when he contemplated the plaster cast which he had made of Newman's bust as placed at last in his studio when finished. He turned to a friend and said, "Those marble busts around us represent some of the most eminent men of our time, and I used to look on them with pride. Something seems the matter with them now.

When I turn from Newman's head to theirs they look *like vegetables*." What he was struck by was the intense personality of Newman's face — a still intensity.

Newman's humility was not more marked in his relations with Mr. Keble than in his relations with Dr. Pusey. In the early years of the "High Church" movement, to which he contributed more than all its other supporters put together, he had no desire to be its head, and was ever pushing Dr. Pusey into that position. And yet with his humility he united a strong belief in his own powers and a conviction that God had imparted to him a high and special mission. That conviction must have been a great support to him during all the numerous trials of his long life. One of the severest of those trials came upon him towards its close. During his last two years the state of his eyes rendered it impossible for him to say Mass. Few of his many afflictions pained him so deeply.

Nothing more characterised Newman than his unconscious refinement. It would have been impossible for him to tolerate coarse society, or coarse books, or manners seriously deficient in self-respect and respect for others. There was also in him a tenderness marked by a smile of magical sweetness, but a sweetness that. had in it nothing of softness. On the contrary, there was a decided severity in his face, that severity which enables a man alike to exact from others, and himself to render, whatever painful service or sacrifice justice may claim. With his early conviction that he had a mission, there had come to him the thought that deliverance is wrought not by the many, but by the few. In his "Apologia" he says,

"I repeated to myself the words which have ever been dear to me from my school-days: *Exoriare aliquis*. Now too Southey's beautiful poem of Thalaba, for which I had an *immense liking*, came forcibly to my mind." The saying, " Out of the strong came forth sweetness," was realised in Newman more than in any one else whom I have known.

In other matters also apparent opposites were in him blended. Thus, while his intellect was pre-eminently a logical one, and while it seemed to him impossible or immoral to discard the authority of logic, when plainly exercised within her legitimate domain, yet no one felt more deeply that both the heart and the moral sense possess their own sacred tribunals in matters of reasoning as well as of sentiment. It was this consciousness which protected him from the narrowing tendencies to which the logical passion or habit, when acting by itself, so often leads. Many a vigorous mind includes but a single section of a mind like his. The logical faculty was in his case most fortunately supplemented by an expansive imagination, which grasped thoughts immeasurably beyond the range of the *mere* logician. The largeness of his intellect thus, as well as his reverence and humility, protected him from the scepticism imputed to him by men, who in his place, would have become not sceptics only, but unbelievers. It was that wide imagination which made him grasp the hidden but substantial analogies between the chief schools of religious thought in the nineteenth century and the corresponding schools in the fifth, analogies which had never revealed themselves to minds perhaps as logical as his own, yet which

he could never repel, however much they distressed
him.

In Newman, again, above both the logical and the
imaginative faculty, there ever hung the spiritual mind,
a firmament full of light, though clouds might at times
oversweep it. These were the characteristics of Newman
which made him write the memorable sentence, "No
number of difficulties *need* produce a single doubt" —
he meant doubt in a mind capable of real convictions.
His mind swung through a wide arc, and thoughts apparently antagonistic often were to him supplemental each
to the other. Thus he tells us in his "Apologia" that
the existence in the world even of such sin and suffering
as sometimes seem to make it incapable of reflecting its
Maker's countenance implies, *for the true Theist*, nothing
disparaging to true Theism. What it teaches *him*, is
that the world cannot have remained what the Creator
made it ; that some dreadful catastrophe must have
overtaken it and wrecked its chief of creatures, Man —
namely, the Fall; that to keep due proportion, a second
mystery, and one not less wonderful than that of a creation, must be true no less, namely, an Incarnation, a
Redemption, a Deliverance; in other words, that not
only Theism is true, but that Christianity, the practical
Theism, is its supplemental Truth.

Another most remarkable union in Newman of qualities
commonly opposed to each other, was that of a daunt-
less courage with profound thoughtfulness. The men of
thought and study are often timid men, and, when not
timid, are indolent and averse to action, a thing which
takes them out of that region in which they can trust

themselves, and into a region in which their battle is a
left-handed one. Men of this order may not on that
account be consciously false to their convictions; but
they wish to serve Truth, a jealous divinity, in their own
way, not hers; and they swerve away from it on specious
pretexts, when approaching near to that point from which
the conclusion must needs be plain, and where there must
remain no other alternative except that of avowed faith-
lessness, or — serious inconvenience. In Newman there
existed the rare union of the contemplative mind and
the heroic soul. Otherwise, he might have pointed out
its way to another generation; but he would not have
'led forth the pilgrimage.'

It would be a mistake to suppose that Newman's imagination, religious as it was, could spare no space for earthly
interests. Had its energies been thus restricted it would
have dealt less vigorously with heavenly subjects. Many
of his writings show how keenly he had studied human
character, and the degree in which it affects that great
drama of Providence called by us "history," in which
whole nations have their entrances and their exits, like
actors, on the stage of life. Nothing except his zeal for
the highest spiritual truths could exceed the sympathy
felt by him with all that concerns the "Humanities"; and
I well remember the look of stern disapproval with which
he spoke to me of the Abbé Gaume's theory of education,
one that must have excluded the Greek and Latin classics
from the schools of Christian youth, or left them but a
small place therein. Another able and excellent man,
Dr. Ward, would, I think, in that matter have sympathised
with the Abbé's opinions more than with Newman's. I

recollect that once, when I had remarked in a letter to
him on the lamentable loss which the world must have
sustained if all the works of Æschylus, and the other
Greek dramatists had perished, as most of them have,
Dr. Ward replied that in the surviving works of those
men, he could really find almost nothing of a character
to be called "ascetic," and that therefore he could not
see what loss would have followed if the whole of them
had disappeared. Newman could heartily admire also,
in spite of its limitations, the heroism of the early world.
His admiration for the greatest of early heroes, Alexander
the Great, was ardently expressed in a letter to me on
my sending him my drama bearing that name. It demanded, "Who was there but he whose object it was
to carry on civilisation and the arts of peace, while he
was a conqueror? Compare him to Attila or Tamerlane.
Julius Cæsar, compared with him, was but a party man
and a great general."

I have thus recorded some of the traits that struck
me as most remarkable in Newman's character.   His
career bore a singular resemblance to that character.
Till his forty-fifth year it was a disturbed one. If, as he
informs us in his "Apologia," his submission to the Roman Catholic Church imparted to his soul a profound
and lasting peace, while as regards things spiritual, far
from chilling or contracting, it greatly stimulated his
genius and energies, it is not less true that the antecedent process of conversion was to him an unusually
painful one.   That conversion meant a separation from
all whom he most loved and honoured, and also, but
only apparently, a desertion of what was then regarded

by many as the battlefield of great principles, and in its
place, at least, an external fellowship with many to whom
he had long felt a strong antipathy on the ground of
their philosophic "liberalism," or of the parts they took
in political "agitation." Newman was an intense loy-
alist, and he had long deemed it a duty of loyalty for
him, as a Churchman, to see matters theological as long
as that was possible from an Anglican point of view.
Eventually he had to choose between thinking independently or discarding those great main principles which
for so many years had been consolidating themselves
both within his intellect and his heart, but which, as
he had reluctantly discovered, could not be realised in
England's Established Church, and were realised, as they
had ever been, in the Roman Catholic Church, notwithstanding the sins or shortcomings of individuals.

Some persons have expressed surprise that a mind
like Newman's should have been so slow in making
that discovery. They forget the difference 'twixt now
and then. They should remember that the wild cry of
"The Mass is idolatry!" had rung for several centuries
over the land, and that its echoes, though dying away
in the distance, had sounded in the ears of Newman's
generation. When passionate polemical errors have lived
their time, and died, so far as the intellect is concerned,
their angry ghosts continue yet for a season to haunt
the imagination. We should also remember that when,
in the sixteenth century, the very idea of the Church
seemed to have been suddenly sponged out of the Northern mind (otherwise the reforms then doubtless much
needed must have been sought in a General Council, not

imposed by local authorities), and when, in the nineteenth century, that idea had been partially restored,
the last part of it to reappear was that of the Church's
visible unity.   That was natural.   The new reformers
thought it sufficient to resist Erastian tyranny, and to
revive the general teaching of Christian antiquity.   In
the latter endeavour they had a great success; in the
former, none at all.   The Civil Power asserted itself more
and more, not from any despotic disposition, but to
defend national "comprehension" at any cost of orthodoxy.   The success and the failure were both of
them necessary to open the eyes of the new reformers;
and the eyes of the most thoughtful opened earliest.
Many of those who remained behind were not less sincere and earnest than those who faced the wilderness.
Few Catholics can doubt the good faith of those noble-
minded men, Pusey and Keble; they were less clear-
sighted than Newman and Manning, Faber and Ward.
Had it been otherwise, a movement would have been
early stopped which, after half a century, is still advancing in conquering progress.

As regards the fast and the slow in religious changes,
it is easier to measure purely intellectual movements than
those of a mixed sort, intellectual and spiritual both;
for in the latter there is a question of Divine grace as
well as of reason, and "the wind bloweth as it listeth."
Few can say whether a religious conversion has been a
rapid or a slow one, and Newman pointedly remarks,
in his "Loss and Gain," that it may err in either way.
Even in scientific enquiries, the philosopher's pace is far
from being a uniform one.   We are rightly warned not

to leap to conclusions; yet the highest scientific conclusions are commonly reached by discoverers who signally differ in pace, one from another. Men of science
do not grudge their labours in making reiterated experiments; but yet they admit that, though a very great
discovery is commonly approached slowly, it is reached
by a bound, the discoverer knows not how. In science
that bound is commonly a lightning flash of that supreme genius which is an inspiration in itself. In religious enquiry it is often an act of that highest and perhaps
latest-won faith which crowns at once the humility and
the insight of faith (that is, its spiritual discernment) by
that heroic courage of faith which qualifies the believer
to become the future martyr. In both cases, to those
who do not accept the conclusion reached, the final act
naturally appears an impulse dictated by an illusion;
and in both cases also a double charge is often brought
against it — that of precipitation, and that of tardiness.

Newman's Anglicanism was killed by his own work on
" Development." That book was written, I believe, within
a year — a very remarkable circumstance; but it was the
result of many years' meditations rapidly brought to a
point. Then the winds of controversy ceased: the waves
fell: and there was a great calm. That spiritual calm
remained with Newman, though of course he had his dif-
ferences with friends on minor matters — till his ninety
years were accomplished, and England was left to lament
the departure of him who had once been one of the most
distrusted and disliked of her sons, but who had gradually
become one of the most venerated.

To that veneration he had preserved his claim inviolate.

He had ever retained a faith, firm and fixed, that the Christian religion came from God, that it was God's chief gift to man and the one hope of the world. He had at last reached a profound conviction that the Catholic faith and Church constituted jointly the authentic and permanent form of that Christian religion, notwithstanding that in their field the tares had from the first been found with the wheat, and must ever be found. He believed that before his England, and before the world there remained greater perils, and also greater possible glories, than at any preceding time; that only through a pure and a complete Christianity, in its integrity and in its unity, those perils could be surmounted, and that glorious inheritance attained. These convictions had long deepened in his mind. The event has already largely proved his sagacity. If, through much of England, and also (though from very different causes) through much of the civilised world besides, one out of the two great main-streams of opinion rolls on in ever widening flood t'wards the rapids of unbelief, it is largely owing to the genius, the courage, and the faithfulness of Newman that there rolls also a counter-tide in the direction of a larger, because humbler knowledge, a firmer faith, and a deeper peace.

And yet all this might have been lost! A single step astray, even in youth, might have transformed his character and career into one its opposite, changing imagination into unreality, intellectual subtlety into scepticism, spiritual ardours into polemical fierceness, heroic courage into a fatal presumption. It was only in their just subordination, the lower to the higher, that all the various elements which had met in that strong nature, and which required a discipline proportionately strong, could have been sustained in equipoise, and taught to correspond with that high Providence which shaped his way.

LINES SUGGESTED BY A VOLUME OF CARDINAL NEWMAN'S POETRY.

Hid in each cord there winds one central strand;
Hid in each breast a panting heart doth lie ;
Hid in the lines that map the Infant's hand
There lurks, some say, a life-long destiny;
Through the dropt leaf, 'gainst wintry sunset scanned
Shines that fine web whose firm geometry
Sustained the nascent frame and each new dye
Fed by spring dews, by autumn breezes fanned.
Stamped on this Book what note we ? One decree
Writ by God's finger on a destined Soul,
That made each thought an act, and, leaving free
The spirit, shaped the life into a whole :
What was that great behest? that mastering vow?
England, God's work completed, answer thou !

CHAPTER XIV

MY first meeting with Cardinal Manning was at a dinner party at the house of the late Earl of Dunraven in 1849. He was ushered into the dining-room some time after we had sat down, and I had a good opportunity of observing a man of whom I had heard so much. I well remember saying to myself, "I see a word written on the forehead of that man, and that word is *Sacerdos*." Later on I wrote of him thus to a friend:

" He is the most venerable, refined, gentle-natured, aspiring, and spiritually ardent man whom I know. He was delighted with Henry Taylor's poem in memory of your husband (Edward Ernest Villiers). ' Did you know him? ' I asked, when he spoke to me of that exquisite elegy. 'Know him?' was the answer; ' we were companions at Merton College, Oxford.' One evening at Lavington we read to each other alternately passages out of Dante's ' Paradiso,' and agreed that there was more theology within the laurelled head of that grand old bard than in the heads of half the bishops now living."

Not long afterwards I passed several days with Manning at his Rectory house at Lavington, of which parish he was then rector. Each day we dined at the palace of the Bishop of Oxford, which was very near the parsonage. One of those days we ascended through the woods to the summit of the Downs, and walked along them, enjoying the magnificent prospect which they command. That night we walked till a very late hour up and down before the hall-door of the parsonage. Our conversation was chiefly on theology, but not a little on poetry also. For that he had plainly a great admiration, provided that the verse was of a severe order, both intellectual and spiritual; but neither he nor Newman ranked Wordsworth as highly as I did. Again he recurred to Dante, and after quoting a remarkable passage, exclaimed vehemently: "There is no poetry like Dante's: it is St. Thomas Aquinas put into verse! Those two were the greatest of human minds!" — a saying recorded by me in a sonnet more than forty years later. Sir Henry Taylor's poetry had a great interest for him, as well as for Cardinal Newman, and for the same reason — namely, its union of compact strength with classic grace and refinement, and its freedom both from the sensational and the effeminate. Neither he nor Newman liked poetry that did not include a strong element of the severe as well as of the thoughtful.

By degrees the chief characteristics which belonged to Manning impressed me with more and more of definiteness. One of these was his extreme intellectual self-possession, a quality in which he was a signal contrast to Carlyle, who seemed to me unable to "do his thinking" until he had worked himself up into an intellectual passion, as the lion is said to prepare himself for action of another sort by first lashing himself into a rage. Manning had also the moral counterpart of this intellectual habit in a self-control which was so marked that no one looking upon him could well imagine his being carried away by any sudden impulse. This singular deliberateness and serenity were sometimes charged upon him as coldness. There are, however, many different sorts of ardour. Archbishop Whately used to speak of his great friend, Dr. Arnold, as one with a heart so warm that his friendships were to him what the closest ties of blood are to others; while mere acquaintance were often to him what friends are to ordinary men. It seemed to me as if a great cause, rather than any individual man, was that which drew out the strongest ardours of Manning's nature. He might easily have preferred the interests of a great friend to his own; but he would certainly have preferred that of a great cause to that of either self or friend. His human affections concentrated themselves on a few, while to the many beyond these he gave respect rather than admiration and a helpful and benevolent regard rather than ardent sympathies. The intensity of his nature, however, could not be doubted by any one who had seen him in church and at prayer. His stillness was one that seemed as if it could not have been shaken if the church had caught fire. Some human affections had also, it is said, acquired with him a character not less intense and indelible; but of these I had not been a witness, and never heard him speak. One of them was directed to his father. Every evening at Lavington he used to walk up to say his vespers in a little church where there were then few or no worshippers, wearing a cloak much the worse for the wear. It had been his father's. His chief friend, I think, was Robert Wilberforce.

He preserved other relics, perhaps more precious, as I learned when travelling with him to Rome. We stopped at Avignon; and a few minutes after our diligence entered the courtyard of our hotel, a small black bag belonging to him was missed. It had been stolen, and all inquiries, whether instituted by the police or the clergy, failed to recover it. He declared that whoever had it in his possession might keep what else it contained, which included £100 in money, if only he restored the letters in it. At the first moment after the discovery of his loss the expression of grief in his face and voice was such as I have seldom witnessed. He spoke little; and when I was beginning to speak, he laid his hand on my arm, and said, "Say nothing! I can just endure it when I keep perfectly silent." The loss probably was that of his most precious memorials; but it did not even at the time make him. negligent of the "casual stranger." After he had given his directions we entered the dining room and he sat down apart. Not long afterwards he observed that at a small table not distant there sat a maid-servant, alone and neglected. The future Cardinal rose and did for her all that her master and mistress had forgotten to do. He brought a waiter to her, became her interpreter, and took care from time to time that nothing should be wanting to her dinner. When all efforts to recover the lost treasure had failed he went to Rome by sea, and I went to Florence. We met again at Rome. He met my inquiries with a brief reply: "No; the loss was probably necessary — necessary to sever all bonds to earth." He once said to me that he feared he had often had to lament great coldness, or apparent coldness, in his bearing to others. Here certainly no such coldness was apparent.

The degree in which Manning had long lived in and for spiritual things threw probably a character of remoteness for him not only over all temporal things, but also over all human ties except the closest. He had been regarded as an Evangelical in his early clerical days, the religion then of most devout men; and when the revived "High Church" doctrine had blended that teaching with a larger one, he became a High Churchman of the most spiritual order. A large proportion of his works in his Catholic days illustrated the gifts of the Spirit, especially the book to which I believe he attached the most import- ance, namely, "The Temporal Mission of the Holy Ghost." I remember his remarking to me that Archbishop Leigh- ton, to whose character and writings he was much attached, had in his youth had some intercourse with the Jesuits, and that their spiritual works had always to a certain degree retained an influence over him. It was thus with himself also. It was his speciality that with the ardent ecclesiastical principles of his mature years there was joined an unmistakable spirituality far higher than that of his early teaching, though quite consistent with it.

The sincerity, and the reality — a different thing — of his ecclesiastical opinions, are amply illustrated in several volumes of his early sermons, the republication of which could not but help, as they did when they first appeared, to advance the cause of Church Principles. These last were, ere long, to be severely tested. Not a few occur- rences took place, and several ecclesiastical judgments were pronounced which were more or less opposed to these principles; but, though he lamented them, they did not abate his profound attachment to the Church of Eng- land — long, indeed, his strongest passion, as it was mine also. At last came the Gorham Judgment, which left the

doctrine of Baptismal Regeneration an open question in
the Anglican fold. A solemn address was almost immediately issued.   It was signed by Manning and fourteen
other prominent High Churchmen, cleric and lay, and
affirmed that that Judgment, unless cancelled, must fix a
gulf between the Church of England and the primitive
Church, and deprive her of all teaching authority. The
Judgment was not cancelled, and Manning surrendered his
Ecclesiastical preferment, though not immediately. Daily
his secession was expected, but it did not come for two
years.   And nothing can be more erroneous than the
imputation that he acted on that occasion under the influence of temper, or precipitately. I remember his saying
to me, during one of my visits to Lavington, — "Leaving
one's Church we ought to regard as the most awful of all
things next to death and judgment"; adding, after a
pause, "yet we have all to die, and all to be judged."
He waited till no hope remained of the Gorham Judgment
being reversed.

My own opinions as to the immense seriousness of the
crisis had been quite as advanced as Manning's from the
time when the Gorham judgment was passed, and it had
become plain that it was not to be cancelled. Many
troubled pamphlets came out from time to time, written
by High Churchmen "perplexed in the extreme," and
propounding theories according to which the condition of
things, bad as it was acknowledged to be, was yet one that
might be borne with under protest. These theories we
both regarded as "jury-mast theories," under which we
were invited to sail while the ship was dragging the mast
recently blown over. I remember Manning meeting them

with a dry remark, "If a man traffics long with such sophisms, he will fall at last into a confirmed habit of babbling and talking nonsense." Old prepossessions and consequent misgivings were, however, strong with me, for I had long thought it a duty of loyalty to read Church history through Anglican spectacles. I remember Manning's quiet answer to a remark of mine. "Our position is not pleasant," I said. "The waves rise; our vessel leaks, and assumes, besides, a good deal the look of a merchant vessel. Near us rides a ship, vast, majestic, and secure. But then there remains an ugly doubt, when we think of the charges brought against her in our youth — namely, may not that stately ship have come from an infected port and have the plague on board?" His face shrivelled up into an expression of humorous vexation as he replied, "Or, at least, bugs!"

Cardinal Manning has often been accused of being ambitious. It seems to me that, as regards that fault, and as regards a very different one, superstition, there are two ways of escaping the snare — namely, that of being above it, and that of being below it. Many, no doubt, are preserved from all temptation to ambition by a noble humility and spirituality, and by the absence of self-love; while others are preserved from it by indolence or frivolity, or the absence of all high aspiration. A man conscious of great powers will generally wish to have a sphere in which he can exercise them for the benefit of mankind, even if he be unusually free from those lower motives which change it into a vulgar ambition. Nay, without any such alloy, or ambition of an unworthy kind, strong faculties may, by a natural instinct, crave a field for their exercise, as bodily energies do without reproach.   Manning would never, I am sure, have desired a position which he knew might be occupied by another with more benefit to mankind; neither would he have been slow to suspect that he might himself be unequal to its duties.   His enemies do not attribute failure to him when tested.   That his promotion to the archbishopric of Westminster was neither sought nor desired seems to be indicated by the enclosed letter:

ST. MARY OF THE ANGELS, May 26, 1865.

MY DEAREST AUBREY, — I write under great pressure.   A few words rather than none.   You were one of the first I thought of when this thing came on me, and I wish I could see you.   It all seems so much like an illusion.   I only trust no personal faults of mine may hinder the work you truly describe.   The way this act of the Holy Father has been received here is as far beyond my thoughts as the act itself.   The consecration is here on June 6.   Next day I hope to start for Rome for the pall, without which I can do nothing.

Always yours very affectionately,

H. E. MANNING.

As little is gratified ambition indicated in the following letter, written when its writer was created Cardinal:

ROME, March 26, 1875.

I wish you were here with me.   You say truly that this is a time of very mixed feeling.   If I can better serve the Church, so be it!   For myself, it is a restraint upon the liberty I have hitherto enjoyed.   Moreover, any one who in the world's eyes rises high is thought to seek it, and love it; and that hinders his work for souls.   God knows whether that has been so with me.   And I will wait for the last day.

St. Andrew's and St. Gregory's are the same. It is a great pleasure to me. I always was drawn to that church, and Bede's 'History of the Anglo-Saxons' gave me always a great love of St. Gregory, besides all that I had for him as Pontiff and Doctor.

One thing I feel, as I said. It is like being told off to fight the persecution which from Berlin will spread wide. And for this I have a good will.

Affectionately yours,

HENRY E., CARDINAL MANNING.

There was the less reason to attribute Cardinal Manning's rise to ambition, in the bad sense of that word, because he manifestly possessed that union of qualities which almost inevitably leads to eminence unless a man is resolved not to accept it. He was, at the same time, a man of great energy and of great circumspection. The practical qualities of a man of business were in him blended with the contemplative faculties necessary for the theologian.. He had ardent convictions; but when events had finally taken a course opposed to them, he was not prevented by temper from accepting the inevitable and making the best of it. This was a thing the more easy for him because he did not attribute bad motives to opponents; he not only admitted, but constantly remembered how often men with equal sincerity and equal capacity see things from the most opposite points of view. He had a profound conviction that the temporal authority of the Pope, however small the territory within which it was to be exercised, is necessary — that is, in the long run necessary — for his independence, and that his independence is an essential part of Christian civ-

ilisation and the well-being alike of all nations, whether
Catholic or Protestant.   This opinion had on various
occasions been strongly expressed on political and philosophical grounds by the most eminent Liberal statesmen,
English and French, such as Palmerston, Brougham, and
Thiers, as well as by the leading Italian patriots of an
earlier day, who believed that the dignity of Italy, as well
as her security, required that the Pope should retain
Rome as its sovereign, and thus not be subjected to, or
supposed to be subjected to, any Civil Power.

Cardinal Manning was, of course, of that opinion.
The following extracts from two letters, the last written
about eighteen years later than the first, show how
deeply he felt on the subject; and at the same time
how far he was from thinking that a remedy was to be
sought for what he deemed a great folly and a great
wrong, through any forcible interference with the rights
or the claims, real or so-called, of the Italian people:

September 21, 1870.

The Italians have forced their way into Rome; and as I
believe that there is a God that judgeth the earth, so sure I
am that their doom will not tarry.   But —— (naming an influential Italian) has poisoned honest, simple, kindly minds, till they
hate the Vicar of Christ, and all that is noble, as false and
base, and love what is base and false, as if it were just and
good.   May God avert the judgment we deserve.

Your affect.   H. E. M.

Again he wrote:

April 19, 1888.

MY DEAR AUBREY, — By all means publish your sonnets on
Rome ("St. Peter's Chains") by themselves, and soon.   I am
watching with anxiety what is passing in Italy, being fully con-

vinced that Rome can only return to the Pope *by the will of the Italian people*, and that armed intervention or diplomatic pressure will only revive and harden the opposition of the Italian people. If it were restored by either of these interventions *ab extra*, it could stand by support *ab extra* over again, from which may Heaven preserve us. I am glad you like the "Religio Viatoris"; the chain of reasoning cannot be broken. The premises may be disputed; but the logic is, I believe, safe. I am reading some of Matthew Arnold's poems with great delight. What I read years ago I did not much take to; but "Thyrsis" and some of the "Paganism" is of a very high order.

Always yours affectionately,

HENRY E., C. ARCHBISHOP.

Looking back on the career of an old friend at his departure, after the question as to how far that career was a noble one, there comes another — namely, how far it was a happy one. Cardinal Manning's was, as far as I can judge, a singularly happy one, not in the sense of having had manifold enjoyments, or of having escaped severe afflictions, but in a higher sense of the word happiness. His life had not, I think, brought him many joys from many sources; yet it had conferred on him much joy from a few, but these the highest. His happiness was almost wholly of a spiritual order, either directly or indirectly. He had a sleepless faith, and one that so penetrated all his faculties that it brought the whole of his life into a unity. Some would have said that his nature was not as wide as it was high. It was not wide in the sense of being, like that of a great dramatist, in strong sympathy with many things of a very contrasted character, some high and some low; but it

was wide in the sense of seeing the same clear light
reflected from many remote objects; and for him it was
not true that only "the low sun makes the colour." He
had, like Cardinal Newman, a keen sense of the humorous,
though the general character of his mind was a severe
seriousness. He had a great love of music, though in
church he could only tolerate ascetic music. The other
arts gave him a deep delight also; but only in those
austerer forms of them in which their highest as well as
their earliest specimens had bravely challenged the human
heart, and but slightly the mere senses; and when, in
early Christian days, the canvas of Cimabue and Giotto
seemed to have caught the sacred shadows flung from
the ensanguined walls and vaulted roofs of the catacombs,
and to have glorified them. When we visited together
the Italian galleries, he passed by, as if he did not see
them, the pictures of the later schools, round which the
larger groups collected, and gazed long upon a Fra
Angelico with a gaze that reminded me of Leigh Hunt's
fine remark, "A great picture is a window. Through
it, we look beyond it — far down long vistas of thought."
His friends scolded him for this exclusiveness. They did
not know that we see many things only through blindness to many things.

The love of literature was in Manning as strong as
the love of art, while to many it seemed to restrict itself
within as narrow limits. Here, too, he was narrow in
one sense, but wide in another. His intellect was a
sternly consistent one, and therefore whatever was opposed, not in form only, but in spirit also, to his strongest
convictions, or to his deepest sympathies, found in him

no acceptance. The lesser merits seemed to him only to wage war on the greater. On the other hand, in what he admired he found more to admire than ordinary admirers find in their wider range. In the case of pagan writers he could make large allowance for the mode in which the subjects they treated must have presented themselves from the pagan point of view. He did not believe that religion required that every book should be didactic; but, on the other hand, he could not forgive those who, in Christian ages and Christian lands, wrote in a strain such as the nobler writers of pagan days would have regarded as a sin not only against decorum but against letters. Among our later poets, I think that the two whom he admired most were Alfred Tennyson and Henry Taylor. Of my father's "Mary Tudor" he wrote thus, several years after its publication: —

"It is work of a mind, high, large, and good: — conception and continuity and intellectual purpose throughout. As to beauty, it is less the beauty of the eye and ear, though there is much of that also, than of the ideal and the spiritual world. And in this its beauty is very great. This is the result of one hasty reading, but I shall not only read it again, but I feel that I have one more book that I can read again and again, as I can the 'Life of St. Thomas of Canterbury.'

"Perhaps my feeling may be tinged by sympathy and the 'Idola Ecclesiastica.' But Gladstone's is not: and we agree in considering 'Mary Tudor' the finest drama since Shakespeare's time. It is to me one more evidence of the injustice or the incapacity of readers and critics, that it should be unknown."

No one can read Manning's numerous volumes, especially those of his later years, without perceiving from the style alone — which, as an Anglican bishop, Dr. Charles Harris, once remarked to me, had " edges as keen as the edge of a knife " — that style must have been with him a careful study.   To that study I only heard him allude once, and then in terms very characteristic.   " In my youth, and when beginning to write, I took great pains with my style.   I am ashamed of this.   It was unworthy." Walter Savage Landor would not have approved that opinion.   He took greater pains himself, and might have replied, " Your humility tramples on the pride of Plato with a greater pride "; or he might have answered: " You are wrong; Bacon, when he published his great work, prefixed to it the words, " These were the thoughts of Francis Bacon, of which that posterity should become possessed he deemed to be their advantage."   High thoughts are a trust for the benefit of others, whose attention, in the absence of a befitting garb for them, they do not adequately challenge.

Landor was proud, not only of his style, but of the pains which he took with it.   That care, he said, should be only in part concealed; light touches of the chisel should remain on the marble.   Newman also wrote with extraordinary care, but his care was only to be plain.

I do not think that beautiful scenery contributed much to the enjoyment either of Manning or Newman; and both of them, I feel sure, would have agreed with Sir Henry Taylor in preferring the wide plains and rich valleys of Italy, bordered by majestic mountains with graceful outlines — mountains that knew how to keep their distance — to the Alpine peaks and precipices. I took him once to Monk Coniston, the exquisite abode of Mr. and Mrs. Garth Marshall, and one of the loveliest regions in England's lake country, but he seemed to me to look on its mountains, and those about Windermere, as he looked on their poet, Wordsworth — that is, with respect, entire approval, and a reasonably warm regard, rather than with enthusiasm. The scenes he most enjoyed were those in which he could most effectually labour for his fellowmen, and especially for their moral interests. In such labours he was indefatigable; nay, they seemed rather to sustain his strength than exhaust it. He had a wonderful gift for administration, systematising all his duties, never being in a hurry, finding out the aptitudes of those about him, and using them to the best advantage. When he had toiled all day, to preach in the evening was a rest to him; it meant simply thinking aloud, often an easier thing than thinking in silence.

He was as much a spiritual utilitarian as if he had been a Jesuit. When a gentleman of great munificence once promised to build a cathedral for him at the cost of £300,000 I can imagine his replying carelessly, " All right "; but he raised, after arduous and unceasing efforts, £20,000 to provide Catholic schools, in place of secular schools, for the Catholic children of his diocese.

Manning was not an enthusiastic man, and it was not from imaginative excitements that his religious happiness was drawn. Neither did it come to him chiefly because submission to authentic authority had led him out of the "strife of tongues," for he was neither an indolent nor a nervous man. Soon after he became a Catholic, I heard that one of his old Anglican friends had written to him, asking what he had found in Catholicism more than he had previously possessed, and that he had answered, "Rest and security," or some words to the same effect. That answer was sharply commented upon. I wrote to him, asking whether he had used those words. His reply was, that his words were "Certainty and Reality." In another letter he said, "I had expected to find in the Church the inexpugnable citadel of Faith; but I have found in it no less the home of Love." So it remained. Religion was the root of that peace which belonged to more than the last forty years of a life that had escaped neither its trials nor its frustrations.

Among the latest of Cardinal Manning's letters to me is one which refers to one of the last of his public acts, that one in which he consented, probably against his will, to take a part as an arbitrator at the time of the great London strikes:

> You must have thought me strangely careless in not thanking you for your affectionate and interesting letter. It came to me in the midst of the strikes. Since then I have been again and again trying to avert new contentions. And now as to the strike: I can only say that I never thought of it till I found myself in it; and I believe that our Lord used me as He did Balaam's ass. I have been so long working with working men that it is no difficulty to me; and somehow I am known to the English working men as well as to any. They listened to me readily from the first. Give my kind regards to your brother Stephen, and my thanks for his excellent version of Horace — a hard task well done.
>
> Christmas, 1889.

It was not all who made the same friendly estimate of Cardinal Manning as was made by his brother archdeacon in their Anglican diocese, Julius Hare, at a clerical meeting held soon after Manning's submission to Rome: "Alas! we shall hear that divine eloquence no more at our meetings." Not long after that submission, I remember hearing three successive reports about him circulated among parties who had a quick ear for whatever illustrated what was called "the deterioration of converts." The first was that he had been seen walking in the Corso at Rome with a hunting-whip in his hand, and in a shooting-jacket opprobrious with large horn buttons; the second was that he had taken an Italian farm; and the third was that he had already manifested such a spirit of insubordination that the Pope had been obliged to send him to prison. In his later life, rumour, which had come in as a lion, went out as a lamb, and limited itself to assertions that his unusually "Liberal" opinions in politics had only been assumed as the best way of playing a Catholic game in England. This assumption was a mistake. His political opinions were more "Liberal" than mine had ever been, for I had ever clung to those convictions which I had learned in my youth from Edmund Burke; but, such as they were, he had expressed them no less in his Anglican than in his Catholic days, opposed in that respect to Newman and Pusey. He might perhaps have echoed an expression attributed to Lacordaire on his death-bed, "I die a penitent Catholic and an impenitent Liberal." All prejudices against him, as against Cardinal Newman, had died away many years before his death. Manning had, I believe, no resentments. Certainly he never confounded the man with the doctrine and, therefore, while uncompromising as regards the doctrine, he was never uncharitable to the individual. No one was more zealously a believer in what is sometimes called "invincible ignorance," but ought to be called "involuntary ignorance" of certain great truths; but he might have also remarked that in our spiritual as in our material heritage, poverty *need* be no more a sin than wealth is, provided that it is "honestly come by." Such a comment upon the poet's "honest doubt" would seem to mean no more than that God alone knows the heart. I remember Manning's saying to me, "We must always remember that no man is lost whom Infinite Power, Infinite Wisdom and Infinite Love can save." He had sympathy with those to whom he appeared very severe. Thus, writing in 1890 of the "Salvation Army," he said, "If General Booth can gather under human influence and guidance those whom all other agencies for good have not yet reached, who shall forbid him?" He was for friendly co-operation where that was practicable, and once he remarked, "It was the Quakers who had originated the Anti-slavery Society."

The charge against him that he was a cold-hearted man certainly was not sanctioned by his known love for children, and his exclamation on one occasion, "A child's needless tear is a blood-blot on this earth."

The most remarkable characteristic of Cardinal Manning's intellect appeared to me to be its pellucid clearness, a clearness by most men attained through effort, but his naturally and inevitably. It was apparently the result of an intensely keen logical faculty, but one not exercised in the common syllogistic form, but after a more transcendental fashion. It is this unconscious form of logic which enables a man to arrange as if by intuition, the whole subject matter of his thought as if from a height, and thus to form a right judgment upon it. Another characteristic of his intellect was its unusual combination of this scientific faculty with imagination. Cardinal Manning had two great favourites among thinkers. Without instituting any comparison between him and them as regards the comparative degree in which he and they possessed those two faculties, which, at all events, he possessed in common with each, the following sonnet expresses that which eminently characterised his intellect also:

CARDINAL MANNING.

LAVINGTON AND ROME.

I learned his greatness first at Lavington.
The moon had early sought her bed of brine,
But we discoursed till now each starry sign
Had sunk. Our theme was one, and one alone,
" Two Minds supreme," he said, " our earth has known;
One sang in science, one served God in song,
Aquinas, Dante." Slowly in me grew strong
A thought: " These two great minds in him are one.
Lord, what shall this man do?" Later, at Rome,
Beside the dust of Peter and of Paul
Eight hundred mitred sires of Christendom
In council sat. I marked him 'mid them all.
I thought of that long night in years gone by,
And cried, " At last my question meets reply."

CHAPTER XV

MY SUBMISSION TO THE ROMAN CATHOLIC CHURCH

THIS event took place in November, 1851. In 1885 I recorded that act and its motives in a letter to one of my earliest and nearest friends. It may have an interest for some. I subjoin most of it.

It is quite true that you could not know either the full grounds or the chief grounds on which, after a youth mainly devoted to theological study, and only in a lesser degree to literature, philosophy, and poetry, I arrived at a final decision on the most important crisis of my life, and acted on that decision. Few of my early friends materially altered their relations with me on my becoming a Catholic; but several of them attributed that act to supposed causes, to which they were doubtless indulgent, but with which it had absolutely no connection whatsoever. On this matter they made few enquiries, if any; and I always abstain from introducing the personal into discussions on subjects of such importance. Some, I know, attributed my change to excitement, impressiveness, imaginative sympathies, or a preference of logical subtleties to common-sense views of things, and others to a great power of deceiving myself by ingenuities after the will had once received a bias. It may please you to know that, whether my final choice was wise or the contrary, none of those things to which it was attributed by such persons had anything to do with it, whereas things of a wholly dissimilar nature had a great deal. Some of the qualities I have named may have been in my character; but persons of the age I had then reached, thirty-seven, have generally learned to be on their guard, on great occasions, against their most mischievous characteristics, and many would have said that my submission to the Catholic Church was out of my character, and stood by itself and apart from all the previous portion of my life. This may be so.

I had an exaggerated love of everything that looked like personal freedom, and never relished binding myself to any final position. If I had acted like an ingenious self-deceiver, it would have been easier for me than for most persons, I believe, to have adopted one of the many "views" under which most of the "High Churchmen" reconciled themselves to their position. The "perverts" considered that those views were sophistries, though com-monly prompted by amiable, and seldom by interested motives, and that they were absolutely opposed to "simple" views, respecting the great religious crisis. All such views had been condemned beforehand by a document published in all the newspapers, which was signed by fifteen of the most eminent of the Anglican leaders, and affirmed that the Gorham decision on baptism was a repudiation of an article in the Nicene Creed, that it disowned the early Church, and that it left the Church of England without any "teaching authority." I had myself arrived at the same conclusion long before, that is, on the hypothesis that the "judgment" would be what it turned out to be. About one-half of those who signed that document remained where they were, and the rest became Roman Catholics. So did I, but not at once, or very soon.

As regards my friends' theory about my imaginative sympathies having led me astray, I may remark that they had been repelled, not attracted by what I thought an excess of ceremonial in the churches and elsewhere when in Italy during past years.   It seemed to me too sensuous; thus I often preferred outline to shaded engravings, and both to pictures except where the colouring was unusually refined.   What was expressed with any touch of exaggeration had always been to me far less impressive than what was skilfully suggested only.   A service rich in detail was often much less to me than a brief description of it.

As regards the precipitation with which I was credited, let me place a fact beside the theory.   Soon after the Gorham case had been decided, I was one of a party of High Churchmen who met at a breakfast in the house of Dr. Wilberforce, Bishop of Oxford.   After he and some of his guests had gone upstairs, we discussed the question what was to be done by those who agreed that the Church of England had formally repudiated High Church Principles, unless she distinctly repudiated that judicial tribunal which had set them at naught — a tribunal to which, whether she approved of it or not, she long remained subject.   Some affirmed that as " Church Principles " had always admitted that the Roman Catholic Church, whatever its defects might be, was a true part of Christ's Church, we had no choice save that of accepting her authority if the Anglican body had

ceased to be a part of it.   Others said that we should
now, on the contrary, learn to distrust "Church Principles," since we had accepted them first in the full belief
that they did not lead to Rome.   I was asked my opinion.
I answered that it seemed to me equally true that "Church
Principles" could no longer be reconciled with the new
position of the English community, and also that many
of us had probably accepted them more easily than we
should otherwise have done in the full belief that that
body sincerely held them, and that they did not lead to
Rome.   Their position, I thought, rendered any precipitate course wrong.   The duty of persons so placed was,
as it seemed to me, to renew a study of "Church principles" themselves, giving a considerable time to it, but
renouncing avowedly at the same time, as a temptation,
what had, till the late Judgment, seemed a duty of loyalty
—namely, all "Anglican" prepossessions.   It would be
our duty as openly to discard those principles if they could
not stand the test of that renewed study; and, in case
they did stand it, then to renounce, at any cost to ourselves, a body which had either practically repudiated
them or had never really held them.   Robert Isaak
Wilberforce (the Bishop's elder brother), whose learning
had earned for him the name of the "walking dictionary
of the Church of England," after a pause, replied to this
effect, "That would be the wise and honest course."   I
gave two years to that renewed study before I took the
final step.

Some of my friends feared that I was at that time in a
state of excitement and agitation.   That was a mistake.
I was much absorbed in it; but it had long been my

custom. to meditate in a somewhat frigid and merely intellectual way on matters which should probably have been otherwise regarded because they also involved moral and spiritual issues, not less than intellectual.

I was profoundly interested in this after-study — for I saw the greatness of the problem — but not the least agitated or distressed. I had early stated openly that on the issue of my study depended my discarding "Church Principles," or realising them in the Roman Catholic Church, which had never ceased to hold them, and with them the full body of Christian Truth. To tell thus much to my friends seemed a duty of frankness to them, and it also left me more entirely free.

The conclusion at which I eventually arrived was this: that "Church Principles" were an essential part of Christianity itself and not an ornamental adjunct of it; and that they were external, not as our clothes are, but as the skin is external to the rest of our body. The Apostles' Creed has affirmed three supreme doctrines which included all others — namely, the Trinity, the Incarnation, and the Church. What God had joined it was not for man to separate. God's Church was created when God's revelation was given. When it was still in the future it was distinctly announced in his parables — the chief subject of his preaching, and in them called generally His "Kingdom." She is the temple of the Holy Spirit Who descended upon her at the Feast of Pentecost. That Pentecost was no transient gift. It is as permanent on earth as the Incarnation of the Divine Son is in Heaven. It is the witness of that Divine Son, and to His whole Revelation; and that witness which alone can be borne to the successive generations so long as a Church, organically and visibly as well as spiritually one, affirms the one Truth through the one Spirit. This is what makes schism a grave offence; apart from this the charge would be unmeaning. It was owing, as I saw, to the Church which maintained Unity that even the separated religious bodies hold the large portion of Revealed Truth which several of them retain, as it is from our planet itself, which is the great magnet, that all the lesser magnets on the earth derive their magnetic power.

Such were the convictions which I had reached. This is not the place for me to state in detail the reasons which led me to them. Many of them I have set forth in published essays.[1] I am not now dealing with theological argument, but with a religious chapter in my own life. For argument this is not the place. When in earlier times friends of mine had become Roman Catholics, I never felt myself competent to criticise them. I could not feel myself alienated from them, because I soon found out that *to them* the change had been, not that they had relinquished any part of their Christianity, but that their belief included much more than before, and was held by them with much more of reality and certainty, to use the language of Cardinal Manning. My own attachment to the "Anglican Church," as we called it, had been from boyhood that ardent thing which Wordsworth tells us that his love for his country had ever been. If from levity or waywardness, not serious misgiving, any one spoke against it, I was much displeased. I had long thought it a duty

[1] Religious Problems of the Nineteenth Century (St. Anselm's Society, 6 Agar Street, Charing Cross, London).

to see things largely through her eyes; and certainly the religious body to which a man owes his earliest Christian hope has strong claims upon him, though not the strongest. At the time of the Gorham judgment, for the Courts to have stood by the teaching of early times and creeds must have driven a large proportion of the Evangelical clergy out of the national establishment. I remembered Cardinal Newman's celebrated saying — namely, " A separated and national Church must be national first, and *after that* as orthodox as it can afford to be." To me it was plain that the " Anglican Church " had been tested and found wanting, and that true loyalty could now be exercised alone toward that Church universal, into which alone, and not into any local Church, the Christian is baptised.

While the Gorham controversy was raging, an eminent statesman read me a sentence in a pamphlet published a few days later. It affirmed that not to repudiate, as a body, a heterodox judgment pronounced by an authority which the Church of England as a body had long since recognised as supreme, was to accept that judgment; and it ended, I think, with words like these, " She has now to choose between the portion of the bride and the mess of potage." Most of the High Churchmen remained with her. I sided with the minority and left her. Which class changed their position, and which changed their principles? It was those who refused to do the latter whom the world stigmatised as weaklings. It was those who affirmed, and acted on that affirmation, that loyalty was due, both to the State in civil things, and also to the Church, one and universal, in spiritual things, whom the world pronounced disloyal.

Some of my friends fancied that in my "conversion to Rome" I had been a victim to polemics, for which they supposed me to have a passion. I had nothing of the sort. I had an immense reverence for theology which (apart from its divine claims) unites whatever is deepest in philosophy, most exalted in poetry, and most fruitful and instructive in history. Polemics, on the contrary, I had always looked upon as a painful and ungracious warfare, from which theology cannot separate itself as long as the Church remains in its present militant condition. The temper is not a good temper, and many who have fought a good fight in it have been the worse for it.

What affected me most during my two years of renewed study respecting "Church Principles" was not found mainly in controversial works. It was found first in the Holy Scriptures. Daily I felt more and more how marvellous was the blindness of the many to the large degree in which the teaching of our Divine Lord, especially in His parables, related to His Church, in them commonly named "His Kingdom." His teaching had evidently been to a great extent a preparatory teaching concerning that Church which was to spring into existence on His Ascension into Heaven, and on the descent of the Holy Spirit — that Church which He had commanded to teach the nations. Not less striking was the degree in which the unity of that teaching was connected with the unity of that Church, and the degree in which both these unities were connected with that one Apostle who was to "strengthen his brethren" by being an abiding principle of organic unity.

The aid I received from uninspired writers came to me

also, not from writers of the polemical but the philosophical school, and chiefly from Coleridge, Bacon, and St. Thomas Aquinas.   For the first of these I had learned from Sir William Hamilton a great reverence, and I saw no reason to discard it (any more than to change my political opinions and throw over Edmund Burke), though of course allowance was to be made for Coleridge's inherited position.   Coleridge had said some hard things of Rome, but his admissions in her favour were much more remarkable.   He had asserted that nearly all her doctrines affirmed great Ideas, but had condensed those Ideas into idols.   That seemed to me his rhetorical way of saying that Catholicism was a religion, and not a mere philosophy.   Coleridge's "Philosophy of Pure Reason" had long before shown me that the so-called philosophical charges against the Church were but cavils proceeding from what Coleridge calls "the Understanding," or the inferior "faculty judging according to sense"; that many of these charges would militate against the chief mysteries of Revelation; and that, though the philosophy of Locke might make much of them, St. Augustine and Plato would have passed them by with the remark that the question really lay deeper down.

Next as to Bacon.   I studied attentively all that Bacon has left to us on the subject of religion, as indeed I had done before.   It seemed most precious and most disappointing.   It has golden sentences as grand and imaginative as anything in Plato.   It is not only great in intelligence, but his heart too was "in the right place" to a degree not universal among philosophers.   But there is an omission in his writings on the subject more wonderful

than all that they include.   The great master of modern
philosophy, often ignored, in questions relating to religion, by those who, in science, "take his name in
vain," had a wholly special vocation and ambition.   As
the father of modern philosophy, his highest ambition had
been, not to gather in the great harvest of thought, but
to show the mode in which the soil was to be cultivated,
so as in future to yield its true increase; and he had
taken to himself, not physical science only, but "all knowledge" as his portion, affirming that spiritual knowledge
— the knowledge of God — was far the highest form
of knowledge.   He was the great teacher of Method.
What was his method in the physical sciences?   We all
know it was Induction.   Next, what was his method in
religion?   He put forward none.   He shirked the subject.   Yet that surely was the great question for the age
of the Reformation.   A Method had been in full operation
on this subject for fifteen centuries and more, and a
thoroughly scientific Method.   The method was not Induction but Deduction.   The deducer of truth from truth was
that Church which St. Paul affirmed to be the pillar and
the ground of Truth, and to the founders of which our
Divine Lord promised that the Holy Spirit would both
recall all things to their minds, and also lead them on into
all truth, upon one condition namely, that they should
always continue to be *one*, even as the Father and the Son
are one.[1]   The great philosopher had no answer respecting "Method" in Theology which did not condemn the

---

[1] I have treated this great question in an essay entitled the "Philosophy
of the Rule of Faith " — " Essays Literary and Ethical " (Macmillan and Co.),
and elsewhere in other essays.

Reformation.   He said things complimentary to the clergy in the reign of Her Most Gracious Majesty.   He indulged in persiflage : —

> " He dallied with his golden chain,
> And, smiling, put the question by."

My third teacher at that great crisis of my life was St. Thomas Aquinas, whom I studied in a compendium of his " Summa Theologiæ " a work written centuries before a polemical war between Protestantism and Catholicism was heard of.   It became daily clearer to me that the objections brought against Catholic teaching were founded on misconceptions caused because portions of it had been considered apart from other portions supplemental to them, just as, in Holy Scripture, text and context are supplemental to each other.   A single illustration of this will suffice.   It is sometimes alleged that the peace promised to man through the Catholic Rule of Faith precludes the ennobling trials connected with "free enquiry," nay, are inconsistent with a state of probation.   But this notion could hardly have occurred to one who knew that, according to other parts of Catholic teaching, full peace is a condition reserved for the Church triumphant, and rests upon the beatific vision ; that Purgatory helps those imperfectly sanctified on earth in a way apart from both action and probation ; while on the other hand, it is the very speciality of the Church militant on earth that it must be ever more the place of trial, action, labour, and probation ; and that all the more in proportion as Christians ascend in sanctity.   The Christian will always have his trials ; but these are not like the pagan's trials.   God has given him aids which the pagan lacked, and the chief of those is revealed truth. Divine truth has been revealed in an intelligible, not an unintelligible, manner. We have been taken out of a spiritual chaos and placed in the midst of a spiritual civilisation, that of the *Civitas Dei.* Its citizens have severe trials, but not the trials of the nomadic tribes. Our feet have been planted on the rock. Does it follow that we are to lie down upon that rock and go to sleep? That is the condition which St. Thomas counts "sloth," and sloth he includes among the mortal sins. If each of the Christian generations, like the first, has received the Truth gratis, it has, like the first, to pay for it by living the truth as well as believing it. The truth has been accorded to Christians when in the normal condition of Christians, with the full certainty of faith; their attitude towards it is not that of discovery (as their attitude is to science), but that of fidelity.

Another thing which I learned from St. Thomas Aquinas was that the Church's "Rule of Faith" could not have been a mere despot's claim, even if she had not been needed as a teacher, because her power to teach is included in her other and still higher attributes. The Church is the dispenser of sacraments, and the truth is a great sacrament. If errors as well as abuses have grown up locally, it is the Church alone, and the Church in its unity which can correct those errors without committing her children first to petty local tyrannies, and then to mere opinions substituted for faith, certain and real.

St. Thomas led me on and up into regions of thought far above the "polemical." He taught me that the real question at issue was not that of a single doctrine, however sacred. It was this. Is Faith Certainty? If so, it can move mountains. Is it but opinion? If so, even when a true opinion, it cannot add a cubit to a man's stature. It was not for mere opinions that the martyrs died.

Returning after a period of independent thought (an independence not challenged by me but forced on me), and after the study of long-honoured and not recent authorities, the arguments used by many of our more eminent writers during this season of distress, acquired for me a character not theirs before, especially the arguments of High Churchmen, which tempted me often to say, "Their poverty and not their will consents." They seemed plainly rhetorical, and often contradictory. Strong statements by which I had once been caught, now appeared but *bravura* phrases, not what was needed — namely, exact thoughts. One old friend, a man of great learning and great rectitude, met my arguments by a statement that he had long since come to the opinion that "scientific theology was an impossible thing." But a great man, Alexander Knox, who by many years had anticipated the Oxford High Church movement, had written that the time was approaching when the test of sound religion would be reached through a sound philosophy, as contrasted (so I understood him) with political considerations, the exigencies of an Establishment, or the traditions of merely local or national bodies, not those of a universal and Apostolic character. His great friend and correspondent, Dr. Jebb, Bishop of Limerick, had said that the reason why Providence allowed the Roman Catholic

Church to stand so long was because, with all her faults, she was the only religious body in the West in which the doctrine of the Holy Trinity was always secure; which seemed to remind one of another statement respecting a body, the earthly head of which was to strengthen his brethren, and against which the gates of hell should never prevail. My honoured friend, F. D. Maurice, had been, like myself, a student of Coleridge, and had in a valuable work, entitled the "Kingdom of Christ," asserted the claims of the Church upon grounds especially connected with Coleridge's philosophy. On this occasion, however, it seemed to me that his aversion to what he called "system" had given him a declamatory mode of speaking, of writing, and of thinking; and that his defence of the then condition of the Anglican Church amounted to little more than the statement that she still retained the power of *witnessing to* certain great ideas, including that of baptismal regeneration. Such a statement, I thought, might have sufficed for a philosophy, but not for a faith or a Church. Mr. Sewell admitted the seriousness of the heterodox Judgment; but could only suggest, when we discussed it, that "the bishops must go to the Queen about it." Another among the chief Anglican leaders, the excellent John Keble, replied to the arguments of a friend that, however the Church of England might err elsewhere, the truth would be found in his parish; and Dr. Pusey had replied, "We do not know what is the answer to these statements, but we know that there must be one." That seemed to me an insufficient answer when the question referred, not to a mystery affirmed by the Church universal, but simply to the present position of a single and isolated community to which no Divine promise had been given, and by which infallibility had never been claimed, but, on the contrary, more than disowned.   That separate Church stood now in a new relation to antiquity and to a primary doctrine of the Nicene Creed.   A new light had been thus thrown on the movement of the sixteenth century, and the real question had now become this — namely, whether a local Church ought not, at that time, to have referred the matters then in dispute to a General Council, not to have separated from the bulk of Christendom and the centre of unity from which she had derived her faith.

I had lay advisers as well as clerical.   I may as well mention that Carlyle was one of those who gave me the most curious form of warning: "I have ridden over here to tell you not to do that thing.   You were born free. Do not go into that hole."   I answered: "But you used always to tell me that the Roman Catholic Church was the only Christian body that was consistent, and could defend her position."   He replied: "And so I say still. But the Church of England is much better notwithstanding, because her face *is turned in the right direction.*"   I answered: "Carlyle, I will tell you in a word what I am about.   I have lived a Christian hitherto, and I intend to die one."

CHAPTER XVI

DURING the later years of a long life I spent less of my time in foreign travel than when young. On the other hand, I occupied myself more with those great political events which have crammed a century of change into a few years. The present chapter records such of those events as I witnessed with deepest interest, and to which I recur most often in recollection — not without apprehension, but also not without hope.

After a long period of comparative security, the year 1848 visited Europe with a series of convulsions such as had not visited the world for a long period. The crowns of ancient monarchies toppled over in rapid succession. Austria, Prussia, the smaller States of Germany and of Italy shared the shock, and the political reforms of Pope Pius the IXth were thus deprived of all chance of success. It seemed as if the new revolution was a universal one, if not one as sanguinary as the great French Revolution. Every day the journals were filled with "wars and rumours of wars"; now a dynasty had fallen; now a republic had been proclaimed; now an unpopular statesman had fled and barely saved his life. Among these last, two of the most eminent, men of very different characters and opinions, took refuge at first in London, Prince Metternich and Guizot. In a short time they met in one of the great social centres of London; and crowds pressed around to hear them as they discussed the situation. The Austrian statesman relieved his wounded feelings by energetic statements that none of the recent misadventures had been to him the slightest surprise. "Years ago, when so-and-so had occurred, my remark on the news was this; two years later I prophesied as follows." The catalogue of his predictions was a long one, and every one of them had been fulfilled to the letter. Guizot's reply was a brief one: "Enfin, mon prince, the only thing which you did not foresee was that you and I would be discussing these matters together in a London salon in the year 1848." I called on M. Guizot the day after; and when we had spoken on other interesting matters he made enquiries about Ireland, and I was very much pleased to find that some of his opinions on that subject coincided with what had long been my own, especially a great measure for State-aided colonisation from Ireland, — a measure on which I had written an article in the "Edinburgh Review." Had such a measure been enacted in time the Repeal agitation might never have arisen; and the great famine would not have fallen on a population dependent almost wholly on agriculture and the potato.

During that crisis the fate and fortunes of England were matters of interest to the whole world, and to none more than to the philosophic mind of Guizot. Would England alone resist the contagion of revolution, or was her greatness at last to be blown over? Of course there was a considerable commotion among the manifold elements of English society. Among the storm-spirits of the time the stormiest was a certain Irishman, Mr.

Feargus O'Connor. It is true that he was generally regarded as mad; but that did not diminish his influence over the masses. That influence helped to procure innumerable signatures to a memorial demanding innumerable absurdities. It was carried in state to the official residence of the Home Secretary — then, I think, Lord Melbourne — who refused to receive it, or even to allow it to remain in his hall. The repulse, however, only stimulated the would-be revolutionists to a fiercer zeal. They had heard of ancient dynasties which had recently fallen like a palace of cards because a mob had marched upon a parliament house. They resolved to try the experiment on a scale hitherto unattempted. They knew possibly that during the French Reign of Terror, the terrorising party in Paris constituted a party of 35,000 only, and the terrorised of 500,000. Perhaps they had heard that in the France of that day a needful and very large measure of reform had already been effected, and that the only reason why it was not completed, with the full consent of all the great powers both of State and of the Church, was because reform was hated by that party which was bent on revolution — and a revolution which should separate for ever the France of the future from the Christian France of the past, in deference to an infidel philosophy and a sensual literature.

They gave notice that on a certain day a body of 200,000 men, carrying a banner, would march through London from that part at the south of the Thames. But on this occasion the party of order, a vast majority, did not leave the game in the hands of the minority. They too had an organisation. They had a great man, and they had the "saving common-sense" of a great tradition. The whole upper class, whether Conservative or Liberal, stood together, and beside them stood the whole remainder of the propertied class; the shopkeepers firmly resolved to protect the shop windows of that city through which old Blucher rode soon after the battle of Waterloo, and which he laughingly pronounced to be "the finest city in the world for a loot." The Government had supplied them all with batons, not firearms, and the Duke of Wellington had drawn up to London about six thousand troops beyond the usual garrison, and placed them in the spots where they would present the least of a threatening appearance, and yet be most able to act if necessary. But the strength of the defence consisted in the absolute unity of action between the higher class and the humbler. Every twenty or thirty of the baton-wielding shopkeepers had at their head some person of note. Before the day of the projected revolution there was a close and genial intercourse between the leaders and the led; and the next day the then Earl of Arundel and Surrey, later Earl Marshal of England, gave a dinner to all those who had been committed to his charge, as doubtless did many others. The army of the revolution marched to the bridges, and on them found a large body of police (backed by a large army of citizens), who quietly forbade them further progress. After a terrible protest and a brief consultation, the invading army executed a brilliant strategical movement towards the rear; and M. Guizot, when informed of the event, exclaimed, "Le monde croule, et l'Angleterre ne croule pas."

The sons of England had cause to be proud of their

country that day. If then, or soon afterwards, the "Church Question" and the "Land Question" had been settled, England and Ireland might have soon been brought into cordial relations. The golden opportunity was lost. An ecclesiastical storm suddenly arose, wholly in consequence of a misconception. A large addition to the number of Roman Catholics had taken place in England, not from conversion, but from recent Irish immigration into England. At last it became natural and expedient to substitute for the system of "Vicars Apostolic," which had placed all ecclesiastical authority in the hands of the Pope, the usual form of Church government — namely, that of local bishops. In Ireland the Roman Catholic bishops had the same titles as the Protestant. In England, in order to avoid giving offence, the new Roman Catholic bishops had been given new territorial titles so as not to clash with those used by the Anglican.

Unfortunately English statesmen of that day imagined that a civil claim in England had been put forward when an ecclesiastical right, valid alone in the Court of Conscience, had been asserted; and when they were assured that in the newly created English Catholic dioceses the authority of the new bishops only existed, and only claimed to exist, *in foro conscientiæ*, and not *in foro externo*, they erroneously assumed that the distinction meant the same thing as the distinction between claims *de jure* and claims *de facto*. Beside this, Cardinal Wiseman, when announcing the new hierarchy, had used a metaphor about a star and its orbit, which was regarded as highly offensive. Nearly twenty years later, when a new hierarchy was created in Scotland, no notice was taken of the "aggression." In England the chief ultimate effect of the uproar was that it served as a great advertisement of the Catholic Church. In Ireland its consequences were of a very serious character. It cancelled in a few months most of what had been effected, since the tardy concession of Catholic Emancipation, in the way of drawing the two countries nearer to each other. It was denounced as a revival of the Penal Laws by the most clear-sighted of the English statesmen who opposed the measure, and it was of course regarded as such by the Irish Catholics, both lay and clerical.

Where England saw her way clearly she walked in it justly. A few years before, she had emancipated her slaves in the colonies, and paid £20,000,000 to their owners, whose position and whose acts, bad as they were, had from first to last possessed the sanction of English law. England had shared the blame, and she decreed that she would bear the penalty. It was by doing this that she struck a blow against slavery from which it can never recover. Her self-sacrifice proved to the world that she was in earnest. If she had simply confiscated the property of those in whose crime and in whose gains she had long had a part, the nations could from such a vicarious penitence have only inferred that she had changed her policy.

It was a sadly different thing in 1851. Statesmen were dealing with a purely theological question of which they knew as little as the clergy commonly knew of political economy. The whole nation was in confusion. The bishops summoned synods or issued pastorals.

Meetings were held everywhere. Our ancient universities despatched their representatives to the sovereign; and yet all this was a misapprehension. The new hierarchy was not intended to be a grand demonstration. It was a business matter, like that restoration of its hierarchy to Holland nearly at the same time. Much less was it intended to inflict either humiliation or injury on a nation whose statesmen had often asked and received political aid from the Holy See in dealing with its Roman Catholic subjects. The new bishops tranquilly stated that their mission was exclusively spiritual, and continued to discharge their functions. No prosecution followed.

Among the statesmen who opposed the Ecclesiastical Titles Act were several of England's ablest, including Sir James Graham, the "Younger Peelites" (who were assured that they would never be returned to Parliament again), and Mr. Gladstone. Mr. Gladstone, who closed his magnificent speech by a solemn statement that, whatever unpopularity he might thus draw down upon his head he would continue to follow that bright star of justice which shone before him, whithersoever it might lead him — a saying which Roman Catholics did not forget even when his Vatican Pamphlets appeared, and which they are bound ever to remember.

An aged statesman, famed for his moderation, who expressed his opposition to the Ecclesiastical Titles Act in the strongest terms, was Lord Aberdeen. As well as I remember, his words were these. I heard them from the Gallery of the House of Lords: "For centuries Catholics were persecuted and tormented by penal laws.

They failed. This measure is a renewal of that persecution; and it will fail again." I remember well the stern severity of his demeanour as he spoke. His language was severely censured by several persons, who, notwithstanding, agreed with his opinions. I heard that censure thus itself censured: "You must have patience with Lord Aberdeen. Though a man of great and acknowledged ability, he has no command of language; none at least like that which more highly educated statesmen boast. When he sees a plain truth, therefore, he has no alternative except that of stating it plainly, or holding his tongue."

The Ecclesiastical Titles Act was never once enforced, and a great commotion in Ireland was thus avoided. Ireland resented it the more, as she had nothing to say to the "papal aggression," though she was to pay the penalty. Every parish priest in Ireland had long used his territorial title prohibited by that measure, which was defended on the ground that it was intended to "give robustness" to laws long dormant. Among such laws were those that prohibited those Religious Orders to which Ireland's "higher education" owed its existence.

Several excellent pamphlets on the Ecclesiastical Titles Act were written by Catholics, while the agitation respecting it was still going on, one of them by my brother, Sir Stephen de Vere. My belief is that if Lord John Russell had seen those pamphlets in time, the cloud of illusion would have been cleared from his eyes, and that measure would never have been heard of. When it had passed, a great blow was unwittingly inflicted (for Lord John was an entire and sincere Liberal) on the

English Liberal party, which had previously made considerable progress in Ireland. Catholic and Protestant Bishops met no more at the Lord Lieutenant's table. Between the castle and the city of Dublin a great gulf had been dug. Men remarked then that between the English Catholics and Cavaliers there had once been much sympathy, and that the Anti-Catholic legislation had originally come chiefly from the Whig party. The decline of that party in Ireland began then; so did the influence of Lord John Russell in both countries. He had struck at Rome, and the blow fell on his own political following. He probably did not know that the New Hierarchy was not a *coup* and had never been a secret. On the contrary, the intention to create it had been stated by Cardinal Wiseman to two eminent English statesmen, who gave him no intimation that it could cause any offence. On the day when the repeal of the Act was sanctioned by the House of Lords, as part of Mr. Gladstone's policy for Disestablishment in Ireland, Earl Russell told me that he did not intend to be present on the occasion. The Ecclesiastical Titles Act, which it took nearly a session to pass, was repealed in an hour or two.

But I must not forget, in politics, some of the more interesting or amusing of those with whom I associated in those old days. One of them was Leigh Hunt. In my boyhood his poetry had given me much enjoyment, and increased that which I had derived from other poetry. The Greeks had, as he felicitously remarked, "invented the poetry of gladness," and by that portion of it his own had been suggested in part. He had a vivid appreciation of Nature as seen from the classical point of view, and his sonnets possess a singular sense of proportion, the finest of them being one entitled "A Thought on the Nile," written, I think, in competition with two composed on the same day by Shelley and Keats.

To these friends he continued to the end devotedly attached; and his conversation was to me always delightful when it turned upon them. He affirmed that if Shelley had lived, he would have been known chiefly as a dramatic poet, notwithstanding the predominance of qualities anything but dramatic in all his poetry written before the "Cenci," one of the few modern dramas which can be pronounced dramatic. When the poetry of Shelley and Keats was generally regarded with unmixed dislike or contempt, Leigh Hunt asserted its greatness with the full courage of his opinions. Byron he much disliked; and had probably been often mortified by his caprices. For Coleridge's poetry he had a high admiration, especially as regards its transcendent metrical merits. I knew also Mr. Procter, better known as Barry Cornwall, whose poetry was once very popular. His daughter's — Adelaide Procter's — poetry had given great pleasure to Montalembert, who requested me to give her his warm thanks for it. Barry Cornwall's wife I met first at a breakfast given by my early friend, Eliot Warburton (whose tragic death was a grief to so many), and thought her one of the most amusing persons in London society. Her wit had sometimes a sharp edge, though sharp only in mirth, not in malice. I remember her telling me once of a brilliant passage-of-arms between herself and a certain clergyman of great ability and well-deserved popularity.

He was well known as a popular preacher, and his sermons happened to be often preached before the class of
people whose names are to be found in the "Blue Book"
of fashionable life.   One day he was severe upon the
frailties and follies of that class, and especially against
detraction, which surprised some of his old friends, who
thought that he was not wholly free from something of the
sort himself.   Among these was Mrs. Procter, who described matters thus.   "I felt so guilty! I was sure
every one would say he was preaching against me!   I
felt myself getting redder and redder.   Besides, no retort
was possible, for you cannot interrupt the preacher.
When the sermon was over, I had to pass close to him,
as he stood in his surplice surrounded by so many clever
people.   As I passed I shook hands with him in a very
frightened but also very sympathetic way, and said, 'Oh,
Mr. ——, did not you and I catch it to-day?'"

Another most amusing friend of mine was Edward
Fitzgerald, an Irishman, the speciality of whose humour
it was that the more comical were his words the more
solemn his face always became.   I remember an illustration of this.   After a large evening party, when nearly all
the guests had departed, the rest remained to smoke.   In
that party was a man celebrated for his passion for titles.
On this occasion he exceeded himself.   All his talk was
of the rich and great.   "Yesterday, when I was riding
with my friend, the Duke of ——."   "On Tuesday last
the Marquis of —— remarked to me."   It went on for a
long time; the party listened, some amused, some bored.
Edward Fitzgerald was the first to rise.   He lighted a
candle, passed out of the room, stood still with the lock

of the door in his hand, and looked back. He could change his countenance into anything he pleased. It had then exchanged in a moment its usual merry look for one of profound, nay hopeless, dejection. Slowly and sadly he spoke: "I once knew a lord, too, but he is dead!" Slowly, sadly he withdrew, closing the door amid a roar of laughter.

To return to things serious. In 1868 a measure was introduced by Mr. Gladstone for the creation of religious equality in Ireland. To such a change I had, long before I was a Roman Catholic, looked forward as the beginning of a new and better era for Ireland, and had written much on the subject. I had looked forward to a measure marked by justice, not by retaliation, one which should remove from Ireland a great opprobrium, and from her poor a grievous loss, while inflicting on the Protestants of Ireland no needless humiliation or needless pecuniary injury. Nothing could be more unjust than the then existing Church settlement of Ireland; but for the creation of that settlement, the Protestants of our day were not responsible. When of old the two Hebrew mothers contended for the child, the true mother preferred that the child should be bestowed upon her rival rather than be cut in two. In this case, to have divided would have been to save, not to destroy. The ancient Church property of Ireland, so long devoted to God and His poor, and so long alienated from their proper functions, should have been restored to Ireland by being equitably divided between the Catholic and the Protestant sons of Ireland for the spiritual weal of both those bodies. This would have been a just course; to alienate the Church property from

all religious purposes could but be a malicious one and a
treacherous one no less; for, while despoiling those who
had migrated to Ireland on England's pledge that they
were to find there a religious provision for themselves and
their descendants, it would impart no religious benefit
whatever to the long-despoiled Catholic majority, the
vested interests of the existing Protestant clergy and
lesser officials alone being respected.

I advocated those convictions in every way open to me,
especially in my intercourse with influential Irish Catholics, clerical and lay, and with English statesmen. I
advocated them also in four successive pamphlets. The
first of these, consisting chiefly of extracts from speeches
or writings of eminent English or foreign Protestants,
was published in 1863, and republished with a preface in
1867. In that year I published also a pamphlet entitled
"The Church Settlement of Ireland."[1] It treated the
subject chiefly in connection with the evil effects political and social generated by secularisation — a course
which, far from retrieving the injustice of centuries,
rendered such a retrieval at any future time an im-
possibility.

The second of those pamphlets was entitled "Ireland's
Church property, and the right use of it"; and another,
by my friend, Doctor Moriarty, Bishop of Kerry, urged
the same course. A strong and most natural jealousy
against State pensions for the Catholic clergy had long
existed, and Edmund Burke had warned Ireland never to
accept them. I had no desire to slight such an instinct or

[1] "The Church Establishment in Ireland illustrated by Protestant
Authorities." Longman, 1867.

to contest such an authority. My pamphlet asserted
that there were other objects wholly distinct from State
pensions to which the Catholic share of " Ireland's Church
property should be devoted, such as aid in proportion to
local contributions to the building of churches, reform-
atories, presbyteries, ecclesiastical seminaries, religious
schools, orphanages and other charitable asylums, as well
as to the purchase of glebes " (p. 33). That pamphlet
maintains that the preservation of Church property for
strictly religious purposes was an imperative duty, on the
ground alike of religion and of the rights of the poor.
Only thus could the poor be benefited by it. This pamphlet affirmed that if Church property were applied to
secular purposes, however beneficent, those purposes would
be but such as must otherwise have been provided for
from other sources, the only gainers being those who had
thus evaded the burthens which must have fallen upon
them.

"The State esurient hungers for Church spoil. Prodigality
and the consequent pressure of impending ruin have been in
general the statesman's incentives to Church spoliation; but
it has so happened that the State has seldom been the richer
for its prey.

" It was a noble thought, and worthy Catholic times, when
a nation devoted a property to God. God kept that property
for the nation. Great hearts could trust great hearts, and each
generation knew that the next would ratify the gift, and partake
the merit. The policy was tender : it provided a spring for
every thirsty life and willed that the ministrations of grace
should surround us like Nature's light and air. It was magnanimous; it gave much that it might receive much; and it
could pardon somewhat. It was profound; it provided for the

clergy a support in one sense fixed, in another sense fluctuating, and thereby it bound up both their sympathies and their interests with those of the people. It was impartial — it neither placed the clergy in dependence on the Government, nor assumed that the normal relation between the Church and State must be one of hate and war."

I quoted largely from what Coleridge says in his noble book "Church and State," on that sacred reserve or "nationalty" which the higher races never allowed to be wholly merged in individual properties.

"This principle," he says, "was common to all primitive races, that in taking possession of a new country, and in the division of the land into heritable estates among the individual warriors or heads of families, a reserve should be made for the nation itself."

Lord Grey and Lord Russell wrote very wise pamphlets at this great crisis, and earnestly recommended that Ireland's Church property should be equitably divided between the Catholics and the Protestants. It was well understood that Mr. Gladstone was of the same opinion. Meaner aspirations went the other way; and it was not to be.

The fate of Ireland has long been decided as regards Church property. That of England hangs still in the balance. If that, too, should be secularised, I wish here to record my conviction that there also a deep injury will be inflicted on religion and on the poor; and that many other great evils will follow in its train — a just retribution. In the case of Ireland at that time, a compromise was made. The ultimate destiny of the Irish Church property was remanded to the deliberations of a future

Parliament.   It was one of those cases in which to deliberate is to be lost.   A time came when the Church question was called "old history" and the "Land Question"
claimed its day.   Somebody remembered that near at
hand lay the troublesome remnant of the Irish Church
property.   The future was sacrificed to a momentary need;
and most of that remnant was tossed into the Irish bog
holes.   The loss was not exclusively one of a spiritual
character.   To it was largely owing the war against property in Ireland during the last fifteen years.   The Irish
demanded why, if no reverence was due to sacred property which had lasted for a thousand years, is any due to
secular property.   Under similar circumstances the same
question will be asked in England.   The Radical section of
the Liberal party would permit no precedent to be created
in Ireland for the preservation of England's Church
property.   The weakest party won the day.

The Irish "Land Question" became imperious.   Many
wild things had been said on the subject in past times —
not, if I remember right, by Mr. O'Connell, who, when
some one at a great Dublin meeting proposed that no
more rent should be paid until "Repeal" had been conceded, rose and moved the immediate expulsion of the
orator.   Among those who advocated large reform on
this subject was Mr. Sharman Crawford, and later Mr.
Napier, Lord Chancellor of Ireland.   But their recom-
mendations included no communistic principle.   Unhappily their counsels were not adopted by Parliament.
Mr. Gladstone's Act of 1870 was a large and bold one,
and in many respects helpful.   For the best thing which
had been done as yet on the Irish land question was the

clause added to that measure by that upright and patriotic man and true orator, Mr. Bright, in order to promote a large addition of peasant proprietors to the existing landed proprietors. The celebrated "clause" was not, it should be remembered, intended to be a levelling-down, but a levelling-up process. The new proprietary of State-aided farmers would have been one not in place of the previous proprietors, but an addition to them, and the tenants thus elevated would have been those whose large contribution to the purchase-money of their farms would have proved their industry and thrift, and thus incited others to the practice of those virtues. They would indeed have won their lands in a manner not wholly unlike that in which lands were won in early days; for fighting was the industry of old times, and the industry of modern times is often exercised in the field of fierce competition, a veritable battlefield.

Yet in Mr. Gladstone's Act of 1870 there were two faults, one of commission and one of omission, which much dissatisfied men habitually acquainted with Ireland. The first of these enacted that in certain cases where what was called *a capricious eviction* had taken place (a rhetorical term wholly incapable of definition) the land-lord should be legally as well as morally bound to com-pensate the outgoing tenant by giving him a sum equiva-lent to a certain number of years' rent. The ministers responsible for that enactment, vehemently and repeatedly affirmed, in defence of it, that it should be regarded as an act of charity alone, and in no sense one of right, and that it recognised on the part of the tenant neither a clan-right derived from ancient usage, nor any claim whatever on the ground of justice. It conferred, they said, on the tenant no claim to any share in the property itself. Wiser men, however, affirmed that at a later time that clause would be appealed to as a proof that the landlord and the tenant were recognised co-proprietors in a single property. And so it turned out. In 1881 the Prime Minister brought forward a wholly new land measure. He had to account for the difference between the two. He said that the Irish tenants had mistaken the meaning of the earlier measure, but that, as the mistake had been made, their view of its provisions must be adopted in the new measure. The Irish proprietors were thus to be subjected to legislation based upon the skilful or fortunate mistake of the tenants; and one of the chief political problems was to be assumed without debate, owing to an accident, but one foretold ten years before. Possibly another accident may have elicited the second principle of the measure of 1881 — namely, the abolition of "Free Contract" (the land principle and not less the commercial principle in England), and elicited also the third principle, then first extemporised — namely, the abolition of the "vested rights" of proprietors, when opposed to rights unknown before to English legislation.

The second fault of the 1870 Land Act, that of omission, militated against the tenant, not the landlord. A Court of Equity should have been created to which the tenant might appeal, if he considered that, by a perversion of law, he had, through an unjust addition to his rent, been deprived of what ought to have been his gain from improvements made by him on his lands, improvements in which the landlord possessed also a great ultimate interest. Such acts on a landlord's part might be rare exceptions, but the law should provide for the exception as well, not less than provide and maintain the sound and salutary rule; and it does so as regards the great rule of parental control, and also in several cases of property. Parental Control continues to be the Law of Households, or else domestic life must have perished long since; but exceptional cases of parental cruelty are punished, and oppressed children are protected.

It should have been thus as regards property. The fundamental principles of "Free Contract" and "Individual Proprietorship" should have been maintained as sacred; while to these were added provisions for the restraining of exceptional abuses, which, even if not directly opposed to law, were plainly perversions of law.

The earlier stages of a revolution are always a period of deep historic interest. I may consequently write of what I have witnessed with a little more of detail than I should otherwise have written with on a subject so painful.

Wise men were not by any means contented with Ireland's condition in 1881. A great work was still needed there. There again a great work was spoilt, and a great opportunity was lost. A considerable change was needed. The land laws in Ireland were substantially the same as in England, but they worked differently, because while in England there existed two industries, agriculture and manufactures, in Ireland the great mass of the people were dependent almost exclusively on agriculture. Competition for farms was therefore in that country painfully severe; while, on the other hand, to abolish competition was plainly a remedy worse than the disease. It was no less than to substitute arbitrary arrangements determined by practically irresponsible authorities for free trade in Ireland's only important industry. It was also to make the primary laws of England and Ireland antagonistic in character thenceforth (as they had already been made in matters ecclesiastical), and that at a time when the cry waxed daily louder that those laws should be assimilated — unless, indeed, it had already been determined that the example set in Ireland, both as regards the Church property and her secular property, should be followed a little later in England. The Irish difficulty had long been patent; what had till then remained unheard-of was the proposed remedy for it. The only rapid remedy, as I must repeat, must have included a very large and State-aided system of emigration, bringing the population of Ireland into proportion to her capital; or else a similar aid to the development of her industrial resources; but each of these would have been a costly proceeding.

In 1881 the Irish land question was dealt with once more, but in a spirit very different from that of the former attempt. The Prime Minister did not justify his new measure by any charges brought against the Irish proprietors. On the contrary, he began his speech by the most distinct affirmation, on the authority of several recent Parliamentary commissions, that they had "been on their trial, and that they had been honourably acquitted." He bade them be of good cheer, as justice would be done, and very few of them would be affected by the measure. No doubt this was his sincere opinion.

What changed it? Not the counter-judgments of the sub-commissioners, for they did not exist until the Land Act of 1881 created them. These gentlemen were a body of men extemporised to meet a need. They were often mere novices in matters connected with land, acting under a formidable pressure and responsible to no tribunal save the court which had appointed them. With all these difficulties in their way the sub-commissioners were sent to solve a problem as hard as finding the longitude or squaring the circle, that is, to ascertain the true value of a farm irrespectively of its actual market value, then nicknamed "rack rent." No principle was explained to them; no rule of action had been prescribed to them. I should be sorry to impute aught of intentional wrong to them for not accomplishing impossibilities. But I know not why their judgments should have been preferred to those which had been successively delivered by successive parliamentary commissions, consisting of experienced men with a limitless power of summoning witnesses acting in quiet times, and with no personal interest in the matter. This has never been explained. It soon became a battle between the Land Court and the "Land League," and before very long the Prime Minister with entire justice denounced the "Land League" party as one advancing "through rapine to revolution." Before the Land Act of 1881 had been introduced, I noted down and showed to a few political friends a brief list of such changes in Ireland's land laws as seemed to meet the real needs of Ireland at that time. Of course they did not include such heroic measures (at the cost of others) as the abolition of freedom of contract,

and the creation of "dual," or rather of plural proprietorship.   My list included the enlargement of Mr. Bright's
clause, and the establishment of a permanent and reliable
"Court of Appeal" for the protection of any tenant who
deemed that the law had been strained so as to deprive
him of what justly was his.   When Mr. W. H. Smith
was the Tory leader of the House of Commons, he was
understood to contemplate a large measure of land purchase, but one in which the vested rights of proprietors
would be guarded as those of the Protestant-Irish clergy,
and even of the West Indian proprietors, had been.

Another provision in my list was that in some cases
landlords should cease to possess some of the extraordinary aids in the collecting of rent, leaving them, of course,
all the ordinary aids for the recovery of debts.

The Land Legislation of 1881, as well as later legislation, included, I think, further provisions for the creation
of a peasant proprietary.   Unfortunately, however, they
were rendered nugatory by being united with a "land
tenure measure," which proposed changes so enormous,
and implied principles so far-reaching and so revolutionary
that those who did the thinking of the Irish farmers at
that time would not allow them to think of anything
besides.   Later those Parnellite leaders themselves may
have come to the conclusion that the two great historical
parties of England, which had recently, to the astonishment of many, joined in passing the Land Act of 1881,
had degenerated into two great factions, themselves no
longer governed by principles, but by party jealousies
and a common faith in the opportune, and that one of
them, if not both, would ultimately prove further com-

pressible. The late Lord Lytton told me that, as he was informed, many members of the House of Lords had been much impressed by assurances which they had received from certain large proprietors in Ulster, that the tenant-right there voluntarily permitted by them had done them no harm. It seems not to have occurred to those counsellors that tenant-right exceptional and by favour was one thing, and that tenant-right rendered universal by law led to consequences of a very different sort. All over Ireland many proprietors had often permitted a conditional tenant-right; but from such compliance the "schoolmen of the State" were not then able to deduce consequences fatal to property.

The Parnellite agitators and their attorneys (for the agitators, the attorneys, and the mob were often united like three strands of a rope) advised their clients not to discard their "plan of campaign" enterprises (the return they had made for the new valuation) for land purchase enterprises till their farms were to be had at a mere nominal price, lest the new landlord, the State, might prove more formidable than the old landlord. Their clients took their advice, and will continue to do so as long as they cherish their present hope. We are bound to remember how long those peasants remained a simple, kindly, and affectionate race as well as one faithful to their engagements. Many things and many men have combined to demoralise them. Tenant-right avows now that it means the right of the tenant to the landlord's property, and that in the absence of Repeal of the Union, the Repeal of the Act of Settlement may suffice. When that is completed the rest will follow. Whether the present Jacobin enterprise will succeed depends upon the wisdom or unwisdom of the present compared with the preceding parliaments during most of the last fifteen years. Dual proprietorship seems to have been "found out." The necessity for freedom of contract will probably be found out later — but perhaps too late.

But it is not easy to predict. The condition of things in Ireland was rendered far more deplorable by the circumstance that a period almost of Revolution was selected as the fittest for the introduction there of such a measure as "Household Suffrage." Even for England a very advanced Liberal, Mr. Gregg, in a pamphlet named "Rocks Ahead," had given a salutary warning. That measure, he said, "places the whole property of England at the disposal of the non-propertied class." I remember that when the bill for household suffrage was introduced into the House of Lords, Lord Derby made an unprecedented confession. He said, "I must confess that the measure is a leap in the dark." It was said that he had adopted it solely owing to his deference for Mr. Disraeli's judgment. When it was passed, and that without the safeguards originally included in it, my then eldest brother, Sir Vere de Vere, puzzled us all by a riddle. "How did Lord Derby feel just after he had taken his leap in the dark?" The propounder of the riddle had himself to furnish the answer to it: "He felt himself a little *dizzy*." The household suffrage, it was said, doubled the English parliamentary constituency, but tripled that of Ireland. I wrote a pamphlet in opposition to that measure. It was termed "Ireland and Proportionate Representation," and contained the following sentence, "Let all true Liberals remember that there exist gifts which are thefts also," an obvious deduction from the scriptural assertion, "Their right hand is full of gifts and lies."

Such, I conceive, were the gifts bestowed on that occasion upon Ireland. To enfranchise, well-nigh in a mass, ignorant cottiers, many of whom could not write their own names, and their servant-boys, is practically to disfranchise the educated and responsible. The anti-revolutionary party were entitled, from their numbers alone, and apart from all reference to the political claims of property, to fully one-third of Ireland's parliamentary representatives. They possess about half that number only, or one-sixth of it. "Proportionate Representation" would eventually redress this wrong, and bring within bounds tyranny in its most fatal form; that is to say, the tyranny of a majority which, uniting an unlimited legal with a boundless physical power, constitutes an illimitable power mitigated by no moral or prudential restraint; and yet is also a power practically wielded by a handful of agitators far more restricted than ever yet constituted either any aristocracy or any oligarchy.

I have been asked what gain could result from "Proportionate Representation" in Ireland if it still left the propertied and educated classes in a minority of merely one-third. The gain to England would be this, that a parliamentary majority created by Ireland, though seated not in Dublin, but in Westminster, would not soon again be able to govern in all essential matters the whole of England and Scotland. That power, had it lasted during but one Parliament more, might at will have either dissolved the British empire or rendered its continuance impossible by rendering it utterly unworthy to continue. The gain to Ireland would be that, in that country, hope would still breathe the vital air; that the sense of wrong would no longer be the excuse for lethargy; that all endeavour to withstand folly and rapine would no longer be paralysed by the sense that all struggle meant but an ignominy the more; that the wisest and best would not be forced to withdraw from public life; that at least irreparable mischief would not have been effected before men now calamitously *désorientés* could again recognise the points of the compass, and see whither they are tending; that time would be given to England to profit by at least recent experience, and for another land, which has both sinned and been sinned against, to return to her better mind.

To a certain class of English politicians the last sentence in this pamphlet was addressed; I trust it may not have been to a large one. "When, some years ago, then somewhat late, you disbanded your English garrison in Ireland, you were not called upon to have subsequently and successively snatched from your kith and kin, who, during so many centuries had sustained there the standard of England, their good name, their lands, their social status, and their political existence."

The line taken by the Roman Catholic clergy during the agitation of the last few years has been by no means as one-sided as has been commonly assumed. Those among them who attended public meetings attracted large attention, whereas those who stayed away from them remained unknown, and the readers of newspapers had no means of knowing at which side was the majority. Those readers little guessed how much was shown of quiet fortitude on the part of those priests who refused to join in the agitation, and who patiently bore up, not alone against a trying unpopularity, but sometimes against very decided boycotting also. Cardinal Cullen had strongly censured illegal courses of all sorts, and also all anti-property movements, as well as Home Rule agitation. On that subject his opinions were of the strongest character. His expressions were these: "France was once as Catholic as Ireland, but the Revolution undermined her faith. Should an Irish parliament, whose strength, I believe, will come from revolutionary sources, pass laws that are subversive of justice, morality, or religion, it will be the duty of the bishops to speak out to warn their flocks, and to condemn such acts. Such a Parliament will at once pass laws to weaken and destroy the Church's action, and to restrain the bishops in the performance of their undoubted duty. With this conviction in my mind, I, for one, can never advocate this revolutionary movement, as I believe it to be, for Home Rule."

If Cardinal Cullen had lived a little longer the whole aspect of affairs would have been very different in Ireland. His successor, Cardinal McCabe, died also prematurely, it is said, of a broken heart, occasioned by the crimes committed during what has been called the Irish "Reign of Terror," to which Mr. Burke and Lord Frederick Cavendish fell victims. The great Dominican preacher, "Father Tom Burke," perhaps the man most venerated in Ireland, then dying of an excruciating malady, continued as long as he could stand to denounce those crimes, though warned that if he persisted in doing so he would be shot in his pulpit. Dr. Moriarty, Bishop of Kerry, and many besides, both among the clergy and laity, spoke out fearlessly. In this matter there were two sides, one of which has been too commonly ignored. Thus the present Bishop of Limerick rebuked the false casuistry, wholly opposed to the teaching of Catholic theology, and that of the present Pope, by which a plea was set up in defiance of the plainest engagements respecting property.

The Catholic clergy have ever been, and now are, Ireland's chief protection against the "Secret Societies," as in the days of the great Bishop Doyle. One of the chief leaders of the attempted revolt of 1845 assured me, long after that date, that it was their influence which alone prevented the people from joining it in large masses.

During those eventful years, the true character of which will be better understood in history than it has yet been, I wrote many essays in our chief periodicals, such as the "Edinburgh" and the "National" reviews, reasserting as far as I was able, and often in his own words, the principles of Edmund Burke, which are now so commonly forgotten, but which effectually rebuked the progress of French Jacobinism in England at the time of the French Revolution. May they rebuke it in his own land! I also published many letters in the newspapers likely to meet the eyes of my fellow-countrymen when passing more and more under the disastrous dominion of the Parnellite body, whose leaders before long vindicated the habitual and undisguised repudiation of the law of the land, by placing in contrast with it "the unwritten

law." Alas, how little do our poor people understand
the deplorable effects which such courses produce upon
their country, its honour, and its faith. I recalled to the
recollections of those led astray the solemn administra-
tions issued at as early a period as June 24, 1880, by the
Catholic archbishops and bishops of Ireland.

"We declare it our duty also to warn our devoted flocks
against allowing themselves to be driven by their sufferings or
persecutions to the employment of unjust or illegal remedies;
and to exhort them to be on their guard against such principles
and projects as are contrary to the teachings of Religion and
Justice." [1]

My freedom of speech drew down on me bitter animad-
versions. I replied to them thus:

"There is an Ireland larger and better than that of the Tenant-
League; and she will yet hold fast the sacred depositions of Irish
traditions, the Ireland of pure homes, not of clamorous meetings;
the Ireland of Catholic principles, not of casuistry misapplied;
the Ireland that suffered during centuries for the faith; the
Ireland that did not confound licence with liberty, that reverenced law, and therefore made no man judge in his own cause.
That Ireland survives. She is my Ireland and I have a right to
remain faithful to what I have loved long, and to resist those
who would set up a Pretender as her rival. Others may, if they
please, set up a new Ireland, and sue her praise. I deem it is a
patriot's duty not to flatter his country, and not to withhold
unpopular counsel when it is needful. If Ireland seeks even
worthy ends by unworthy means, she will miss them, or win
them at a heavy cost."

[1] Hodges and Figgis, Dublin, 1885; and "Essays Literary and Ethical,"
Macmillan, 1889.

The gentlemen of Ireland have within the last few years received hard usage at the hands of many among their fellow-Irishmen, who, during a long period previously, had felt, for I will not say professed, a strong attachment to them. They have received also during the same years of trial, from many of their English friends in both Houses of Parliament, a treatment different from that which they had expected. What proportion of that property which they received from their ancestors and had hoped to bequeath to their descendants will remain with them we know not. It is only certain that their duties will remain. Their first duty as Christians will be to allow no vindictive or selfish instinct to determine their course. Their highest duty to Ireland will be to remain among their poor, no matter how wronged or defamed, there or elsewhere, so long as they can continue to benefit them, even with means so often reduced to one-half or less, and to resist the progress of that Jacobinism from which Ireland has suffered so much. Their duty to both countries will be to cement their union and make it become at last, if possible, a union alike of hearts and of interests.

CHAPTER XVII

IT is generally supposed that, among a poet's Recollections, some remain with him long in connection with the special object and aim with which a few of his poems were composed. Several such Recollections are here preserved in connection with poems intended to illustrate religious philosophy or early Irish history.

I. INISFAIL.

In the year 1861 I published a chronicle poem entitled "Inisfail," illustrating Irish annals during about six centuries, from the Norman Conquest of Ireland to the repeal of the Penal Laws. When the poem appeared, Ireland was in a condition of great depression.

Irish history had always possessed a deep interest for me. My father, while thoroughly an Imperialist in his politics, had written a touching poem entitled "The Lamentation of Ireland," and used to tell us in our young days pathetic stories taken often from the "Pacata Hybernia," a book written by the secretary of Sir George Carew, Queen Elizabeth's President of Munster. Later, what struck me was that, while the details of Irish history were obviously so full of significance, the history itself was nowhere to be found except in fragments. It appeared to lack all unity. Again and again it seemed as if England must have lost her hold upon Ireland, but she did not; as if the Irish chiefs and Norman lords, "more Irish than the Irish," must have at last combined against her, but they did not; as if France or Spain must have found their advantage in fighting England on Irish soil, but their aid did her far more mischief than good. It was after the lapse of many years that the meaning of Irish history flashed upon me. It possessed unity, although not a political one. Religion was Ireland's unity. That had not been a series of frustrations. A great destiny had been working itself out, not from the time of Strongbow, but from that of St. Patrick. The Norman time and the time of the Penal Laws had both of them been but episodes. When a few of that great Norman race which had conquered England, and much of Europe besides, subjected about half her Irish princes, probably without the knowledge of the Irish, to an English suzerain; when, at a later period, those Irish vassal princes had quarrels with their English suzerain, as English kings in their character of Norman dukes often had with their suzerain, the King of France; when those Irish vassal princes and their Gaelic clans had been nicknamed rebels; and when, in their turn, the Norman Palatines had been lawlessly deprived of those palatine rights acknowledged for centuries; and when Norman nobles were deprived of their lands because they would not surrender their Faith — these things doubtless were frustrations. But these things constituted but an inferior part of Irish history. When St. Patrick preached and the people believed, and again when the believing nation sent out its missionaries to far lands and planted the Faith of Christ, here were

no frustrations.   Alone among the northern nations Ireland was faithful.   But had her earlier calamities nothing to do with that later fidelity?   Much every way.   When
a new Faith was backed by penal laws, by whom were those
penal laws to be obeyed?   Not by Norman barons, whose
law had ever been their own will.   Not by Gaelic serfs,
from whom their native law had been taken, and to
whom the English had been denied.

One of the lessons taught to us by Irish history is
this: that to the different nations different vocations are
assigned by Providence; to one, an imperial vocation, to
another, a commercial one; to Greece an artistic one, to
Ireland, as to Israel, a spiritual one.

I often call to mind a sermon preached in Limerick by
Father Faber of the Oratory, who had been passing some
days at Tervoe, one in which he dwelt much on the past
of Ireland, and much on her future.   "Do not imagine,"
he said, "that Ireland will ever be a nation with a
splendid political or a prosperous commercial career, like
those of Genoa or Venice of old.   It is no material
obstacle, no historical accident, that stands in her way.
It is a holier greatness, a more exalted destiny, that forbid a lower one.   Ireland's vocation is, as it has ever
been, an Apostolic one.   She may be true to it, or she
may be false to it; but if she forgets it or discards it, she
will meet with success in no other for ever.   As at the
time of her only real greatness — her missionary greatness — the heathen are her inheritance: let her remember
that first, and then all that she needs beside will be
'added unto her!'"   I remember the looks, some of
amusement, and some of displeasure, which were exchanged

by many persons in that church as he spoke; but I remember also that when the preacher was taking his departure, many of the humbler class rushed forward and kissed the hem of his garment. They at least made no mistake as to his meaning, though they had never heard him say, "Those who travel in Ireland have one great joy. They cannot but see that the great majority of the poor are living in the grace of God."

No other poem of mine was written more intensely, I may say more painfully, from my heart than "Inisfail." Some of its English readers were displeased at Irish history being thus interpreted, though one of them, I remember, exclaimed on reading it, "Either this is the true meaning of Irish history or else it never had a meaning." If those who were displeased imagined that the book was one likely to excite Irish political passions, they must have been very simple. The book was addressed not to the many, but to the thoughtful and the few, and at least as much to English statesmen as to Irish patriots.

II. The Legends of St. Patrick.

The conversion of Ireland had been effected without a drop of martyr blood by that great-hearted apostolic man whose soul, like St. Paul's, was ever filled with a passionate love for God and man. It was effected with little aid resembling that which England had received from several English kings.

St. Patrick addressed himself more to the people than to the chiefs, and their conversion was like an inspiration. It resulted larg   from the character of the

people.   When confronted by greatness and by truth they
could see both and they could love both.   In several of
their national characteristics there was doubtless an
oppugnancy to the Faith, but there was more often a sympathy with it.   The race was barbaric, but not savage.
It had the barbaric virtues as well as vices.   It had
no corrupt civilisation.   Nature remained, and Nature,
though often fiercely opposed to Grace, has also great
analogies to it, and is its needful supplement.

I wished in my poems to illustrate the different
modes in which Christianity presented itself to different
countries.   I selected England and Ireland.   They are
signally unlike.   The Irish, as a race, are the more
impulsive, more sanguine, more imaginative, tenderer in
love, and fiercer in hate.   The English are stronger,
more reliable, and juster.   The Irish are more sympathetic; the English more benevolent.   The Irish are
more elastic; the English robuster.   The Irish regard
the family most; the English the State.   The philosophic
poet tells us that "we live by animation, hope, and love;
these are eminently among the virtues of children; and
we are told by a higher authority that it is as little children that we enter into His kingdom.   It is in their
childhood that the nations have commonly received the
"glad tidings" and understood them.   Some have remarked that we little know how much man is learning
in the first few years, nay, in the first few months of his
life.   Something like this may be said of nations.   Their
legends are fragments of their earliest knowledge.   Only
a few of them remain; but these are such among them as
carried most significance with them.

The children of Foeclut Wood commemorate that "cry of the children" by night which dragged St. Patrick back from a free land to Ireland, where he had long lived as Milcho's slave. In that awful wood the misery of pagan Ireland had reached its utmost height; but even there one hope remained. Men said that some "Unknown God" had lost his children there, and that he would return to them there; that he would find them and take them home with him. This legend illustrates the pathetic character of early Irish Christianity. The stranger — St. Patrick — visits them and confirms that hope, and those who hear him believe.

The proof that they believe is that they at once discard their chief national sin, that of vindictiveness. They launch their ships, cross the straits to the north, and bring the "good tidings" to their immemorial enemies, — a glorious example to their descendants. St. Patrick at Cashel was selected in part to illustrate the passionate loyalty of the early Irish to princes loyal to their people no less. "St. Patrick and King Eochaid" was an attempt to draw the character of a Gaelic chief. It was copied in part from that of one whom I knew well, and who might, I believe, be called the last Irish chief.

Eochaid is brave yet cautious, generous yet exacting; subtle, but simple also; full of penetration, yet absolutely unreasonable; sagacious, blinded at times by a little self-love; ardent in belief, but much more proud of his shrewd-ness; and inflexibly obstinate when contradicted. He becomes a Christian, but out of a whim refuses to be baptised, and dies as he has lived.

The greatest by far of the Irish legends is "The Striving of St. Patrick on Mount Cruecham." The apostle's great work is completed; but in the hour of victory a fear falls upon him. He knows that Ireland has great trials before her. Will she prove equal to them? Mount Cruecham rose on Ireland's western coast, the chief fortress of all those evil Spirits that had so long held her in subjection. It was believed that from its summit, a corresponding force must be accorded to Prayer. The saint advances to the battle with those spirits and to pray one great prayer — namely, that Ireland may remain faithful to Christ's truth so long as the world lasts. He advances on through the forest that girds the base of the mountain, and the first being whom he meets there is St. Victor, his guardian angel, who had accompanied him wherever he went, and strengthened him for each successive enterprise. On this occasion alone the angel warns him that the boon he demands is one too great to be granted, and commands him to depart from the Mountain of Prayer. For the first time the saint disobeys him. He continues his ascent. The demons flock around him from all parts of Erin. Three times the battle is renewed. At last the prayer is granted, and the demons flee for ever from the land. The angel then informs St. Patrick that his own apparent opposition was but to kindle in the saint to a greater height the spirit of faith and of prayer.

III. ALEXANDER THE GREAT AND SAINT THOMAS
OF CANTERBURY.

These two dramas were written with a kindred aim. "Alexander the Great" was published in 1874. Though primarily a drama, it was meant also to be a philosophic poem. A few remarks may make the meaning plainer in both capacities.

As a drama it was intended to delineate the one great Greek who devoted himself mainly to action, not thought.

As a poem, it was intended to illustrate one of the chief of those historic periods on which have rested the destinies of the world. Four such epochs existed recognised antecedent to the Christian era. Four great kingdoms (we should call them empires) were seen in vision by the Hebrew prophets. Of these the Babylonian was the first and the worst, representing little more than wealth and material greatness. Rome was the fourth, the kingdom of war and of law, with which was blended a pale reflex of Greek philosophy and letters. Rome was the great road-making empire, thus pointing to a universal dominion realised later, but in a spiritual, not political, form. To it succeeded that spiritual kingdom foretold by the prophets as the "Mountain of the Lord's House," destined to be "exalted to the summit of the mountains." Between the first and the last of those kingdoms — namely, the Babylonian and the Roman, there intervened the Persian and the Greek, the latter founded by Alexander the Great.

It soon became plain to me that, whether the work was regarded as a philosophical poem or as a drama, its interest must become identified with the destiny of Alexander, and above all with his character, and with the changes gradually made in that strong character by subsequent events carefully delineated. The chief characteristic of Alexander was pride; but, as he was a pagan, pride did not prevent that character from being cast in an

heroic mould.   On the contrary, pride had a large place
in pagan heroism, though a small place in Christian,
such as that of Charlemagne or of Godfrey of Bulloign,
as delineated by Tasso in the only Christian epic, both
of those warriors having been strong in the grace of
humility.   The events crowded into Alexander's brief
career belonged to a twofold order, an outward one, visible to all, and an inward one neither discerned by those
around him nor suspected by himself.   The rapid train
of his successes were externally successes only; but
internally what they meant was the development of his
characteristic chief fault and the consequent accomplishment of his destiny.   They but deepened the black spot
in his being.   His successes rendered his final success impossible.   This is indicated by a remarkable event dating
from the time when, standing in the Temple of Jerusalem,
Alexander rejected a command which yet he knew to be
Divine.   He had got upon the wrong road, and advanced
along it the more swiftly because it was the downward
way.   Alexander's visit to Jerusalem is recorded by
Josephus, and it is one of the most memorable things in
his career.   The scene in this drama may be easily over-
looked, for it is short.   When that visit took place it is
to be remembered that Alexander's true mission in the
East had already been fully accomplished: for the Persian
empire had become his.   The Jewish high priest tells
him plainly that God has granted to him that Persian
empire, but expressly forbidden him to seek that of the
world:

> " He who claims that must be the Prince of Peace.
> Thy portion lies in bounds.   Limit and Term
> Govern the world."

Alexander replies that he will *deliberate;* the high priest departs.

Hephestion, the good angel of Alexander's life, was "then far away" — a man whose mere instincts had a wisdom about them that all the intelligence of Ptolemy, "our wisest," lacked. Ptolemy was near and at hand. From that early moment all Alexander's successes were but so many snares. He confided to Ptolemy that just before the Persian war had begun, he had for once felt Fear: that at that hour a vision had fallen upon him in which the high priest, the same with whom he had just conversed, encouraged him to persevere because God would be his protector and his guide.

Immediately after his disobedience two great events took place — namely, first, the consent of Alexander to the sentence of death against Parmenio. This was Alexander's one great offence against justice. The second was his march to the remote East — a barren victory, as he discovers when dying at Babylon.

> " I have a secret; one for thee alone
> 'T was not the mists from that morass disastrous
> Nor death of Him that died; nor adverse Gods;
> Nor the Fates themselves ; 't was something mightier yet
> And secreter in the great night that slew me."

Many passages were introduced into this drama to indicate that while Alexander's fortunes were apparently always mounting, his character was in decline. Before his pride had fully culminated he denounced that legend so dishonourable to his mother — namely, that Jupiter was his father. Later he adopts it. Early he commanded that

his tomb should be made in "Macedonian Pella." When
dying he ordains that it should be

> " Mid sands Egyptian, by the Ammonian grove,
>   In my great Father's fane."

The assumption of divine honours extorted by him
from all the Grecian States shortly before his death con-
trasts sadly with his reverence, when, standing beside
the tomb of Achilles, his great ancestor, he renounced
for himself, and dedicated to him all his own expected
triumphs. Towards the end of his work he speaks of it
as that of one more than mortal, and one who feels
himself to be

> " Less a person than a Power,
> Some fateful wheel, that, rolling round in darkness,
> Knows this — its work ; but not that work's far scope."

Later he speculates on the possibility of men passing
by heroic merit into gods.

That the purer greatness of Alexander's earlier day
had returned to him in part at death may be inferred on
historical grounds when we call to mind his memorable
answer to the question demanded of him at that moment
— namely, Who should wear his crown? "The worthiest
head." To suggest that his great solitary friendship
had survived ambition, and lasted to the end, he is here
made to murmur also in death words not then spoken for
the first time:

> " Patroclus died. Achilles followed soon."

He had first spoken those words at the proud beginning
of his career, when he and Hephestion stood side by side
before the tombs of Patroclus and Achilles at Troy.

IV. St. Thomas of Canterbury.

"St. Thomas of Canterbury" was intended to be in some respects a work analogous to Alexander the Great," and in others to be a contrast to it. Each was to be at once a philosophical poem, and also a drama, the interest of which should rest mainly on the gradual evolution of a character; but the two characters were selected with the desire of illustrating two opposite forms of greatness, "Alexander's" being a pagan greatness, and Becket's a Christian. The two poems were also designed to illustrate two utterly dissimilar states of human society, "St. Thomas of Canterbury's" being that of the middle ages.

At that period a great conflict was raging in the Western world, that between the *régale* and the *pontificale*. On both sides there were exaggerated demands; but, in the long run, during most of those ages the Church succeeded, not in all that some popes had claimed, but at least in the maintenance of her liberties, the destruction of which must have not only grievously dimmed the great Christian civilisation, but have also reduced Western society to the abject condition of an Oriental Caliphate. Nor would the evil have ended there. The far future too would have been strangled before its birth. The debased condition of the New Europe would have proved a barren soil wholly incapable of germinating modern civilisation. After the destruction of all spiritual, and consequently of all moral freedom, the restoration of the best arts, letters, and political ideas of the ancient world would have been as impossible as the growth of corn upon rock. A secular tyranny would at the time have affected to patronise these arts, but it could not have inspired them.

The chief dangers to the freedom of religion in the middle ages came from the inordinate wealth heaped upon the clergy by a munificence which later provoked the cupidity of the baronage. A worse evil remained.

If there were despotic kings there were also priests without a true vocation. Such there must ever be where excessive ecclesiastical wealth bribes parents to push their sons into holy orders.

A few remarks may be necessary here to render intelligible an age often calumniated but also often over-admired. Among the clergy at the time of Becket there existed many of very different characters. One of the nobler was represented by John of Salisbury, devout, accomplished, with a culture not confined to religious studies, a man of the world as well as a man of God, but not a worldly man. John of Oxford is the type of the diplomatic ecclesiastic not then uncommon, to whom the playing of an ambitious game was not only the business of his life, but an amusement so absorbing that he might have devoted himself to it even if it had promised no reward; a hard man with a heart made harder from the sanctities he daily profaned. Henry of Blois, King Stephen's brother, was the Prince Bishop, upright, magnanimous, fearless, not scrupulous but faithful to his primary duties, though neither a saint nor affecting sanctity. Gilbert Foliot, originally not without strong leanings towards ascetic virtue, but turned by an exaggerated reputation for it into a self-deceiver as well as a hypocrite. Herbert of Bosham, a saint and mystic both; simple as a child, pure, benign, humble, with faith unflawed, and with that "single eye" of the Gospel which enables a man to see, almost without an effort, what genius alone could never detect, and also to see in all things the symbols of the things invisible. Such a character is often called a visionary, and often turns out to be more practical than its censors.

In Becket my design was to illustrate the greatest of that lion-race, those earlier Archbishops of Canterbury, who fought for the freedom of God's Church — "Ut Ecclesia Anglicana libera sit," as Magna Charta expresses it. He was not a man of the highest ability, but he had in the highest degree the great virtue of fidelity. Reluctantly he had become a man in charge; and he had vowed that, while that charge was his, his master should not suffer wrong. He had begun life as a brave and honourable man of the world while free from its vices, though too regardful of its applause. This unsought elevation forced him on and up through the strenuous airs of painful duties to a spiritual height made daily greater by the machinations of unscrupulous foes, and the desertion of false friends. In the grades of merit he had proceeded "Hero" before long, and the next degree was that of "Saint." It came to him through suffering.

Herbert of Bosham had long watched his friend's progress in sanctity with an experienced insight, and rejoiced less in his occasional triumphs than in those desolations which deepened his patience and humility. The desertion of false friends was the least of these trials. The severest was that one at Montmirail, for there he was

abandoned even by the good French king, and by the
papal legates themselves. Becket's victory there was
solely that of endurance. Herbert thus describes it :

> " In patient sadness
> With neck a little bent, and forward head,
> Six hours he stood before that storm of tongues
>   .   .   .   .
> I saw that God had sent his soul that hour
> A soul's supremest trial — Dereliction :
> The fountains of the mighty deep of woe
> Were broken up; the joy of Faith was dead :
> Yet Faith itself lived on : 'mid storm and darkness
> He clung to God as limpet to the rock.
> *He 's greater than he was.*"

Once again, only once, that terrible dereliction falls
on him, as he treads the shore near Boulogne just before
his return to England; but it is dissipated by the near
approach of personal danger, with which dereliction has
no connection, that trial being only in the spirit, not
in the body. Becket had at last reached to the Saint's
degree. He was then fit for death, martyrdom, and
martyrdom's legacy.

Alexander and Becket were opposites. Alexander was
born in the purple, was endued with a genius the greatest
ever accorded to a prince, and had for his preceptor the
chief philosopher of his age, Aristotle. St. Thomas of
Canterbury was a man of humble birth, no extraordinary
ability and no unusual culture. Alexander had brooded
from his boyhood over a single design, that of founding
an empire extending over the whole earth, and replete
with all the wisdom of Greece. St. Thomas had no
ambition save that of discharging some ordinary duty,

but discharging it with entire honesty. Alexander advanced from triumph to triumph; and his intellect was ever expanding; but his moral being was ever degenerating. St. Thomas was ever passing after his first exaltation from humiliation to humiliation; but spiritually he was ever growing higher and higher. Alexander died and his empire died with him. St. Thomas died also, and his death preserved from bonds, first in England, and as a consequence, throughout the world, the kingdom whereof its founder had promised that "the gates of Hell should not prevail against it." The warfare of the emperors and the anti-popes against His Church had begun and was in rapid progress. If the conspiracy had proved then triumphant in England it must have advanced rapidly over the rest of the world, "Like chaos o'er creation, uncreating."

V. The Legends of the Saxon Saints.

Upon these legends, as I read or wrote, there seemed ever to rest the shadow of Odin, that heroic prince, the chief action of whose life is set forth in the first Legend of the Saints, entitled "Odin the Man," and again in the last, after his prophecy had been fulfilled, and pagan Rome had undergone the penance he had invoked upon her head centuries before.

In "The Saxon Saints" my aim was to present to the reader a picture both of the early British and Anglo-Saxon England during the seventh century. Of course I followed the footsteps of the venerable Bede. That century gave to England's chief race her Christianity, on which has ever since rested her liberty, civilisation, and greatness. The poem was meant to illustrate the chief types, pagan and Christian, of society, from the cowherd to the minstrel, the warrior, the king, and the prophet, and among them the graver figures of the Roman missionaries and the Saxon saints. These Saxon saints were very different from the Irish. So were the races; the English differed much from the Irish. There was less of the wild and strange about them, but more dignity; less of the child but more of the man; less of the missionary but more of the Christian subject and citizen.

The unity which belongs to a drama or to an epic is of course neither to be found or to be sought in a collection of legends; but a certain degree of unity must sometimes be found where those legends are not the creations of fancy, but rest upon authentic history. The chief religious legends of Anglo-Saxon history stand in close connection with a far earlier pagan legend — perhaps of all such the most memorable. I refer to the wonderful legend which even the sceptical Gibbon speaks of as not improbably true — that of Odin. He was a prince whose kingdom lay near Ararat, and who, finding it impossible further to resist the advance of the Roman arms under Pompey, resolved that if he could not preserve their country for his people, he would at least preserve his people from servitude. He led them forth into the great German forest. He had been a traveller in youth through that vast tract, and he had also sojourned at Rome. He told his people when leading them forth that Rome was already so corrupted and enervated that within a few centuries more it could make no defence, and that within the same period their descendants would be so hardened and strengthened by the terrible climate of the North that they could then with certainty accomplish their destiny, force their way to the sunny South, execute the divine vengeance on Rome, and break up for ever its immeasurable empire.

That pagan legend reappears again and again in the "Legends of Saxon Saints."

The mandate of that patriotic king, the high instrument of Providence, had been in a great part obeyed by his race, yet after a time it had degenerated, not indeed like Rome, by corruption of morals, but by cruelty and a perpetual thirst for battle. Their heaven itself was to be, they thought, not eternal peace, but eternal war. Their household morals retained that purity ascribed to the Germans by Tacitus; but their religion had insensibly changed. Before their migration they had, as many believe, held much in common with other Eastern races and with early Eastern religious traditions of a highly Theistic character. In part these had remained to them, and later had facilitated their conversion to Christianity; but in part they had disappeared. The descendants of Odin's subjects had committed a great crime against Odin. They had made him a god. He had been a mighty warrior; and their life thenceforth was war. Into about the centre of my poem I introduced a legend entitled "King Sigibert and Heida the Prophetess," recalling Odin's high design, but implying its partial frustration. The purer spirits among the worshippers of the Scandinavian Gods were beginning to grow dissatisfied with them, and were beginning to listen to the Christian monks of St. Columba from Iona. An ancient Scandi-

navian book had been discovered, making a confession
never made by any other religion, namely that all the
gods then worshipped were one day to perish, and one
great God of sanctity and peace was to take their place
for ever.   So said "The Völuspá" or primeval prophecy.

The final legend, entitled "The Banquet Hall of
Wessex," or "The King who could see," decides for ever
between the true representatives of Odin, and those who
only dishonoured the great king whom they professed to
adore.   Kenwalk, King of Wessex, was a pagan, but
refused to persecute the Christians.   Wessex is conquered by the sovereign of Mercia, but after a time it is
delivered from this yoke, and Kenwalk is restored.   A
great banquet is held to which throng all the Scandinavian
nobles, priests, and bards intent on the destruction of
the Christian faith, and those who hold it.   When the fury
of the pagan host is at its height, and the destruction of
the Christians seems imminent, Birirnus, the bishop from
Rome, rises and at once quells the tumult.   "Odin," he
affirms, disowns them.

> " True Man was He: ye changed him to false God;
> That Odin, when the destined hour had pealed,
> Beckoned to Alaric, marched by Alaric's side."

Alaric had fulfilled the prophecy of Odin when he led
his people forth into the German forest.   Alaric had
inflicted the Divine vengeance on Rome.   Alaric was
the great chief of the barbaric race which worshipped
Odin.   But this high triumph had not been conceded to
Alaric until he had become a Christian; so speaks the
Bishop Birirnus.   King Kenwalk then rises from his
throne, declares that during his exile he had often delib-

erated as to whether he should or should not become a Christian, and that what he had that day seen had made him resolve to do so without delay. The next day, at the king's baptism, Birirnus prophesies of King Alfred, and announces that Wessex, one of the smallest kingdoms of the Heptarchy, will, under his rule, become its head, and eventually bequeath the noblest of empires to the race of Odin, itself delivered over to Christ.

VI. The Foray of Queen Meave.

In 1880 I passed much pleasant time among the collections of the Royal Irish Academy in Dublin. Those collections included several manuscript translations into English prose of remarkable poems belonging to Ireland's Heroic Age. Several of these translations, among others "The Tripartite Life of St. Patrick," had been translated by Mr. W. Hennessy, one of the best recent Irish scholars; another had been translated by Prof. Eugene O'Curry, and published; and I had the advantage also of reading Professor O'Looney's manuscript translation of what is regarded as the greatest of the early Irish epics, or, as some would say, its finest fragment. To me it seemed the "fragment of a lost world," as Landor said of Homer's poems; and I resolved to try at least whether the substance of that Irish epic, "The Foray of Queen Meave," believed to have been orally transmitted from a period antecedent to the Christian era, might not be preserved to the English and Irish reader in poetic form.

The greatness of early Irish poetry, and of the age that produced it is brought home to us by its immense superiority to Ireland's medieval poetry, called "Ossianic," because it relates chiefly to Ossian. These later poems combine truth to nature with vigour and pathos, but they do not possess the breadth or the force of the epic fragments belonging to a far earlier date. They have not the same inventive imagination or passion, nor are the characters as sharply delineated.

The poetry of that first age, though very unequal, was great because the age was great. The "Heroic Age" of Ireland anticipated by some five or six centuries the "Saintly Age." To the first century belonged Cachullam, by far the noblest of the Irish warriors; and Fordia, his sworn friend, though a Firbolg, not a Gael. To it belonged Conell Carnach. To it belonged one of their wisest kings, Conor Mac Nessa, and a far nobler one, Fergus Mac Roy, so royal-hearted, though so indifferent to power, that he abandoned his throne on discovering that his subjects preferred his step-son. To him was attributed the great Irish epic, "The Tain," commemorating the war in which he had taken so large a part. Deirdrè, the chief female representative of that heroic age, had in her also many traits of noblest Irish character still found in our own.

The poetry that illustrates a "Heroic Age" is quickly recognised. It is both great-hearted and light-hearted. It abounds in wild mirth, sure that such mirth will meet with sympathy, and that no critic will complain because close to the comic he finds passages that challenge "pity or terror." The poet of that age sets forth what he sees, and he sees that which is, because he comes to the great drama of human life without preoccupations. Nature bears with strange mixtures, and the poet bears with them also. The early chronicler thus supplies the later dramatist with material, for he noted facts as they occurred, and without the gloss of theory, political or ethical. The facts he meets walk naked and are not ashamed. The modern historian seldom inspires the dramatist, because what he records has, in his hands, taken a shape not its own. Nature disowns them thus transformed, and true Art will not live on Nature's leavings. Those old Irish poems bore for me plainly the stamp of reality. The poet was a witness, and did not set himself up as a judge. He did not look down upon them from a height, real or imaginary, but encountered them face to face as he moved along the paths and by-paths of men.

There is often in those old Irish legends a sense of honour, even in the midst of the most lawless enterprises. For example, the Firbolg race had complained that the Gaelic hosts had landed on Erin's coasts *by night*. Their complaint was submitted by the Gaels to their chief bard, Amergin. He commanded his fellow-countrymen to re-embark and sail over the sea "nine waves," return to the land by day, and keep it if they could. They obeyed him. The military laws which ruled the standing army of Ireland under Fionn are marked by the high reverence for woman, for the Druid, for the bards.

As I read each prose translation of ancient Irish song, there rose before me a vision of a "Heroic Age," such as has long ceased to exist. The men then living had strong nerves as well as strong hearts. Deirdrè, "The Child of Destiny," when she sang the dirge of the three far-famed Brothers, wailed for them only, not for herself, though when that dirge was over she fell dead at their feet.

I read on and felt less and less disposed to contest the assertion of Prof. Eugene O'Curry that "The Tain" is to Irish history what "The Argonautic Expedition" and "The Seven against Thebes" were to that of Greece. Behind those Irish warriors there stood a background in harmony with them — structures not like those which glorified the age of Pericles and Phidias, but one resembling the tomb of Agamemnon and the huge ruins at Mycenè. The Irish structures that rose before me as I read were the huge fortifications on Aran Isle, Dun Angus, and Dun Connor, works of the Firbolg race, whose cyclopean walls still outbrave the Atlantic waves with their long courses of uncemented stone. Another such background is presented in the marvellous sepulchral remains on the banks of the Boyne, the monuments of a race earlier still than the Firbolg, namely, that of the Tuatha De Danann — such monuments as New Grange, Knowth, and Dowth, — and the earlier monuments of Ireland's third race, the Gael, such as the huge fort close to Emania now Armagh, or the lonely cairn on one of the summits of Howth, the grave of Oscar's wife, so familiar to the readers of Sir Samuel Ferguson's bravely pathetic poem, "Aideen's Grave."

THE END.

JOHN WILSON & SON

University Press

.

MR. EDWARD ARNOLD'S
New Books & Announcements.

LONDON: 37 BEDFORD STREET.
NEW YORK: 70 FIFTH AVENUE.

Telegraphic Addresses : 'Scholarly, London '; 'Scholarly, New York.'

Dedicated by Special Permission to Her Majesty the Queen.

OLD ENGLISH GLASSES.

𝔄n 𝔄ccount of 𝔊lass 𝔇rinking-𝔙essels in 𝔈ngland from 𝔈arly 𝔗imes to the end of the 𝔈ighteenth 𝔗entury.

With Introductory Notices of Continental Glasses during the same period, Original Documents, etc.

By ALBERT HARTSHORNE,
Fellow of the Society of Antiquaries.

Illustrated by nearly 70 full-page Tinted or Coloured Plates in the best style of Lithography, and several hundred outline Illustrations in the text. Super royal 4to., price Three Guineas net.

The plates and outline illustrations are prepared for reproduction by Mr. W. S. Weatherly and Mr. R. Paul respectively, from full-size or scale drawings by the author of the actual drinking-vessels in nearly every instance. The text is printed in the finest style, and the lithographic work executed by Messrs. W. Griggs and Son. The volume is now ready for delivery.

A full prospectus, giving a complete account of the principal contents of this elaborate and magnificent work, which treats of a subject never before comprehensively undertaken for England, can be had post free on application.

THE AUTOBIOGRAPHY AND LETTERS

OF THE

RT. HON. JOHN ARTHUR ROEBUCK,

Q.C., M.P.

Edited by ROBERT EADON LEADER.

With two portraits, demy 8vo., 16s.

The late Mr. Roebuck was a man of remarkable independence and strength of character. He lived through some of the most exciting periods of recent political history, and always made his presence felt. He was on terms of close intimacy with John Stuart Mill, and among his friends was Francis Place, a man who had far more influence on the politics of his time than is commonly supposed. Mr. Roebuck's early years were spent in Canada, where he educated himself in the habit of original speculative thought and independent action that made his subsequent career so remarkable. The autobiographical portion of the book closes with his youth, but the subsequent letters are unusually valuable as discussing subjects of universal and permanent interest.

RECOLLECTIONS OF AUBREY DE VERE.

In one volume, demy 8vo., with portrait, 16s.

It is not often that we have the privilege of publishing the reminiscences of a man who, a distinguished poet himself, can look back upon a personal acquaintance with Wordsworth. Mr. Aubrey de Vere was born and bred in a literary atmosphere, and has known nearly all the greatest thinkers and writers of our time, not merely from casual meetings in society, but as friends enjoying a sympathetic communion of intellectual tastes. But Mr. de Vere's reminiscences are not confined to literary circles. As a Catholic he was on terms of intimacy with Cardinal Newman and Cardinal Manning. As an Irishman he witnessed many exciting political changes, and has numerous anecdotes and good stories to tell, pervaded with the racy humour characteristic of the country.

A MEMOIR OF ANNE J. CLOUGH,

Principal of Newnham College, Cambridge.

By her Niece, BERTHA CLOUGH.

In one volume, 8vo., 12s. 6d.

The name of Miss Clough, Principal of Newnham College, Cambridge, is familiar to all who are interested in women's education. The story of her life is, indeed, synonymous with the story of the marvellous development which has taken place during the past fifty years in the provision of higher teaching for girls and women. The earlier portion of the book contains a singularly interesting fragment of autobiography which gives a key to the high motives and strong principles that ordered and governed the whole of Miss Clough's long life. The rest of the work has been written by a niece, Miss Bertha Clough, who acted as her aunt's secretary at Newnham for several years, and lived with her on terms of the closest intimacy. Many valuable reminiscences have also been contributed by former pupils of Miss Clough's. The work is furnished with two admirable portraits, reproduced in photogravure, one from the well-known picture by J. Shannon, R.A., in Newnham College, the other from a photograph by Mrs. Frederick Myers. 'To know Miss Clough is to love her,' were the words of one who had ample opportunities of judging, and they may well serve as a comprehensive motto for this volume.

THE CITY OF BLOOD.

An Account of the Benin Expedition.

By R. H. BACON, Commander R.N.

Illustrated by W. H. OVEREND.

In one volume, demy 8vo., 7s. 6d.

Commander Bacon was the Naval Intelligence Officer to the Benin Expedition, 1897. He gives in this volume an interesting and lucid account of the incidents of the expedition, of the country and its people, and of the city which has been till now the capital of unenlightened paganism and of superstitious barbarity. Mr. Overend has illustrated the work from sketches and descriptions by the author.

STYLE.

By WALTER RALEIGH,

Professor of English Literature at University College, Liverpool ;

Author of ' Robert Louis Stevenson,' etc.

One vol., crown 8vo., 5s.

Professor Raleigh's work is a masterly review of style in literature. It deals with the problems and functions of style, the meaning of style and its elements. It surveys Romantic and Classic styles, the value of synonyms, of variety of expression, of metaphor. It considers the relation of the author to his audience, the uses of quotation, rhetorical corruptions.

ROME : THE MIDDLE OF THE WORLD.

By ALICE GARDNER,

Lecturer in History at Newnham College ;

Author of ' Friends of the Olden Time,' etc.

With Illustrations and Map. Crown 8vo., 3s. 6d.

CONTENTS :

i. How Rome became the Middle of the World.—ii. Augustus, and what he did for Rome.—iii. Nero and his Times.—iv. Trajan and Hadrian.—v. The Severi.—vi. Constantine the Great.—vii. The Goths and the Huns.—viii. Theodoric and Justinian.—ix. Renewal of the Empire in Rome.—x. Emperors and Popes.—xi. Kings and Popes.— xii. Rienzi the Tribune.—xiii. The Medici Popes.—xiv. The World without a Middle.

FIFTY SUPPERS.

By Colonel KENNEY HERBERT,

Author of ' Common-sense Cookery,' etc.

Crown 8vo., cloth, 2s. 6d.

A companion volume to the popular booklets, ' Fifty Dinners,' ' Fifty Breakfasts,' and ' Fifty Lunches.'

THE CHIPPENDALE PERIOD IN ENGLISH FURNITURE.

By K. WARREN CLOUSTON.

With over 150 Illustrations by the Author.

Demy 4to., handsomely bound.   One guinea, net.

CONTENTS :

i. Introduction.—ii. Sir William Chambers.—iii. Thomas Chippendale.—iv. Chippendale's Contemporaries.—v. The Brothers Adam.—vi. Thomas Shearer.—vii. A. Hepplewhite.—viii. Thomas Sheraton.

LESSONS IN OLD TESTAMENT HISTORY.

By the VENERABLE ARCHDEACON AGLEN.

One vol., crown 8vo., 4s. 6d.

The Archdeacon of St. Andrews is known to literature for his scholarly contributions to the ' Encyclopædia Britannica,' for his translation of the Odes of Horace, and as the editor of ' Selections from the Writings of Dean Stanley.'

BALLADS OF THE FLEET.

By RENNELL RODD, C.B., C.M.G.

One vol., crown 8vo., cloth, 6s.

A new volume of poems by the poet-diplomatist, Mr. Rennell Rodd.

MORE BEASTS
(FOR WORSE CHILDREN).

By H. B. and B. T. B.,

Authors of ' The Bad Child's Book of Beasts.'

One vol., 4to., 3s. 6d.

This is a companion volume to the book by the same authors which appeared last Christmas and was very warmly received. It is hoped that the present work will be equally acceptable, from the irresistible drollery of its illustrations and its fascinating 'nonsense verses.'

FIRE AND SWORD IN THE SUDAN.

By SLATIN PASHA.

Translated and Edited by COLONEL WINGATE, C.B.,

Chief of the Intelligence Department Egyptian Army.

A new, revised, and cheaper edition of this famous work.

Illustrated.   Price 6s.

In this edition the book has been thoroughly revised by the authors, omitting certain matters of temporary interest, and making it as far as possible a standard work of permanent value for young and old.   The striking illustrations by Mr. Talbot Kelly have been retained.

' The story of the experiences of Slatin Pasha as a ruler, a soldier, and a captive in the Sudan is one of the most striking romances of modern times.   The return of this distinguished officer, after a disappearance of eleven years and more, from what Father Ohrwalder with bitter recollections calls a "living grave," and the perilous incidents of his escape and flight, form in themselves an extraordinary tale.   But the interest of the book is much increased by the importance which, in the minds of English people, attaches to the melancholy events in which he bore a part, and by the narrative in which this witness risen from the dead reopens the story of the great tragedy of Khartoum.'—*Speaker.*

' Whether Slatin's work is more important and attractive as a powerful exhortation on a subject of the greatest political importance and of special national significance from the noble English blood spilt in the Sudan, or as a chapter of human experience wherein truth far surpassed fiction in hair-breadth escapes and deeds of daring beyond what seemed possible, it would be difficult to decide ; but the whole result is one that places this volume on a shelf of its own, not merely as the book of the day, but as the authority for all time on the great Mahommedan upheaval in the Sudan, which was accompanied by an amount of human slaughter and suffering that defies calculation.' —*Times.*

𝔑ew 𝔑ovels.

PAUL MERCER.

𝔄 𝔗ale of 𝔯epentance among 𝔐illions.

By the Hon. and Rev. JAMES ADDERLEY.

Author of 'Stephen Remarx.'

One vol., crown 8vo., 3s. 6d.

Another story from the pen of the author of 'Stephen Remarx' is certain to attract widespread interest and attention among the thousands of every rank of society who have read that brilliant sketch. This story is one of the same character, dealing, as did 'Stephen Remarx,' with the bearing of religion upon every-day life. It is written in the same epigrammatic style which no doubt contributed to render the serious purpose of Mr. Adderley's earlier story popular with the general reading public.

JOB HILDRED.

𝔄rtist and 𝔠arpenter.

By Dr. RICHARDS.

Edited by ELLEN F. PINSENT.

Author of 'Jenny's Case,' 'No Place for Repentance,' etc.

One vol., crown 8vo., 3s. 6d.

The work of Mrs. Pinsent has already attracted the attention of the reading public and of literary critics for the strength of her writing and her faithful rendering of country life and character. This novel is well calculated to add to the reputation she has already attained by 'Jenny's Case,' and 'No Place for Repentance.'

THE KING WITH TWO FACES.

By M. E. COLERIDGE,

Author of ' The Seven Sleepers of Ephesus,' etc.

One vol., crown 8vo., 6s.

Readers who recollect the remarkable interest of Miss Coleridge's first novel, 'The Seven Sleepers of Ephesus,' will be glad to know that in this novel she again bases the story upon a romantic incident of history, taken, on this occasion, from the history of Sweden. The characters of the story are drawn with force and dexterity, and the work is one of striking originality.

THE SON OF A PEASANT.

By EDWARD McNULTY,

Author of ' Misther O'Ryan,' etc.

One vol., crown 8vo., 6s.

'Misther O'Ryan' was the author's first attempt at fiction, and attracted attention for the cleverness of its satire, and as a faithful and humorous sketch of Irish life. 'The Son of a Peasant' is a story of greater length—a novel rather than a sketch of Irish life, but it exhibits the same rich appreciation of the humorous and pathetic side of Irish character.

NETHERDYKE.

By R. J. CHARLETON,

Author of ' Newcastle Town,' etc.

One vol., crown 8vo., 6s.

'Netherdyke' is a romance of the rebellion of 'forty-five.' It gives a stirring and picturesque account of the adventures of Prince Charles, which will be likely to be acceptable both to boys and to all lovers of adventure.

The Sportsman's Library.

Edited by the RT. HON. SIR HERBERT MAXWELL, BART., M.P.

TWO NEW VOLUMES.

REMINISCENCES OF A HUNTSMAN.

By the HON. GRANTLEY F. BERKELEY.

With a Coloured Frontispiece and the original Illustrations by JOHN LEECH, and several Coloured Plates and other Illustrations by G. R. JALLAND.

Large 8vo., handsomely bound, 15s.   Also a Large-Paper Edition, limited to 200 copies, two guineas net.

These reminiscences, by one well known among sportsmen of his day, consist of an interesting medley of records of the chase, observations on men and manners of the time, notes on natural history, and experiences in shooting and fishing.   The author was a bit of a character, and his peculiarities are faithfully reflected in his pages.   As a master of hounds he forms a curious link with a bygone state of things, when his father hunted the whole country between Bristol and Kensington Gardens.

THE ART OF DEER-STALKING.

By WILLIAM SCROPE.

With Frontispiece by EDWIN LANDSEER, and 9 Photogravure Plates of the original Illustrations.

Large 8vo., handsomely bound, 15s.   Also a Large-Paper Edition, limited to 200 copies, two guineas net.

The author of this book, which has long been in the first rank of literature of the forest, was an example of the best kind of sportsman. A highly cultivated scholar and a painter far more accomplished than most amateurs, Scrope had a keen eye for a great deal more than the mere pursuit of game.   He filled his notebook with traditions and anecdotes collected among stalkers and gillies in an age before compulsory education had driven old-world lore out of their heads, and wove them into his treatise on deer-stalking wth great taste and literary skill.

The Sportsman's Library.

Edited by the RIGHT HON. SIR HERBERT MAXWELL, BART., M.P.

A Re-issue, in handsome volumes, of certain rare and entertaining books on sport, carefully selected by the Editor, and illustrated by the best sporting artists of the day, and with reproductions of old plates.

Library Edition, 15s. a Volume.

Large Paper Edition (limited to 200 copies), 2 guineas a volume.

The EARL OF COVENTRY writes : 'I think the idea of a "Sportsman's Library" an excellent one. So many now follow various sports that a library of the old books brought out again will be very attractive.'

Sir RALPH PAYNE-GALLWEY, Bart., writes: 'Just the class of work to be popular, whether in the shelves or lying on the smoking-room table. A pleasure to read, see, and handle.'

VOLUME I.

THE LIFE OF A FOX, AND THE DIARY OF A HUNTSMAN.

By THOMAS SMITH, Master of the Hambledon and Pytchley Hounds.

With Illustrations by the Author, and Coloured Plates by
G. H. JALLAND.

' It will be a classic of fox-hunting till the end of time.'—*Yorkshire Post.*

VOLUME II.

A SPORTING TOUR THROUGH THE NORTHERN PARTS OF ENGLAND AND GREAT PART OF THE HIGHLANDS OF SCOTLAND.

By COLONEL T. THORNTON, of Thornville Royal, in Yorkshire.

With the Original Illustrations by GARRARD, and other Illustrations and Coloured Plates by G. E. LODGE.

' Sportsmen of all descriptions will gladly welcome the sumptuous new edition issued by Mr. Edward Arnold of Colonel T. Thornton's "Sporting Tour," which has long been a scarce book.'—*Daily News.*

VOLUME III.

THE SPORTSMAN IN IRELAND.

By a COSMOPOLITE.

With Coloured Plates and Black and White Drawings by P. CHENEVIX TRENCH, and reproductions of the Original Illustrations drawn by R. ALLEN and engraved by W. WESTALL, A.R.A.

' The book is one to be read and enjoyed.'—*Saturday Review.*

Volumes of Sport, Travel and Adventure.

RECENTLY PUBLISHED.

WILD NORWAY:

With Chapters on the Swedish Highlands, Jutland, and Spitzbergen.

By ABEL CHAPMAN, Author of 'Wild Spain,' etc.

With seventeen full-page Illustrations and numerous smaller ones by the
Author and CHARLES WHYMPER.

Demy 8vo., 16s.

'There is not a chapter in this book which would not be missed.'—*Spectator.*
'A very good, very accurate, and deeply interesting book of wild life and natural history.'—*Illustrated Sporting and Dramatic News.*
'Will be read with keen interest by the angler, the hunter of wild game, and the student of bird life.'—*Scotsman.*
'It will be found not only an invaluable but a delightful companion by the sportsman, the angler, and the ornithologist.'—*Times.*

THROUGH UNKNOWN AFRICAN COUNTRIES.

The First Expedition from Somaliland to Lake Rudolf and Lamu.

A Narrative of Scientific Exploration and Sporting Adventures.

By A. DONALDSON SMITH, M.D., F.R.G.S.

With nearly thirty full-page Plates and numerous smaller Illustrations by
A. D. McCORMICK, CHARLES WHYMPER, etc., and detailed Maps
of the countries traversed.

Super royal 8vo., One Guinea net.

'Will be of the greatest interest to sportsman, traveller, and man of science.'—*Pall Mall Gazette.*
'Since the publication of Stanley's "Across the Dark Continent," there has been no work of African travel equal, in scientific importance and thrilling interest, to Dr. Donaldson Smith's book. As a book of exciting sport, apart from its geographical and ethnological usefulness, it deserves to stand alongside the best experiences of the toughest Anglo-Indian shikaris.'—*Daily Telegraph.*
'While to the large class of people interested in African exploration this book is indispensable, sportsmen will find in its pages a wealth of exciting incidents rarely equalled in similar works.'—*St. James's Gazette.*

ON VELDT AND FARM:

In Cape Colony, Bechuanaland, Natal, and the Transvaal.

By FRANCES McNAB.

With Map. Crown 8vo., 300 pages, 3s. 6d.

'Well worth the study of those interested in the agricultural and general development of South Africa.'—*Saturday Review.*
'A delightful book, and we can confidently recommend it as far more worth reading than many a work of infinitely greater pretensions. The whole work is full of interest, and is, moreover, written in a style that compels the attention of the reader.'—*Globe.*
'Abounds in interesting and useful information.'—*Daily News.*

SOLDIERING AND SURVEYING IN BRITISH EAST AFRICA, 1891-1894.

An Account of the Survey for the Uganda Railway, and the various Campaigns in the British Protectorate during the last few years.

By Major J. R. MACDONALD, R.E.

Illustrated from Sketches and Photographs by the Author and numerous Plans and a Map.

Demy 8vo., 16s.

' No country in the world has had greater need of an impartial historian than Uganda, and, strange to say, though the bitter feelings engendered by the struggles of the past ten years have not had time to cool, one has been found among the actors in these stormy scenes—Major Macdonald. . . . No one who reads this exciting book of adventure can regret that we are spending £3,000,000 on the railway. Major Macdonald writes with considerable literary and historical skill, and his sketches and maps are all excellent.'—*Pall Mall Gazette.*

' The illustrations from photographs and sketches are better than any we have seen of this part of the Dark Continent, and the maps are distinctly good.'—*Daily Chronicle.*

MEMORIES OF THE MONTHS.
Leaves from a Field Naturalist's Note-book.

By the Right Hon. Sir HERBERT MAXWELL, Bart., M.P.

Crown 8vo., with four Photogravure Illustrations, 6s.

' It is a very long time since we have read so pleasant a book as this.'—*Daily Chronicle.*
' Most agreeably and freshly written.'—*Field.*
' Few books will fill the idle moments of a country-loving man more pleasantly.'—*British Review.*
' The easy style, the graphic descriptions of bird-life, and of the ways of beasts and fishes, the clever sketches of sport, the happy introductions of plant-lore and of fragments of myth and legend, will ensure a warm welcome for this delightful volume.'—*Daily News.*

FISH TAILS AND SOME TRUE ONES.

By BRADNOCK HALL, Author of ' Rough Mischance.'

With an original Etching by the Author, and twelve full-page Illustrations by T. H. McLACHLAN.

Crown 8vo., 6s.

' This is one of the best books of angling reminiscences I have ever come across.'—*Fishing Gazette.*
' A pleasant companion for an angler's holiday.'—*Glasgow Herald.*
' Witty, in the best taste, and abounding with sympathetic interest to the angler. . . . The illustrations are exceedingly good. . . . The stories are capital, every one.'—*Field.*

Volumes of Travel, Sport, and Adventure.

Bacon—THE CITY OF BLOOD. (*See page* 3.)

Balfour—TWELVE HUNDRED MILES IN A WAGGON. A Narrative of a Journey in Cape Colony, the Transvaal, and the Chartered Company's Territories. By ALICE BLANCHE BALFOUR. With nearly forty original Illustrations from Sketches by the Author, and a Map. Demy 8vo., cloth, 16s.

Beynon—WITH KELLY TO CHITRAL. By Lieutenant W. G. L. BEYNON, D.S.O., 3rd Goorkha Rifles, Staff Officer to Colonel Kelly with the Relief Force. With Maps, Plans, and Illustrations. Demy 8vo., 7s. 6d.

Bottome — A SUNSHINE TRIP: Glimpses of the Orient. Extracts from Letters written by MARGARET BOTTOME. With Portrait, elegantly bound, 4s. 6d.

Bull—THE CRUISE OF THE 'ANTARCTIC.' To the South Polar Regions. By H. J. BULL, a member of the Expedition. With frontispiece by W. L. WYLLIE, A.R.A., and numerous full-page illustrations by W. G. BURN-MURDOCH. Demy 8vo., 15s.

Chapman—WILD NORWAY. (*See page* 11.)

Colvile—THE LAND OF THE NILE SPRINGS. By Colonel Sir HENRY COLVILE, K.C.M.G., C.B., recently British Commissioner in Uganda. With Photogravure Frontispiece, 16 full-page Illustrations and 2 Maps. Demy 8vo., 16s.

Custance—RIDING RECOLLECTIONS AND TURF STORIES. By HENRY CUSTANCE, three times winner of the Derby. One vol., crown 8vo., cloth, 2s. 6d.

Freshfield — THE EXPLORATION OF THE CAUCASUS. By DOUGLAS W. FRESHFIELD, lately President of the Alpine Club and Honorary Secretary of the Royal Geographical Society. With Contributions by H. W. HOLDER, J. G. COCKIN, H. WOOLLEY, M. DE DÉCHY, and Prof. BONNEY, D.Sc., F.R.S. Illustrated by 3 Panoramas, 74 full-page Photogravures, about 140 Illustrations in the text, chiefly from Photographs by VITTORIO SELLA, and 4 Original Maps, including the first authentic map of the Caucasus specially prepared from unpublished sources by Mr. FRESHFIELD. In two volumes, large 4to., 600 pp., Three Guineas net.

Gordon—PERSIA REVISITED. With Remarks on H.I.M. Mozuffered-Din Shah, and the Present Situation in Persia (1896). By General Sir T. E. GORDON, K.C.I.E., C.B., C.S.I. Formerly Military Attaché and Oriental Secretary to the British Legation at Teheran, Author of 'The Roof of the world,' etc. Demy 8vo., with full-page illustrations, 10s. 6d.

Hall—FISH TAILS AND SOME TRUE ONES. (*See page* 12.)

Hole—A LITTLE TOUR IN AMERICA. By the Very Rev. S. REYNOLDS HOLE, Dean of Rochester, Author of 'The Memories of Dean Hole,' 'A Book about Roses,' etc. With numerous Illustrations. Demy 8vo., 16s.

Hole—A LITTLE TOUR IN IRELAND. By 'OXONIAN' (the Very Rev. S. REYNOLDS HOLE). With nearly forty Illustrations by JOHN LEECH. Large crown 8vo., 6s.

Knight-Bruce—MEMORIES OF MASHONALAND. By the late Right Rev. Bishop KNIGHT-BRUCE, formerly Bishop of Mashonaland. 8vo., 10s. 6d.

Macdonald—SOLDIERING AND SURVEYING IN BRITISH EAST AFRICA. (*See page* 12.)

Mcnab—ON FARM AND VELDT. (*See page* 11.)

Maxwell—THE SPORTSMAN'S LIBRARY. (*See pages* 9 *and* 10.)

Maxwell—MEMORIES OF THE MONTHS. (*See page* 12.)

Pike—THROUGH THE SUB-ARCTIC FOREST. A Record of a Canoe Journey for 4,000 miles, from Fort Wrangel to the Pelly Lakes, and down the Yukon to the Behring Sea. By WARBURTON PIKE, Author of 'The Barren Grounds of Canada.' With illustrations by CHARLES WHYMPER, from Photographs taken by the Author, and a Map. Demy 8vo., 16s.

Pollok —FIFTY : YEARS' REMINISCENCES OF INDIA. By Lieut.-Colonel POLLOK, author of 'Sport in Burmah.' Illustrated by A. C. CORBOULD. Demy 8vo., 16s.

Portal—THE BRITISH MISSION TO UGANDA. By the late Sir GERALD PORTAL, K.C.M.G. Edited by RENNELL RODD, C.M.G. With an Introduction by the Right Honourable LORD CROMER, G.C.M.G. Illustrated from photos taken during the Expedition by Colonel RHODES. Demy 8vo., 21s.

Portal—MY MISSION TO ABYSSINIA. By the late Sir GERALD H. PORTAL, C.B. With Map and Illustrations. Demy 8vo., 15s.

Slatin—FIRE AND SWORD IN THE SUDAN. (*See page* 6.)

Smith—THROUGH UNKNOWN AFRICAN COUNTRIES. (*See page* 11.)

Stone—IN AND BEYOND THE HIMALAYAS : A Record of Sport and Travel. By S. J. STONE, late Deputy Inspector-General of the Punjab Police. With 16 full-page Illustrations by CHARLES WHYMPER. Demy 8vo., 16s.

AMERICAN SPORT AND TRAVEL.

These books, selected from the Catalogue of MESSRS. RAND MCNALLY & CO., *the well-known publishers of Chicago, have been placed in* MR. EDWARD ARNOLD'S *hands under the impression that many British Travellers and Sportsmen may find them useful before starting on expeditions in the United States.*

Aldrich—ARCTIC ALASKA AND SIBERIA; or, Eight Months with the Arctic Whalemen. By HERBERT L. ALDRICH. Crown 8vo., cloth, 4s. 6d.

AMERICAN GAME FISHES. Their Habits, Habitat, and Peculiarities ; How, When, and Where to Angle for them. By various Writers. Cloth, 10s. 6d.

Higgins—NEW GUIDE TO THE PACIFIC COAST. Santa Fé Route. By C. A. HIGGINS. Crown 8vo., cloth, 4s. 6d.

Leffingwell—THE ART OF WING-SHOOTING. A Practical Treatise on the Use of the Shot-gun. By W. B. LEFFINGWELL. With numerous Illustrations. Crown 8vo., cloth, 4s. 6d.

Shields—CAMPING AND CAMP OUTFITS. By G. O. SHIELDS ('Coquina'). Containing also Chapters on Camp Medicine, Cookery, and How to Load a Packhorse. Crown 8vo., cloth, 5s.

Shields—THE AMERICAN BOOK OF THE DOG. By various Writers. Edited by G. O. SHIELDS ('Coquina'). Cloth, 15s.

Thomas—SWEDEN AND THE SWEDES. By WILLIAM WIDGERY THOMAS, Jun., United States Minister to Sweden and Norway. With numerous Illustrations. Cloth, 16s.

𝔚orks of 𝔉iction.

RECENTLY PUBLISHED.

A DEVOTEE:

An Episode in the Life of a Butterfly.

By MARY CHOLMONDELEY, Author of 'Diana Tempest,' 'The Danvers Jewels,' etc.

Crown 8vo., 3s. 6d.

'The many readers and admirers of that fine novel "Diana Tempest" will welcome a new book by Miss Cholmondeley with interest and high expectation, and it is pleasant to be able to inform them that they will not be disappointed. A most original and truthful sketch.'—*Westminster Gazette.*

'Another of Miss Cholmondeley's clever social sketches from the world about her.'—*Manchester Guardian.*

'Miss Cholmondeley's sketches of young men and women belonging to fashionable society are as clever as ever.'—*Athenæum.*

'The story is written with Miss Cholmondeley's usual vigour, brilliancy, and delicacy.'—*Guardian.*

A RELUCTANT EVANGELIST,
AND OTHER STORIES.

By ALICE SPINNER,

Author of 'Lucilla,' 'A Study in Colour,' etc.

Crown 8vo., 6s.

'Good, too, is Miss Spinner's budget of short stories. "Buckra Tommie" is an exquisitely pathetic story.'—*Pall Mall Gazette.*

'Vivid and suggestive studies.'—*Spectator.*

'Remarkably clever studies of life and character.'—*Lady.*

INTERLUDES.
By MAUD OXENDEN.

Crown 8vo., 6s.

'An admirably written book. The author is to be congratulated on the strength with which she portrays men and women, and describes the passions of love or of grief that sometimes fill the mind.'—*Scotsman.*

THE BAYONET THAT CAME HOME.

By N. WYNNE WILLIAMS,

Author of 'Tales of Modern Greece.'

Crown 8vo., 3s. 6d.

'Well worth reading.'—*Liverpool Mercury.*

'Enthrals the reader to the end.'—*Manchester Courier.*

Works of Fiction.

'Adalet'—HADJIRA : A Turkish Love Story. By 'ADALET.' 1 vol.,
crown 8vo., cloth, 6s.

Adderley—STEPHEN REMARX. The Story of a Venture in Ethics.
By the Hon. and Rev. JAMES ADDERLEY, formerly Head of the Oxford House and
Christ Church Mission, Bethnal Green. Twenty-Second Thousand. Small 8vo.,
elegantly bound, 3s. 6d. Also, in paper cover, 1s.

Adderley—PAUL MERCER. (*See page* 7.)

Blatchford—TOMMY ATKINS. A Tale of the Ranks. By ROBERT
BLATCHFORD, Author of ' A Son of the Forge,' ' Merrie England,' etc. New Edition.
Crown 8vo., cloth, 3s. 6d.

Charleton—NETHERDYKE. (*See page* 8.)

Cherbuliez—THE TUTOR'S SECRET. (Le Secret du Précepteur.)
Translated from the French of VICTOR CHERBULIEZ. One vol., crown 8vo., cloth, 6s.

Cholmondeley—A DEVOTEE. By MARY CHOLMONDELEY. (*See
page* 15.)

Clifford—LOVE-LETTERS OF A WORLDLY WOMAN. By Mrs.
W. K. CLIFFORD, Author of ' Aunt Anne,' ' Mrs. Keith's Crime,' etc. One vol.,
crown 8vo., cloth, 2s. 6d.

Coleridge—THE KING WITH TWO FACES. (*See page* 8.)

Collingwood—THE BONDWOMAN. A Story of the Northmen in
Lakeland. By W. G. COLLINGWOOD, Author of ' Thorstein of the Mere,' ' The Life
and Work of John Ruskin,' etc. Cloth, 16mo., 3s. 6d.

Crane—GEORGE'S MOTHER. By STEPHEN CRANE. Author of
' The Red Badge of Courage.' Cloth, 2s.

Dunmore—ORMISDAL. A Novel. By the EARL OF DUNMORE,
F.R.G.S., Author of ' The Pamirs.' One vol., crown 8vo., cloth, 6s.

Ford—ON THE THRESHOLD. By ISABELLA O. FORD, Author of
' Miss Blake of Monkshalton.' One vol., crown 8vo., 3s. 6d.

Gaunt—DAVE'S SWEETHEART. By MARY GAUNT. One vol.,
8vo., cloth, 3s. 6d.

Hall—FISH TAILS AND SOME TRUE ONES. (*See page* 12.)

Hutchinson—THAT FIDDLER FELLOW : A Tale of St. Andrews.
By HORACE G. HUTCHINSON, Author of ' My Wife's Politics,' ' Golf,' ' Creatures
of Circumstance,' etc Crown 8vo., cloth, 2s. 6d.

Knutsford—THE MYSTERY OF THE RUE SOLY. Translated by Lady KNUTSFORD from the French of H. DE BALZAC. Crown 8vo., cloth, 3s. 6d.

McNulty—MISTHER O'RYAN. An Incident in the History of a Nation. By EDWARD McNULTY. Small 8vo., elegantly bound, 3s. 6d.

McNulty—SON OF A PEASANT. (*See page* 8.)

Montrésor—WORTH WHILE. By F. F. MONTRÉSOR, Author of ' Into the Highways and Hedges.' Crown 8vo., cloth, 2s. 6d.

Oxenden—INTERLUDES. (*See page* 15.)

Pinsent—JOB HILDRED. (*See page* 7).

Prescott—A MASK AND A MARTYR. By E. LIVINGSTON PRESCOTT, Author of ' Scarlet and Steel.' Cloth, 6s.

Spinner—A RELUCTANT EVANGELIST. (*See page* 15.)

Williams—THE BAYONET THAT CAME HOME. (*See page* 15.)

Tales of Adventure for Boys.

Clowes—THE DOUBLE EMPEROR. By W. LAIRD CLOWES, Author of 'The Great Peril,' etc. Illustrated. Crown 8vo., 3s. 6d.

Fawcett—SWALLOWED BY AN EARTHQUAKE. By E. D. FAWCETT. Illustrated. Crown 8vo., 3s. 6d.

Fawcett—HARTMANN THE ANARCHIST; or, The Doom of the Great City. By E. DOUGLAS FAWCETT. With sixteen full-page and numerous smaller Illustrations by F. T. JANE. Crown 8vo., cloth, 3s. 6d.

Fawcett—THE SECRET OF THE DESERT. By E. D. FAWCETT. With numerous full-page Illustrations. Crown 8vo., cloth, 3s. 6d.

Hervey—THE REEF OF GOLD. By MAURICE H. HERVEY. With numerous full-page Illustrations, handsomely bound. Gilt edges, 5s.

Hervey—ERIC THE ARCHER. By MAURICE H. HERVEY. With numerous full-page Illustrations. Handsomely bound, crown 8vo., 5s.

Munroe—THE FUR SEAL'S TOOTH. By KIRK MUNROE. Fully illustrated. Crown 8vo., cloth, 5s.

Munroe—SNOW-SHOES AND SLEDGES. By KIRK MUNROE. Fully illustrated. Crown 8vo., cloth, 5s.

Munroe—RICK DALE. By KIRK MUNROE. Fully illustrated. Crown 8vo., cloth, 5s.

Nash—BAREROCK; or, The Island of Pearls. By HENRY NASH. With numerous Illustrations by LANCELOT SPEED. Large crown 8vo., handsomely bound, gilt edges, 5s.

Works on Science and Philosophy.

RECENTLY PUBLISHED.

WASTED RECORDS OF DISEASE.

By CHARLES E. PAGET, Lecturer on Public Health in Owens College, Medical Officer of Health for Salford, etc.

Crown 8vo., 2s. 6d.

' We welcome Mr. Paget's attempt to indicate the lines on which efforts at reform may be successful.'—*British Medical Journal.*
' An admirable common-sense statement of the case.' —*Yorkshire Post.*
' An interesting summary of what has been done to register diseases.'—*Sanitary Journal.*
' The importance of disease registration is lucidly and ably discussed.'—*Pall Mall Gazette.*

THE RELIGIONS OF INDIA.

By E. W. HOPKINS, Ph.D. (Leipzig), Professor of Sanskrit and Comparative Philology in Bryn Mawr College.

One volume, demy 8vo., 8s. 6d. net.

' Ought to meet a very distinct want. Professor Hopkins has ample learning. He knows the sacred books as few men do. He is also an independent student and critic. . . . A valuable bibliography, with works and articles classified under subjects, and a good index should be mentioned.'—*Manchester Guardian.*

A TEXT-BOOK OF NURSING FOR HOME AND HOSPITAL USE.

By C. WEEKS SHAW.

Revised and largely re-written by W. RADFORD, House Surgeon at the Poplar Hospital, under the supervision of Sir DYCE DUCKWORTH, M.D., F.R.C.P.

Fully Illustrated, crown 8vo., 3s. 6d.

' A careful perusal of its pages has convinced us that at present the book has no equal. . . . May justly be described as a standard work of its kind, and one for which we foresee an extensive circulation.'—*Hospital.*
' The teaching in the book is modern and thoroughly practical.'—*Scottish Medical and Surgical Journal.*
' The book is invaluable alike in the home and in the hospital ward.'—*Cape Times.*
' Should be in the hands of every nurse who is anxious to qualify herself in her profession.'—*Nurses' Journal.*
' We can recommend the book to nurses and practitioners alike.'—*Lancet.*

THE CHANCES OF DEATH, AND OTHER STUDIES IN EVOLUTION.

By KARL PEARSON, F.R.S., Author of 'The Ethic of Free Thought,' etc.

In two vols., demy 8vo., with Illustrations, 25s. net.

CONTENTS OF VOL. I.—The Chances of Death—The Scientific Aspect of Monte Carlo Roulette—Reproductive Selection—Socialism and Natural Selection—Politics and Science—Reaction—Woman and Labour—Variation in Man and Woman.

CONTENTS OF VOL. II.—Woman as Witch—Ashiepattle; or, Hans seeks his Luck —Kindred Group Marriage—The German Passion Play—Index.

'We have pleasure in welcoming a new work of extreme scientific value and of deep popular interest.'—*Saturday Review.*

'Worthy of the high reputation which Mr. Pearson has already earned.'—*British Review.*

'All of these essays are well worth reading.'—*Times.*

'Full of interest as regards their subject, and of animation in point of style.'—*Daily Telegraph.*

'These brilliant volumes contain the most satisfactory work that Professor Pearson has yet done.'—*Speaker.*

HABIT AND INSTINCT.

A Study in Heredity.

By C. LLOYD MORGAN.

Author of 'Animal Life and Intelligence,' 'The Springs of Conduct,' etc.

Demy 8vo., 16s.

'A valuable book on a fascinating subject.'—*Times.*

'An exceedingly interesting volume.'—*British Review.*

'It is a book that no one interested in the larger problem of existence can afford to neglect.'—*Academy.*

'An admirable introduction to the study of a most important and fascinating branch of biology.'—PROFESSOR A. R. WALLACE in *Natural Science.*

THE CALCULUS FOR ENGINEERS.

By Prof. JOHN PERRY, F.R.S.

Crown 8vo., 380 pp., cloth, 7s. 6d.

'A great diversity of most instructive exercises are suggested.. . . . A good index enhances the value of the book. . . . The author has been successful in retaining all that liveliness and originality of illustration which distinguishes him as a lecturer.'—*Electrician.*

'Elle mérite tous les éloges.'—M. ALIAMET in *L'Electrician.*

Bryan—THE MARK IN EUROPE AND AMERICA. A Review of the Discussion on Early Land Tenure. By ENOCH A. BRYAN, A.M., President of Vincennes University, Indiana. Crown 8vo., cloth, 4s. 6d.

Burgess—POLITICAL SCIENCE AND COMPARATIVE CONSTITUTIONAL LAW. By JOHN W. BURGESS, Ph.D., LL.D., Dean of the University Faculty of Political Science in Columbia College, U.S.A. In two volumes, demy 8vo., cloth, 25s.

Fawcett—THE RIDDLE OF THE UNIVERSE. Being an Attempt to determine the First Principles of Metaphysics considered as an Inquiry into the Conditions and Import of Consciousness. By EDWARD DOUGLAS FAWCETT. One vol., demy 8vo., 14s.

Hopkins—THE RELIGIONS OF INDIA. *(See page* 18.)

Ladd—LOTZE'S PHILOSOPHICAL OUTLINES. Dictated Portions of the Latest Lectures (at Göttingen and Berlin) of Hermann Lotze. Translated and edited by GEORGE T. LADD, Professor of Philosophy in Yale College. About 180 pages in each volume. Crown 8vo., cloth, 4s. each. Vol. I. Metaphysics. Vol. II. Philosophy of Religion. Vol. III. Practical Philosophy. Vol. IV. Psychology. Vol. V. Æsthetics. Vol. VI. Logic.

THE JOURNAL OF MORPHOLOGY. Edited by C. O. WHITMAN, Professor of Biology in Clark University, U.S.A. Three numbers in a volume of 100 to 150 large 4to. pages, with numerous plates. Single numbers, 17s. 6d. ; subscription to the volume of three numbers, 45s. Volumes I. to XII. can now be obtained, and the first number of Volume XIII. is ready.

Morgan—ANIMAL LIFE AND INTELLIGENCE. By Professor C. LLOYD MORGAN, F.G.S., Principal of University College, Bristol. With 40 Illustrations and a Photo-etched Frontispiece. Second Edition. Demy 8vo., cloth, 16s.

Morgan—HABIT AND INSTINCT. *(See page* 19.)

Morgan—THE SPRINGS OF CONDUCT. By Professor C. LLOYD MORGAN, F.G.S. Cheaper Edition. Large crown 8vo., 3s. 6d.

Morgan—PSYCHOLOGY FOR TEACHERS. By Professor C. LLOYD MORGAN, F.G.S. With a Preface by J. G. FITCH, M.A., LL.D., late one of H.M. Chief Inspectors of Training Colleges. One vol., crown 8vo., cloth, 3s. 6d. net.

Paget—WASTED RECORDS OF DISEASE. *(See page* 18.)

Pearson—THE CHANCES OF DEATH. *(See page* 19.)

Perry—CALCULUS FOR ENGINEERS. *(See page* 19.)

THE PHILOSOPHICAL REVIEW. Edited by J. G. SCHURMAN, Professor of Philosophy in Cornell University, U.S.A. Six Numbers a year. Single Numbers, 3s. 6d. ; Annual Subscription, 14s. post free. The first number was issued in January, 1892.

Shaw—A TEXT-BOOK OF NURSING. *(See page* 18.)

Young—A GENERAL ASTRONOMY. By CHARLES A. YOUNG, Professor of Astronomy in the College of New Jersey, Associate of the Royal Astronomical Society, Author of *The Sun*, etc. In one vol., 550 pages, with 250 Illustrations, and supplemented with the necessary tables. Royal 8vo., half morocco, 12s. 6d.

Works in General Literature.

RECENTLY PUBLISHED.

A TREASURY OF MINOR BRITISH POETRY.

Selected and Arranged, with Notes, by J. CHURTON
COLLINS, M.A.

Handsomely bound, crown 8vo., 7s. 6d.

' The idea is an admirable one, and it has been admirably carried out. The book is a valuable contribution to poetical literature.'—*Manchester Guardian.*
' A choice and beautiful book.'—*Standard.*
' Few, if any, living critics have a knowledge of English literature so accurate and exhaustive as Mr. Churton Collins. When we take up an anthology compiled by him, we may be sure that no poem has been omitted from ignorance of its existence. . . . It contains an abundance of most interesting verse.'—*Saturday Review.*
' In this handsome volume Mr. Collins has undoubtedly succeeded in presenting to readers many exquisite poems for which they would search in vain in other collections.'—*Academy.*

THE TREATMENT OF NATURE IN DANTE'S 'DIVINA COMMEDIA.'

By L. OSCAR KUHNS.

Professor in Wesleyan University, Middleton, U.S.A.

Crown 8vo., cloth, 5s.

' Should it fall into the hands of a student in the early stages of his acquaintance with Dante, it will delight and amaze him by the scope, the variety, and the minuteness of the references to natural objects and phenomena which it records.'—*Manchester Guardian.*
' Critical and erudite . . . a valuable commentary.'—*Pall Mall Gazette.*

A BOOK ABOUT ROSES.

By the Very Rev. S. REYNOLDS HOLE, Dean of Rochester.

Author of 'A Book about the Garden,' 'A Little Tour in Ireland.'

Illustrated by H. G. Moon and G. Elgood.

The Presentation Edition, with coloured plates, etc., handsomely bound,
10s. 6d. ; Popular Edition, with frontispiece, 3s. 6d.

The call for a fifteenth edition of this popular work enabled Dean Hole to thoroughly revise and largely to rewrite the book, bringing the information in it well up to date. Advantage has also been taken of the opportunity to respond to the frequently expressed wishes of many admirers of the book for a more handsome and illustrated edition ; it has therefore been reprinted, and beautifully Coloured Plates have been drawn by Mr. H. G. Moon, while Mr. G Elgood contributes charming black-and-white pictures. There is also a facsimile of a sketch by John Leech given to Dean Hole, and never before published.

THE BEGGARS OF PARIS.

Translated from the French of M. LOUIS PAULIAN.
By Lady HERSCHELL.

Crown 8vo., paper boards, 192 pages, 1s.

Not only contains a great many amusing and instructive anecdotes, but formulates a definite scheme for the entire suppression of begging as a trade. Lady Herschell's excellent translation should be read by all who are interested in the vexed question of charity-giving, and even to those who read but for amusement it will prove vastly interesting.'—*Times.*

'One of the most interesting books which have appeared during recent years on the subject of mendicancy.'—*National Observer.*

'Lady Herschell's translation is worthy of M. Paulian's interesting manner.'—*Pall Mall Gazette.*

'A fascinating book.'—*Spectator.*

WAGNER'S HEROINES:
BRUNHILDA—SENTA—ISOLDA.

By CONSTANCE MAUD,
Author of 'Wagner's Heroes.'

Illustrated by J. W. MAUD.   Crown 8vo., 5s.

'Miss Maud's poetical and successful attempt at embodying the fantasies of Wagner in the form of tales. . . . She has made a clear advance in her second volume. . . . This is, in fine, really a beautiful casket of stories.'—*Spectator.*

'The volume is capitally illustrated by some really beautiful drawings from the pencil of Mr. W. T. Maud.'—*Westminster Gazette.*

'We recommend everyone who likes moving and lovely stories to read them.'—*Saturday Review.*

THE PLANT-LORE AND GARDEN-CRAFT OF SHAKESPEARE.

By HENRY N. ELLACOMBE, M.A., Vicar of Bitton,
Author of 'In a Gloucestershire Garden,' etc.

Fully Illustrated by Major E. BENGOUGH RICKETTS.

Large Crown 8vo., handsomely bound, 10s. 6d.

'A very useful work. We find an account of all the plants mentioned in Shakespeare, and quotations of all the passages in which such mention is made.'—*Saturday Review.*

'Mr. Ellacombe has produced a fascinating book.'—*Church Times.*

THE GOSPEL THE POWER OF GOD, AND OTHER SERMONS.

By CHARLES D. BELL, D.D., Honorary Canon of Carlisle.

Crown 8vo., cloth, 3s. 6d.

'A good example of the sound, old-fashioned Evangelical Churchmanship.'—*Guardian.*

Aglen—OLD TESTAMENT HISTORY. (*See page* 5.)

Bell—DIANA'S LOOKING GLASS, and other Poems. By the Rev. CANON BELL, D.D., Rector of Cheltenham, and Hon. Canon of Carlisle. Crown 8vo., cloth, 5s. net.

Bell—POEMS OLD AND NEW. By the Rev. CANON BELL, D.D. Cloth, 7s. 6d.

Bell—THE NAME ABOVE EVERY NAME, and other Sermons. By the Rev. CANON BELL, D.D. Cloth, 5s.

Bell—THE GOSPEL AND POWER OF GOD. (*See page* 22.)

Bell—KLEINES HAUSTHEATER. Fifteen Little Plays in German for Children. By Mrs. HUGH BELL. Crown 8vo., cloth, 2s.

Most of these little plays have been adapted from the author's 'Petit Théâtre,' the remainder from a little book of English plays by the same writer entitled 'Nursery Comedies.'

Butler—SELECT ESSAYS OF SAINTE BEUVE. Chiefly bearing on English Literature. Translated by A. J. BUTLER, Translator of 'The Memoirs of Baron Marbot.' One vol., 8vo., cloth, 5s. net.

Clouston—EARLY ENGLISH FURNITURE. (*See page* 5.)

Collingwood—THORSTEIN OF THE MERE : a Saga of the Northmen in Lakeland. By W. G. COLLINGWOOD, Author of 'Life of John Ruskin,' etc. With Illustrations. Price 10s. 6d.

Collins—A TREASURY OF MINOR BRITISH POETRY. (*See page* 21.)

Cook—THE DEFENSE OF POESY, otherwise known as An APOLOGY FOR POETRY. By Sir PHILIP SIDNEY. Edited by A. S. COOK, Professor of English Literature in Yale University. Crown 8vo., cloth, 4s. 6d.

Cook—A DEFENCE OF POETRY. By PERCY BYSSHE SHELLEY. Edited, with notes and introduction, by Professor A. S. COOK. Crown 8vo., cloth, 2s. 6d.

Davidson—A HANDBOOK TO DANTE. By GIOVANNI A. SCARTAZZINI. Translated from the Italian, with notes and additions, by THOMAS DAVIDSON, M.A. Crown 8vo., cloth, 6s.

Ellacombe—THE PLANT-LORE AND GARDEN-CRAFT OF SHAKESPEARE. (*See page* 22.)

Fleming—THE ART OF READING AND SPEAKING. By the Rev. Canon FLEMING, Vicar of St. Michael's, Chester Square. Third edition. Cloth, 3s. 6d.

Garnett—SELECTIONS IN ENGLISH PROSE FROM ELIZABETH TO VICTORIA. Chosen and arranged by JAMES M. GARNETT, M.A., LL.D. 700 pages, large crown 8vo., cloth, 7s. 6d.

Goschen — THE CULTIVATION AND USE OF IMAGINATION. By the Right Hon. GEORGE JOACHIM GOSCHEN. Crown 8vo., cloth, 2s. 6d.

GREAT PUBLIC SCHOOLS. ETON — HARROW — WINCHESTER — RUGBY — WESTMINSTER — MARLBOROUGH — CHELTENHAM — HAILEYBURY — CLIFTON — CHARTERHOUSE. With nearly 100 Illustrations by the best artists. Cheaper edition. One vol., large imperial 16mo., handsomely bound, 3s. 6d.

Gummere—OLD ENGLISH BALLADS. Selected and Edited by FRANCIS B. GUMMERE, Professor of English in Haverford College, U.S.A. Crown 8vo., cloth, 5s. 6d.

Harrison—STUDIES IN EARLY VICTORIAN LITERATURE. By
FREDERIC HARRISON, M.A., Author of 'The Choice of Books,' etc. New and
Cheaper Edition, large crown 8vo., cloth, 3s. 6d.

Hartshorne—OLD ENGLISH GLASSES. (*See page* 1.)

Herschell—THE BEGGARS OF PARIS. (*See page* 22.)

**Hole—ADDRESSES TO WORKING MEN FROM PULPIT AND
PLATFORM.** By the Very Rev. S. REYNOLDS HOLE, Dean of Rochester. One vol.,
crown 8vo., 6s.

**Hudson—THE LIFE, ART, AND CHARACTERS OF SHAKE-
SPEARE.** By HENRY N. HUDSON, LL.D., Editor of *The Harvard Shakespeare*,
etc. 969 pages, in two vols., large crown 8vo., cloth, 21s.

**Hudson — THE HARVARD EDITION OF SHAKESPEARE'S
COMPLETE WORKS.** A fine Library Edition. By HENRY N. HUDSON,
LL.D., Author of 'The Life, Art, and Characters of Shakespeare.' In twenty volumes,
large crown 8vo., cloth, £6. Also in ten volumes, £5.

Hunt—Leigh Hunt's 'WHAT IS POETRY?' An Answer to the
Question, 'What is Poetry?' including Remarks on Versification. By LEIGH HUNT.
Edited, with notes, by Professor A. S. COOK. Crown 8vo., cloth, 2s. 6d.

Lang—LAMB'S ADVENTURES OF ULYSSES. With an Intro-
duction by ANDREW LANG. Square 8vo., cloth, 1s. 6d. Also the Prize Edition, gilt
edges, 2s.

Maud—WAGNER'S HEROES. Parsifal—Tannhauser—Lohengrin—
Hans Sachs. By CONSTANCE MAUD. Illustrated by H. GRANVILLE FELL. Second
Edition, crown 8vo., 5s.

Maud—WAGNER'S HEROINES. (*See page* 22.)

Morrison—LIFE'S PRESCRIPTION, In Seven Doses. By D.
MACLAREN MORRISON. Crown 8vo., parchment, 1s. 6d.

Raleigh—STYLE. (*See page* 4.)

Rodd—FEDA. and other Poems, chiefly Lyrical. By RENNELL
RODD, C.M.G. With etched Frontispiece. Crown 8vo., cloth, 6s.

Rodd—THE UNKNOWN MADONNA, and other Poems. By
RENNELL RODD, C.M.G. With Frontispiece by RICHMOND. Crown 8vo., cloth, 5s.

Rodd—THE VIOLET CROWN, AND SONGS OF ENGLAND. By
RENNELL RODD, C.M.G. With Photogravure Frontispiece. Crown 8vo., cloth, 5s.

Rodd—THE CUSTOMS AND LORE OF MODERN GREECE. By
RENNELL RODD, C.M.G. With 7 full-page Illustrations. 8vo., cloth, 8s. 6d.

Rodd—BALLADS OF THE FLEET. (*See page* 5.)

Schelling—A BOOK OF ELIZABETHAN LYRICS. Selected and
Edited by F. E. SCHELLING, Professor of English Literature in the University of
Pennsylvania. Crown 8vo., cloth, 5s. 6d.

Schelling—BEN JONSON'S TIMBER. Edited by Professor F. E.
SCHELLING. Crown 8vo., cloth, 4s

Sichel—THE STORY OF TWO SALONS. Madame de Beaumont
and the Suards. By EDITH SICHEL, Author of 'Worthington Junior.' With Illustrations. Large crown 8vo., cloth, 10s. 6d.

Thayer—THE BEST ELIZABETHAN PLAYS. Edited, with an
Introduction, by WILLIAM R. THAYER. 612 pages, large crown 8vo., cloth, 7s. 6d.

WINCHESTER COLLEGE. Illustrated by HERBERT MARSHALL.
With Contributions in Prose and Verse by OLD WYKEHAMISTS. Demy 4to., cloth,
25s. net. A few copies of the first edition, limited to 1,000 copies, are still to be had.

Works of History and Biography.

Benson and Tatham—MEN OF MIGHT. Studies of Great Characters. By A. C. BENSON, M.A., and H. F. W. TATHAM, M.A., Assistant Masters at Eton College. Second Edition. Crown 8vo., cloth, 3s. 6d.

Boyle—THE RECOLLECTIONS OF THE DEAN OF SALISBURY. By the Very Rev. G. D. BOYLE, Dean of Salisbury. With Photogravure Portrait. 1 vol., demy 8vo., cloth, 16s.

Cawston and Keane—THE EARLY CHARTERED COMPANIES. A.D. 1296-1858. By GEORGE CAWSTON, barrister-at-law, and A. H. KEANE, F.R.G.S. Large crown 8vo., with Frontispiece, 10s. 6d.

Clough—MEMOIRS OF ANNE CLOUGH. (*See page* 3.)

De Vere—RECOLLECTIONS OF AUBREY DE VERE. (*See page* 2.)

Fowler—ECHOES OF OLD COUNTY LIFE. By J. K. FOWLER, of Aylesbury. Second Edition, with numerous Illustrations, 8vo., 10s. 6d. Also a Large-paper edition, of 200 copies only, 21s. net.

Gardner—ROME : THE MIDDLE OF THE WORLD. (*See page* 4.)

Gardner—FRIENDS OF THE OLDEN TIME. (*See page* 28.)

Hare—MARIA EDGEWORTH : her Life and Letters. Edited by AUGUSTUS J. C. HARE, Author of 'The Story of Two Noble Lives,' etc. Two vols., crown 8vo., with Portraits, 16s. net.

Hole—THE MEMORIES OF DEAN HOLE. By the Very Rev. S. REYNOLDS HOLE, Dean of Rochester. With the original Illustrations from sketches by LEECH and THACKERAY. Twelfth thousand, crown 8vo., 6s.

Hole—MORE MEMORIES : Being Thoughts about England Spoken in America. By the Very Rev. S. REYNOLDS HOLE, Dean of Rochester. With Frontispiece. Demy 8vo., 16s.

Kay—OMARAH'S HISTORY OF YAMAN. The Arabic Text, edited, with a translation, by HENRY CASSELS KAY, Member of the Royal Asiatic Society. Demy 8vo., cloth, 17s. 6d. net.

Lecky—THE POLITICAL VALUE OF HISTORY. By W. E. H. LECKY, D.C.L., LL.D. An Address delivered at the Midland Institute, reprinted with additions. Crown 8vo., cloth, 2s. 6d.

Le Fanu—SEVENTY YEARS OF IRISH LIFE. By the late W. R. LE FANU. New and Popular Edition. Crown 8vo., 6s.

Macdonald—THE MEMOIRS OF THE LATE SIR JOHN A. MACDONALD, G.C.B., First Prime Minister of Canada. Edited by JOSEPH POPE, his Private Secretary. With Portraits. Two vols., demy 8vo., 32s.

Milner—ENGLAND IN EGYPT. By Sir ALFRED MILNER, K.C.B., Governor of Cape Colony and High Commissioner to South Africa. Popular Edition, with Map, and full details of the British position and responsibilities, 7s. 6d.

Milner—ARNOLD TOYNBEE. A Reminiscence. By Sir ALFRED
MILNER, K.C.B., Author of.' England in Egypt.' Crown 8vo., paper, 1s.

Oman—A HISTORY OF ENGLAND. By CHARLES OMAN, Fellow
of All Souls' College, and Lecturer in History at New College, Oxford; Author of
' Warwick the Kingmaker,' ' A History of Greece,' etc. Crown 8vo., cloth, 5s.
Also in two parts, 3s. each. Part I., to A.D. 1603; Part II., from 1603 to present time.

Pilkington—IN AN ETON PLAYING FIELD. The Adventures
of some old Public School Boys in East London. By E. M. S. PILKINGTON. Fcap.
8vo., handsomely bound, 2s. 6d.

Pulitzer—THE ROMANCE OF PRINCE EUGENE. An Idyll under
Napoleon the First. By ALBERT PULITZER. With numerous Photogravure
Illustrations. Two vols., demy 8vo., 21s.

Raleigh—ROBERT LOUIS STEVENSON. By WALTER RALEIGH,
Professor of English Literature at Liverpool University College. Second edition.
Crown 8vo., cloth 2s. 6d.

Ransome—THE BATTLES OF FREDERICK THE GREAT. Ex-
tracted from Carlyle's ' History of Frederick the Great,' and edited by CYRIL
RANSOME, M.A., Professor of History at the Yorkshire College, Leeds. With
numerous Illustrations by ADOLPH MENZEL. Square 8vo., 3s. 6d.

Rochefort—THE ADVENTURES OF MY LIFE. By HENRI
ROCHEFORT. Second Edition. Two vols., large crown 8vo., 25s.

Roebuck—AUTOBIOGRAPHY AND LETTERS. (*See page 2.*)

Santley—STUDENT AND SINGER. The Reminiscences of
CHARLES SANTLEY. New Edition. Crown 8vo., cloth, 6s.

Sherard—ALPHONSE DAUDET: a Biography and Critical Study.
By R. H. SHERARD, Editor of ' The Memoirs of Baron Meneval,' etc. With Illustrations. Demy 8vo., 15s.

Tollemache—BENJAMIN JOWETT, Master of Balliol. A
Personal Memoir. By the Hon. LIONEL TOLLEMACHE, Author of ' Safe Studies,' etc.
Third Edition, with portrait. Crown 8vo., cloth, 3s. 6d.

Twining—RECOLLECTIONS OF LIFE AND WORK. Being
the Autobiography of LOUISA TWINING. One vol., 8vo., cloth, 15s.

Practical Science Manuals.

GENERAL EDITOR: PROFESSOR RAPHAEL MELDOLA, F.R.S.

STEAM BOILERS. By GEORGE HALLIDAY, late Demonstrator at the
Finsbury Technical College. With numerous Diagrams and Illustrations. Crown
8vo., 400 pages, 7s. 6d. [*Ready.*

AGRICULTURAL CHEMISTRY. By T. S. DYMOND, of the County
Technical Laboratory, Chelmsford. [*In preparation.*

ELECTRIC TRACTION. By ERNEST WILSON, Wh. Sc., M.I.E.E.,
Lecturer and Demonstrator in the Siemen's Laboratory, King's College, London.
[*In preparation.*

Works upon Country Life and Pastimes.

Brown—PLEASURABLE POULTRY-KEEPING. By E. BROWN, F.L.S. Fully illustrated. One vol., crown 8vo., cloth, 2s. 6d.

Brown—POULTRY-KEEPING AS AN INDUSTRY FOR FARMERS AND COTTAGERS. By EDWARD BROWN. Fully illustrated. Second edition. Demy 4to., cloth, 6s.

Brown—INDUSTRIAL POULTRY-KEEPING. By EDWARD BROWN. Illustrated. Paper boards, 1s. A small handbook chiefly intended for cottagers and allotment-holders.

Brown—POULTRY FATTENING. By E. BROWN, F.L.S. Fully illustrated. New Edition. Crown 8vo., 1s. 6d.

Clouston.—EARLY ENGLISH FURNITURE. (*See page 5.*)

Cunningham—THE DRAUGHTS POCKET MANUAL. By J. G. CUNNINGHAM. An Introduction to the Game in all its branches. Small 8vo., with numerous diagrams, 2s. 6d.

Ellacombe—IN A GLOUCESTERSHIRE GARDEN. By the Rev. H. N. ELLACOMBE, Vicar of Bitton, and Honorary Canon of Bristol. Author of ' Plant Lore and Garden Craft of Shakespeare.' With new illustrations by Major E. B. RICKETTS. Second Edition. Crown 8vo., cloth, 6s.

Gossip—THE CHESS POCKET MANUAL. By G. H. D. GOSSIP. A Pocket Guide, with numerous Specimen Games and Illustrations. Small 8vo., 2s. 6d.

Hartshorne—OLD ENGLISH GLASSES. (*See page 1.*)

Hole—A BOOK ABOUT THE GARDEN AND THE GARDENER. By the Very Rev. S. REYNOLDS HOLE, Dean of Rochester. Second edition. Crown 8vo., 6s.

Hole—A BOOK ABOUT ROSES. (*See page 21.*)

Holt—FANCY DRESSES DESCRIBED. By ARDERN HOLT. An Alphabetical Dictionary of Fancy Costumes. With full accounts of the Dresses. About 60 Illustrations by LILLIAN YOUNG. Many of them coloured. One vol., demy 8vo., 7s. 6d. net.

Kenney - Herbert — FIFTY BREAKFASTS : containing a great variety of New and Simple Recipes for Breakfast Dishes. By Colonel KENNEY-HERBERT (' Wyvern '). Small 8vo., 2s. 6d.

Kenney - Herbert — FIFTY DINNERS. By Colonel KENNEY-HERBERT. Small 8vo., cloth, 2s. 6d.

Kenney - Herbert — FIFTY LUNCHES. By Colonel KENNEY-HERBERT. Small 8vo., cloth, 2s. 6d.

Kenney-Herbert—FIFTY SUPPERS. (*See page 4.*)

Kenney - Herbert — COMMON - SENSE COOKERY : based on Modern English and Continental Principles, Worked out in Detail. By Colonel A. KENNEY-HERBERT (' Wyvern '). Large crown 8vo., over 500 pp., 7s. 6d.

Shorland—CYCLING FOR HEALTH AND PLEASURE. By L. H. PORTER, Author of ' Wheels and Wheeling,' etc. Revised and edited by F. W. SHORLAND, Amateur Champion 1892-93-94. With numerous Illustrations, small 8vo., 1s.

White—PLEASURABLE BEE-KEEPING. By C. N. WHITE, Lecturer to the County Councils of Huntingdon, Cambridgeshire, etc. Fully illustrated. One vol., crown 8vo., cloth, 2s. 6d.

WILD FLOWERS IN ART AND NATURE. By J. C. L. SPARKES, Principal of the National Art Training School, South Kensington, and F. W. BURBIDGE, Curator of the University Botanical Gardens, Dublin. With 21 Full-page Coloured Plates by H. G. MOON. Royal 4to., handsomely bound, gilt edges, 21s.

Books for the Young.

FIVE SHILLINGS EACH.

SNOW-SHOES AND SLEDGES. By KIRK MUNROE. Fully illustrated. Crown 8vo., cloth, 5s.

RICK DALE. By KIRK MUNROE. Fully illustrated. Crown 8vo., cloth, 5s.

ERIC THE ARCHER. By MAURICE H. HERVEY. With numerous full-page Illustrations. Handsomely bound, crown 8vo., 5s.

THE FUR SEAL'S TOOTH. By KIRK MUNROE. Fully illustrated. Crown 8vo., cloth, 5s.

HOW DICK AND MOLLY WENT ROUND THE WORLD. By M. H. CORNWALL LEGH. With numerous Illustrations. Foolscap 4to., cloth, 5s.

HOW DICK AND MOLLY SAW ENGLAND. By M. H. CORNWALL LEGH. With numerous Illustrations. Foolscap 4to., 5s.

DR. GILBERT'S DAUGHTERS. By MARGARET HARRIET MATHEWS. Illustrated by CHRIS. HAMMOND. Crown 8vo., cloth, 5s.

THE REEF OF GOLD. By MAURICE H. HERVEY. With numerous full-page Illustrations, handsomely bound. Gilt edges, 5s.

BAREROCK; or, The Island of Pearls. By HENRY NASH. With numerous Illustrations by LANCELOT SPEED. Large crown 8vo., handsomely bound, gilt edges, 5s.

THREE SHILLINGS AND SIXPENCE EACH.

TALES FROM HANS ANDERSEN. With nearly 40 Original Illustrations by E. A. LEMANN. Small 4to., handsomely bound in cloth, 3s. 6d.

THE SNOW QUEEN, and other Tales. By HANS CHRISTIAN ANDERSEN. Beautifully illustrated by Miss E. A. LEMANN. Small 4to., handsomely bound, 3s. 6d.

HUNTERS THREE. By THOMAS W. KNOX, Author of 'The Boy Travellers,' etc. With numerous Illustrations. Crown 8vo., cloth, 3s. 6d.

THE SECRET OF THE DESERT. By E. D. FAWCETT. With numerous full-page Illustrations. Crown 8vo., cloth, 3s. 6d.

JOEL: A BOY OF GALILEE. By ANNIE FELLOWS JOHNSTON. With ten full-page Illustrations. Crown 8vo., cloth, 3s. 6d.

THE MUSHROOM CAVE. By EVELYN RAYMOND. With Illustrations. Crown 8vo., cloth, 3s. 6d.

THE DOUBLE EMPEROR. By W. LAIRD CLOWES, Author of 'The Great Peril,' etc. Illustrated. Crown 8vo., 3s. 6d.

SWALLOWED BY AN EARTHQUAKE. By E. D. FAWCETT. Illustrated. Crown 8vo., 3s. 6d.

HARTMANN THE ANARCHIST; or, The Doom of the Great City. By E. DOUGLAS FAWCETT. With sixteen full-page and numerous smaller Illustrations by F. T. JANE. Crown 8vo., cloth, 3s. 6d.

ANIMAL SKETCHES: a Popular Book of Natural History. By Professor C. LLOYD MORGAN, F.G.S. Crown 8vo., cloth, 3s. 6d.

TWO SHILLINGS EACH.

THE CHILDREN'S FAVOURITE SERIES. A Charming Series of Juvenile Books, each plentifully Illustrated, and written in simple language to please young readers. Price 2s. each; or, gilt edges, 2s. 6d.

My Book of Wonders.
My Book of Travel Stories.
My Book of Adventures.
My Book of the Sea.
My Book of Fables.
Deeds of Gold.
My Book of Heroism.

My Book of Perils.
My Book of Fairy Tales.
My Book of History Tales.
My Story Book of Animals.
Rhymes for You and Me.
My Book of Inventions.

ONE SHILLING AND SIXPENCE EACH.

The Children's Hour Series.

All with Full-page Illustrations.

THE PALACE ON THE MOOR. By E. DAVENPORT ADAMS. 1s. 6d.

TOBY'S PROMISE. By A. M. HOPKINSON. 1s. 6d.

MASTER MAGNUS. By Mrs. E. M. Field. 1s. 6d.

MY DOG PLATO. By M. H. CORNWALL LEGH. 1s. 6d.

FRIENDS OF THE OLDEN TIME. By ALICE GARDNER, Lecturer in History at Newnham College, Cambridge. Second Edition. Illustrated. Square 8vo., 2s. 6d.

THE INTERNATIONAL EDUCATION SERIES.

THE INTELLECTUAL AND MORAL DEVELOPMENT OF THE CHILD. By GABRIEL CAMPAYRE. 6s.

TEACHING THE LANGUAGE-ARTS. Speech, Reading, Composition. By B. A. HINSDALE, Ph.D., LL.D., University of Michigan. 4s. 6d.

THE PSYCHOLOGY OF THE NUMBER, AND ITS APPLICATION TO METHODS OF TEACHING ARITHMETIC. By JAMES A. McLELLAN, A.M., and JOHN DEWEY, Ph.D. 6s.

THE SONGS AND MUSIC OF FROEBEL'S MOTHER PLAY. By SUSAN E. BLOW. 6s.

THE MOTTOES AND COMMENTARIES OF FROEBEL'S MOTHER PLAY. By SUSAN E. BLOW and H. R. ELIOT. 6s.

HOW TO STUDY AND TEACH HISTORY. By B. A. HINSDALE, Ph.D., LL.D. 6s.

FROEBEL'S PEDAGOGICS OF THE KINDERGARTEN; or, His Ideas concerning the Play and Playthings of the Child. Translated by J. JARVIS. Crown 8vo., cloth, 6s.

THE EDUCATION OF THE GREEK PEOPLE, AND ITS INFLUENCE ON CIVILIZATION. By THOMAS DAVIDSON. Crown 8vo., cloth, 6s.

SYSTEMATIC SCIENCE TEACHING. By EDWARD G. HOWE. Crown 8vo., cloth, 6s.

EVOLUTION OF THE PUBLIC SCHOOL SYSTEM IN MASSACHUSETTS. By GEORGE H. MARTIN. Crown 8vo., cloth, 6s.

THE INFANT MIND; or, Mental Development in the Child. Translated from the German of W. PREYER, Professor of Physiology in the University of Jena. Crown 8vo., cloth, 4s. 6d.

ENGLISH EDUCATION IN THE ELEMENTARY AND SECONDARY SCHOOLS. By ISAAC SHARPLESS, LL.D., President of Haverford College, U.S.A. Crown 8vo., cloth, 4s. 6d.

EMILE; or, A Treatise on Education. By JEAN JACQUES ROUSSEAU. Translated and Edited by W. H. PAYNE, Ph.D., LL.D., President of the Peabody Normal College, U.S.A. Crown 8vo., cloth, 6s.

EDUCATION FROM A NATIONAL STANDPOINT. Translated from the French of ALFRED FOUILLÉE by W. J. GREENSTREET, M.A., Head Master of the Marling School, Stroud. Crown 8vo., cloth, 7s. 6d.

THE MORAL INSTRUCTION OF CHILDREN. By FELIX ADLER, President of the Ethical Society of New York. Crown 8vo., cloth, 6s.

THE PHILOSOPHY OF EDUCATION. By JOHANN KARL ROSENKRANZ, Doctor of Theology and Professor of Philosophy at Königsberg. (Translated.) Crown 8vo., cloth, 6s.

A HISTORY OF EDUCATION. By Professor F. V. N. PAINTER. 6s.

THE VENTILATION AND WARMING OF SCHOOL BUILDINGS. With Plans and Diagrams. By GILBERT B. MORRISON. Crown 8vo., 4s. 6d.

FROEBEL'S 'EDUCATION OF MAN.' Translated by W. N. HAILMAN. Crown 8vo., 6s.

ELEMENTARY PSYCHOLOGY AND EDUCATION. By Dr. J. BALDWIN. Illustrated, crown 8vo., 6s.

THE SENSES AND THE WILL. Forming Part I. of 'The Mind of the Child.' By W. PREYER, Professor of Physiology in the University of Jena. (Translated.) Crown 8vo., 6s.

THE DEVELOPMENT OF THE INTELLECT. Forming Part II. of 'The Mind of the Child.' By Professor W. PREYER. (Translated.) Crown 8vo., 6s.

HOW TO STUDY GEOGRAPHY. By FRANCIS W. PARKER. 6s.

A HISTORY OF EDUCATION IN THE UNITED STATES. By RICHARD A. BOONE, Professor of Pedagogy in Indiana University. Crown 8vo., 6s.

EUROPEAN SCHOOLS; or, What I Saw in the Schools of Germany, France, Austria, and Switzerland. By L. R. KLEMM, Ph.D. With numerous Illustrations. Crown 8vo., 8s. 6d.

PRACTICAL HINTS FOR TEACHERS. By GEORGE HOWLAND, Superintendent of the Chicago Schools. Crown 8vo., 4s. 6d.

SCHOOL SUPERVISION. By J. L. PICKARD. 4s. 6d.

HIGHER EDUCATION OF WOMEN IN EUROPE. By HELENE LANGE. 4s. 6d.

HERBART'S TEXT-BOOK IN PSYCHOLOGY. By M. K. SMITH. 4s. 6d.

PSYCHOLOGY APPLIED TO THE ART OF TEACHING. By Dr. J. BALDWIN. 6s.

THE SCHOOL SYSTEM OF ONTARIO. By the Hon. GEORGE W. ROSS, LL.D. 4s. 6d.

FROEBEL'S EDUCATIONAL LAWS FOR ALL TEACHERS. By JAMES L. HUGHES. 6s.

SCHOOL MANAGEMENT AND SCHOOL METHODS. By Dr. J. BALDWIN. 6s.

THE NATIONAL REVIEW.

Edited by L. J. MAXSE.

Price Half-a-crown Monthly.

The 'National Review' is the leading Unionist and Conservative Review in Great Britain. Since it passed into the control and editorship of Mr. Leo Maxse, most of the leaders of the Unionist Party have contributed to its pages, including the Marquis of Salisbury, Mr. Arthur Balfour, Mr. J. Chamberlain, and Lord George Hamilton. The episodes of the month, which give a masterly review of the important events of the preceding month, form a valuable feature of the Review, which now occupies a unique position among monthly periodicals.

PUBLICATIONS OF THE INDIA OFFICE AND OF THE GOVERNMENT OF INDIA.

Mr. EDWARD ARNOLD, having been appointed Publisher to the Secretary of State for India in Council, has now on sale the above publications at 37 Bedford Street, Strand, and is prepared to supply full information concerning them on application.

INDIAN GOVERNMENT MAPS.

Any of the Maps in this magnificent series can now be obtained at the shortest notice from Mr. EDWARD ARNOLD, Publisher to the India Office.

The following Catalogues of Mr. Edward Arnold's Publications will be sent post free on application :

CATALOGUE OF WORKS OF GENERAL LITERATURE.

GENERAL CATALOGUE OF EDUCATIONAL

WORKS, including the principal publications of Messrs. Ginn and Company, Educational Publishers, of Boston and New York, and of Messrs. E. L. Kellogg and Company, of New York.

CATALOGUE OF WORKS FOR USE IN ELE-

MENTARY SCHOOLS. With Specimen Pages.

ILLUSTRATED LIST OF BOOKS FOR PRESENTS

AND PRIZES.

Index to Authors.